V1

By
KENNETH ANAND
&
JARED GOLDSTEIN

SNEAKER LAW has created this publication to provide you with accurate and authoritative information concerning the subject matter covered. SNEAKER LAW is not engaged in rendering legal or other professional advice, and this publication is not a substitute for the advice of an attorney. If you require legal or other expert advice, you should seek the services of a competent attorney or other professional.

No part of this publication may be reproduced in whole or in part, or stored in a retrieval system, or transmitted in any form or by any means, electronic, mechanical, photocopying, recording, or otherwise, without written permission from Sneaker Law LLC. For information regarding permission, or other inquiries, please contact info@sneakerlaw.com.

COPYRIGHT © 2020 SNEAKER LAW LLC

All rights reserved.

Library of Congress Control Number: 2021902049

ISBN 9781735782003

Acknowledgements

Sneaker Law — Safia Anand and Jake Goldstein, for their contributions to the book; Stadium Goods, for providing the majority of our sneaker photos; The Ronin and Elle Park, for their assistance with marketing and design; Prof. Nana Sarian, for inviting us to teach Sneaker Law at Harvard Law School; and Rylan Brook and Daphne Spector, our OG legal interns.

Kenneth — Safia, Alex, and Deven, for their love and support; my parents, for teaching me the importance of education and empathy; my brother, for being a true artist; Kanye West, for his inspiration; and 3 8 0.

Jared — My beautiful wife, Rosalind, for her constant love and support and for always pushing me; my baby girl, Sylvia. Daddy loves you so much (and will always make sure you have the freshest kicks); and my parents, brothers, step-siblings, and in-laws.

Source: Stadium Goods

CONTENTS.

Acknowledgements	iii
Table of contents	iv

Introduction

What is *Sneaker Law*?	6
About the Authors	7
Kenneth Anand	8
Jared Goldstein	10
What Will You Get Out Of This Book?	11
What You Won't Get Out of This Book (A Disclaimer)	14

1 History of the Sneaker Business

The Creation of the Sneaker — 20
Paleolithic Times
Ancient Greece
Great Britain
United States
Great Britain — 21
United States
Germany
Japan
Boston — 22

Influential Sneaker Companies to Know Today — 23
Reebok — 24
adidas — 26
Puma — 27
Nike — 28
New Balance — 29
Converse — 30

Major Sneaker Deals — 31
Michael Jordan x Nike — 32
LeBron James x Nike — 33
Kanye West x adidas — 34
Off-White x Nike — 35

Sneakers That Changed the Game for Good — 36
Stan Smith (by adidas) — 37
Air Force 1 (by Nike)
Air Jordan XI (by Nike and Jordan)
Chuck Taylor All Star (by Converse) — 38
The Pump (by Reebok)
Suede (by Puma)
990 (by New Balance)

2 Starting Your Own Business

Entity Types & Formation	**44**
Sole Proprietorship	45
Partnership	47
Limited Liability Company	49
Corporation	52
Writing a Business Plan	54
Branding	**58**
Intellectual Property Essentials	59
Hiring Contractors & Employees	**66**
Independent Contractors	67
Employees	68

3 Design

What Makes a Good Sneaker Design?	**76**
What Does a Sneaker Designer Do?	77
Knowing Styles and Trends versus Making Your Own Waves	
Rough Design Drawings	
Research and Development	
Sample Sneakers	78
Quality Control and Assurance	
How to Become a Sneaker Designer	**79**
Attend a Notable Design School	80
Other Options	87
Famous Sneaker Designers You Should Know	**91**
Virgil Abloh	92
Yoon Ahn/Ambush	93
Tiffany Beers	94
Salehe Bembury	95
Don C	96
Nike Doernbecher Designs by Children	97
Dr. D'wayne Edwards	98
Ronnie Fieg	99
Hiroshi Fujiwara	100
Tinker Hatfield	101

3 Design (cont'd)

Stephanie Howard	102
Jerry Lorenzo	103
Sergio Lozano	104
Cynthia Lu	105
Aleali May	106
Mark Miner	107
Nigo	108
Rick Owens	109
Jason Petrie	110
Raf Simons	111
Steven Smith	112
Christian Tresser	113
Kanye West	114
Pharrell Williams	115
Sean Wotherspoon	116
Giuseppe Zanotti	117

4 Manufacturing & Distribution

Manufacturing	**124**
Sneaker Components & Materials	125
The Sneaker Manufacturing Process	128
Other Manufacturing Concerns	132
Sustainable Manufacturing	138
Best Countries for Sneaker Manufacturing	140
Navigating Factories	
Third-Party Production Companies	141
Distribution	**142**
Direct to Consumer (D2C)	144
Retail	150
Wholesale	156

5 Licensing & Collaborations

Licensing	**164**
Typical Licensing Arrangements	165
Benefits of Licensing	
Risks of Licensing	167
Collaborations	**168**
How Did the Term Collaboration Get Coined with Sneakers?	169
License Deals versus Collaborations	
What Is the Impact of a Collaboration on the Sneaker Market?	170
Athlete Collaborations	**171**
Musician Collaborations	**190**
Fashion Brand Collaborations	**202**
Other Collaborations	**218**

6 Marketing

The Four Ps of the Marketing Mix — 232
Product — 233
Price
Place or Placement
Promotion

Traditional Marketing Channels — 235
Print — 236
Television and Film — 239

Digital Marketing Channels — 241
Online Marketing — 243

Social Media — 248
Instagram — 250
Facebook — 252
Twitter — 253
Snapchat — 254
Reddit — 255
LinkedIn — 256
TikTok

Blogs, Vlogs, Podcasts, & Other Content Conglomerates — 257
Blogs — 258
Vlogs
Podcasts
Content Conglomerates — 259
Sneaker Conventions — 260
Influencers & Sponsored Posts — 261
The Growth and Economics of Influencer Marketing
Who Are Influencers in the Sneaker Business?
Use of Influencers to Endorse Sneakers
Disclosures & FTC Requirements — 262

7 The Law of Sneakers Part 1: The Law & Litigation

Intellectual Property — 269
Trademarks — 270
Trade Dress — 276
Notable Trademark and Trade Dress Cases — 279
Copyrights — 291
Notable Copyright Cases — 293
Patents — 298
Notable Patent Cases — 304
Trade Secrets — 314

Employment Law — 316
History of US Employment Law — 317
Wage and Hour Laws — 323
Discrimination — 324
Classification: Employees versus Independent Contractors — 327
Employment Contracts & Offer Letters — 328
Work-for-Hire Agreement and Clauses — 330
Nondisclosure Agreements and Confidentiality

8 The Law of Sneakers Part 2: The Art of the Sneaker Deal

Types of Deals	336
Standard Clauses	**337**
Intellectual Property Ownership	338
Name/Likeness	343
Trade Secrets	
Compensation	344
Design Approval	345
Distribution	349
Marketing and Promotion	350
Counterfeiting	353
Employment	
Confidentiality	
Term & Termination	354

9 Reselling & Counterfeits

Reselling & Reseller Basics	360
Types of Resellers	
Acquiring Inventory	**361**
Copping at Retail	362
Bots	366
Cook Groups	368
Buying on the Secondary Market	
The Plug	369
Strategies to Prevent Resale	
Flipping Your Inventory	**370**
Major Resale Platforms	373
Mom-and-Pop Shops	376
Hand to Hand	
Violence in Sneakers	**377**
Release Date	378
Resale Transactions	
Counterfeits	**379**
What Is the Harm in Counterfeiting?	380
What Is Being Done about Counterfeiting?	381
What Does the Future Hold for Sneaker Counterfeits?	382

Conclusion   384

Introd

uction

Source: Stadium Goods

> "We try to evolve with each shoe. We try to make it even better… it's always about evolution."
>
> *—KOBE BRYANT*

INTRODUCTION

Sneakers. What do they mean to you? If you are a sneakerhead like us, sneakers mean more than you can articulate. Sneakers are not only an extension of yourself; they are a rite of passage. Sneakers are a common language. No matter your age, gender, race, ethnicity, religion, or sexuality, all sneakerheads have a common bond: our love and passion for sneakers. Even if you do not consider yourself a sneakerhead, sneakers still play a key role in your everyday life. After all, where would you be without the rubber soles beneath your feet as you carry out your days?

Like humans, sneakers have evolved over time. The concept of the sneaker and its surrounding culture, including its diversity, technology, creativity, marketing, and imagination, have made significant strides. The Converse Chuck Taylor All Star, released in 1917, was the first basketball sneaker ever made. At the time, the Chuck Taylor was radical and unprecedented in its style, design, and technology; it featured a high-top, single-piece back that wrapped around the ankle for support. The Chuck Taylor was an instant commercial success and has since sold more than a billion pairs worldwide, revolutionizing the sneaker business.

Flash forward to today: radical, unprecedented sneakers continue to define the industry. The adidas YEEZY Boost 350 V2, released in February 2017, a hundred years after the Chuck Taylor, has a flexible woven Primeknit upper and ultra-cushiony BOOST midsole. The 350 has sold millions of pairs and continues to be released in a myriad of colorways. Who knows how many pairs will be sold over the next hundred years, but the 350 is undoubtedly one of the most highly regarded sneakers of the century.

The Converse Chuck Taylor All Star and the adidas YEEZY Boost 350 V2, although only grains of sand on a beach of important sneakers, are both prime examples of the timelessness of sneakers. Throughout history, sneakers have remained relevant and constant, and we believe they always will.

Like sneaker style, design, and technology, the business of sneakers has also evolved. The sneaker business began many years ago to create a functional product that provided support and comfort to help people get through their daily lives. Today, it comprises an assortment of business and legal areas that expand well beyond support, comfort, style, design, and technology. This massive and ever-growing world is shaped by designers, developers, manufacturers, business owners, retailers, entrepreneurs, lawyers, resellers, marketers, analysts, sneakerheads, everyday consumers, and many, many others. By 2025, the sneaker business is expected to be a $95 billion industry.

INTRODUCTION

Prior to now, no single book has explained all areas of the sneaker business in a friendly and understandable way. Enter *SNEAKER LAW.*

WHAT IS SNEAKER LAW?

Sneaker Law is all you need to know about the sneaker business.

As of 2020, the US footwear industry rakes in over $90 billion annually, mainly from millennial consumers. The average sneaker enthusiast spends a considerable portion of their disposable income on sneakers. Most do this knowing very little about the business. Isn't that shocking? We think so!

Knowing this staggering information, we decided to write this book. Through *Sneaker Law*, we hope to educate and empower our readers so they can have a more meaningful understanding of exactly what goes into the sneaker business. We've taken all of our legal and business experience, research and passion, and of course undying love for sneakers, and bundled it all into *Sneaker Law: All You Need to Know about the Sneaker Business.* We've packed our book with information you'll need to structure and fire up your own sneaker business, if that's your goal. If your dream is to design the next iconic sneaker, we've laid out your options for getting started. But we're not just writing this for sneakerhead entrepreneurs or future Tinker Hatfields. Whether you are a collector, designer, aspiring business owner, brand, reseller, law student, lawyer, or just someone who is curious about sneakers, we will explain to you the latest business trends, legalities, and practices that shape this rapidly growing and highly lucrative industry. We hope this book not only teaches you but also inspires you to gain a more profound understanding of everything that makes sneakers so influential and fundamental to our everyday lives.

Kenneth & Jared at Harvard Law School
- January 2020

> We are not just lawyers; we are true sneakerheads. Even though we may be some years apart in age, our combined experience, knowledge, and passion for sneakers and the sneaker industry is extensive. What's more, we are true friends, and Sneaker Law is turning our childhood dreams into reality. Here's a little bit more about us.

Kenneth Anand

I have been doodling on my Converse Chuck Taylors and scuffing my Nike Air Delta Forces since the mid-1980s. In 1990, I convinced my parents to buy my first pair of Jordans—the white, grape-ice, and teal Air Jordan V, which I cleaned daily with a toothbrush and believed made me jump higher. My love for Jordans turned into an obsession for Air Maxes and Dunks. With the sneakers came a similar obsession for hip-hop music and music production, which I studied relentlessly. In college at Virginia Tech, I paired a minor in Computers and Music with a Communications major.

After trying to shop my beats to rappers and major record labels with little success, I applied to law school in 1999 with the goal of helping creatives protect their intellectual property rights. By that time, I had more streetwear gear and pairs of kicks than I could keep in my tiny Brooklyn studio apartment. In fact, after I met my wife in law school, got married, and moved to her apartment in Brooklyn Heights, I had to get rid of half my sneaker collection just so we could share two small closets. Now that's true love!

After graduating from Brooklyn Law School in 2002, I practiced law at New York City firms for over fifteen years, advising hundreds of companies, executives and entrepreneurs in employment, intellectual property and entertainment matters, including everything from federal court litigation to contract negotiations.

In 2017, I decided to make a shift, and left law firm life to become General Counsel & Head of Business Development at YEEZY Apparel, Kanye West's sneaker and fashion house. My career had finally come full circle; I had found a job that would blend together my love for sneakers, fashion, and music. Working for Kanye inspired me to continue to chase my dreams, going back to school and obtaining my Executive MBA so that I could supplement my legal training with a primer in business.

Today, I am one of the co-founders of 3 8 0 Group, a fashion licensing company specializing in the manufacture and distribution of premium apparel, footwear and accessories. At 3 8 0, I continue my lifelong work of helping creatives as a leading business and legal expert and regularly lecture on topics involving sneakers and fashion.

INTRODUCTION

Jared Goldstein

When I was ten years old and in the third grade, I heard "Air Force Ones" by Nelly on the radio. The song immediately resonated with me, so I asked my mom if she could buy me a pair for my birthday. Before I knew it, I had multiple pairs of Air Force 1s, along with Jordans, Iversons, T-Macs, and many other sneakers. Sneakers became my obsession, ruling my life along with hip-hop, fashion, streetwear, and basketball. As far back as I can remember, I read *Complex*, *Vibe*, *Sole Collector*, *Slam*, and other magazines on a daily basis. I couldn't get enough. The culture became my lifestyle—and still is to this day.

In 2012, while in college at the University of Central Florida, I was fortunate enough to turn my passion for sneakers into a business. At first, I was lucky enough to cop two pairs of Nike Air Yeezy 2s and decided to flip them for a sizable profit. From that point on, I knew that reselling sneakers could be a good way to make money on a consistent basis. I went on to build a strong sneaker resale business and learned a great deal about the business of sneakers along the way.

After graduating from college in 2014, I moved to New York to attend Brooklyn Law School. While there, I began searching for a way to fuse my love of sneakers with the law. I researched legal areas in connection with sneakers, but did not find much. Thus, after joining *Brooklyn Law Review*, I knew that I had to write my note about sneakers—and I ended up writing more than forty pages about the lack of legal protection for sneaker designs. I thought my note was fire, but the executive board must've felt differently and chose not to publish it. That only motivated me to get my note out to the world through a different medium.

A short time later, I landed a legal internship at Complex Media, Inc. As I mentioned earlier, I'd read *Complex* magazine as a kid, and was always an enormous fan, so working for the company was a dream come true. Not only did I gain invaluable legal skills and experience, I was also able to rock kicks to work every day instead of a suit and tie like most legal jobs! One day, I thought of using *Complex* as a platform to get my law review note out to the world. I pitched the idea to the head sneakers editor; he loved it and gave the green light for me to condense and publish it as a *Complex* article. I went on to write two additional published articles for *Complex* related to legal issues applied to sneakers.

After interning at Complex for almost half of my law school career, I graduated and joined Undertone, an ad-tech and media company, where I would become the sole in-house legal counsel. At Undertone, among other things, I negotiated various agreements related to advertising, technology, data, privacy, intellectual property, and other areas. I also ensured company compliance with privacy and data protection laws. After Undertone, I joined LiveIntent, an ad-tech, marketing, and media company, as the sole in-house legal counsel, where I continue to handle business and legal matters related to advertising, marketing, and technology. I have also represented various clients in the entertainment, music, and fashion industries. Most importantly, at both Undertone and LiveIntent, I still rock sneakers to work!

Crazily enough, without those *Complex* articles, it is quite possible that *Sneaker Law* wouldn't exist. Kenneth read the articles and reached out to me on LinkedIn. We ended up meeting, shared our love for sneakers, and became good friends. A short time after, we came up with *Sneaker Law*. Now, we're here!

INTRODUCTION

What Will You Get Out of This Book?

Now that you know more about us, here is an overview of what you will find in this book:

1 History of the Sneaker Business

Consider this chapter Sneakers 101; here, we discuss the history of the sneaker business, some influential sneaker companies, major sneaker deals, and specific sneakers we feel have changed the game. After you read this chapter, you will have the sneaker basics mastered.

2 Starting Your Own Business

In this chapter, we cover all you need to know in order to start your own sneaker business. First, we discuss entity formation and how to decide which entity type is right for your company. Next, we dive into branding, the essentials of intellectual property, and how to apply for a copyright and a trademark. Finally, we discuss how to hire employees so that your business can grow properly.

5 Licensing & Collaborations

In this chapter, we explore the world of sneaker licensing, including how your favorite sneaker collaboration deals are put together, and what we consider some of the most famous collabs in the history of sneakers. If you want to know what goes on behind the scenes of some of the biggest deals in sneakers, read this chapter!

6 Marketing

Don't believe the hype! In chapter 6, we cover how sneakers are marketed and promoted. After this chapter, you will understand the most common techniques used by sneaker companies to make their products sell. From global ad campaigns, viral social media posts, to billion-dollar endorsement deals—it is all here!

9 Reselling & Counterfeits

Finally, we close out the book with an in-depth look at the secondary sneaker market, including the $2 billion sneaker reselling industry and the $450 billion counterfeit industry. Our book would not be complete without explaining how to flip sneakers and avoid fakes. The information in this chapter alone justifies your investment in *Sneaker Law*—one flip could cover the cost!

3 Design

In this chapter, we take an in-depth look at the design process, including what sneaker designers do, the most influential designers in the sneaker game today, and how you can become a sneaker designer. Anyone who's interested in sneaker design will benefit from the wealth of information in this chapter.

4 Manufacturing & Distribution

We then turn to manufacturing, including the essential components of sneakers, and how and where you can make and mass produce them. We also discuss the various channels of distribution and how sneakers make their way to consumers. After this chapter, you will have a full understanding of how sneakers go from factory to foot.

7 The Law of Sneakers, Part 1

Chapters 7 and 8 are a two-part extravaganza (it's lit!), where we teach you all you need to know about the law of sneakers. In Part One, we explain the most important areas of law that shape the sneaker business and some major litigation and disputes related to them. After reading this chapter, you should be ready to argue your first sneaker case!

8 The Law of Sneakers, Part 2

Here, we dive into the art of the sneaker deal. Whether you are a designer looking to protect your next big sneaker idea, a brand that wants to ensure that it is legally protected, or an aspiring sneaker lawyer, chapter 8 has something for you. We will cover all aspects of intellectual property and other sneaker-related laws so that you can navigate through the sneaker industry with some serious legal skills.

What You Won't Get Out of This Book (A Disclaimer):

Although it is important to understand what this book is about, it is equally important to understand what it is not about. *Sneaker Law* is not a compendium of every sneaker ever made. Nothing makes us happier than talking about our favorite sneakers, and this book certainly explores the history of sneakers and major sneaker brands, but *Sneaker Law* is more about the business behind the sneakers than sneakers themselves. So please, do not be offended if we left out your favorite Jordan, the latest celebrity collaboration, or if we failed to mention an indie sneaker brand that's poised to be the next adidas or New Balance. There are plenty of other amazing sneaker books out there that cover these things.

Last, and most importantly, this book is also not a substitute for legal advice. We will address many areas of law that surround and impact the business of sneakers, but in no way is this book intended to take the place of competent legal counsel. For example, we have a whole section on how to file your own trademark and another on how to negotiate a licensing deal, but it is always advisable to consult an attorney, especially on complex matters that could drastically affect your career in sneakers.

Now that we've gotten that out of the way, let's get into SNEAKER LAW!

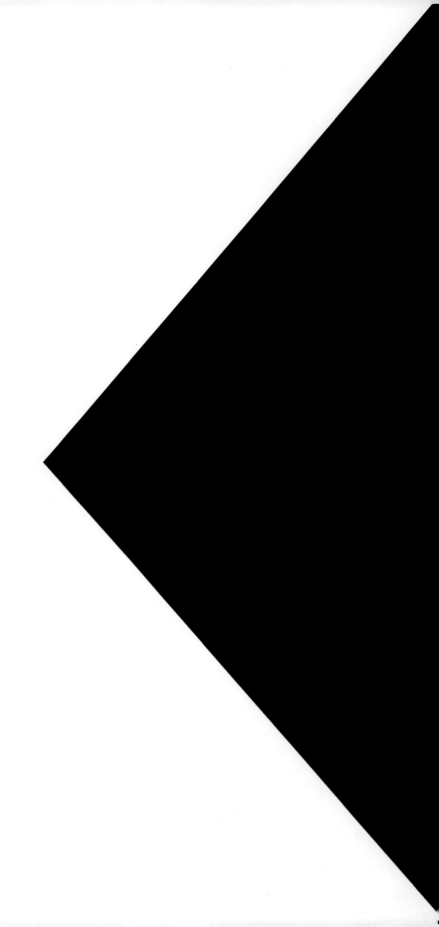

1

History of the Sneaker Business

"My adidas, walk through concert doors, and roam all over coliseum floors."

—*RUN DMC*

Sneakers are more prevalent than ever, and that's not stopping anytime soon. The global athletic footwear market is expected to grow from $80 billion in 2020 to $95 billion in 2025. We should all expect the industry to experience continuous growth for several years, if not decades, to come.

Sneakers have been around forever, but why are they so popular today? It goes deeper than the fact that sneakers provide arch support and are athletic necessities. Rather, the sneaker surge can be attributed to a few other reasons.

People Just Love Sneakers

Historically, sneakers were reserved for comfy walks, errands, and sporting events. Now sneakers are part of everyday life and are even heralded as a fashion statement, featured everywhere from Paris runways to Instagram mirror selfies. And sneakerheads are not the only ones vested in the industry—people from all different backgrounds and walks of life find joy and purpose in a fresh pair of kicks.

Sports and Entertainment

Thanks to the digital age, when major sporting and entertainment events take place, or celebrities are spotted wearing a certain sneaker, sneakers are purposefully promoted through social and digital channels, reaching billions of people instantaneously. If LeBron James walks from the team bus to the locker room in a pair of Nike Air Force 1s that drop on Nike's SNKRS app, the sneaker is likely to sell out.

When Kanye West performs in an unreleased YEEZY, that sneaker is going to be highly sought after and heavily discussed from that moment on. Whether at Coachella, Wimbledon, the NBA Finals, TMZ paparazzi shots, or the FIFA World Cup, sneakers are at the forefront of sports and entertainment, and that has significantly contributed to the flourishing state of the sneaker business.

Social Media Presence

Everyone loves to show off (or flex) on social media. For many, sneakers are the ultimate flex (no GRs). Social media provides a platform that facilitates news, content, discussion, and commerce, all related to sneakers. As a whole, social media has accelerated the growth of the sneaker business.

The Culture

Over the years, sneakers have become a global obsession. Sneaker enthusiasts have forged a culture that perplexes many non-sneakerheads. For sneakerheads, sneakers are a part of everyday life and you either get it or you don't. (If you don't get it, this book will definitely help.) What you have on your feet is of the utmost importance!

So how did we get from an idea to a worldwide movement? Let's get into the history of sneakers, as well as their rise to current times.

The Creation of the Sneaker

Paleolithic Times

Sneakers technically owe their creation to the very first humans who walked with footwear. Although researchers and historians may argue over the official start date, there is evidence of human beings wearing footwear during Paleolithic times, which means some type of sneaker has been a part of our history for over 40,000 years.

Ancient Greece

Fast forward a few thousand years, and we arrive at the Olympics. What were the Olympic athletes rocking? Well, at first—around 776 BC—they competed in their bare feet. Over time, athletes who joined the competition from different regions started to wear leather sandals to protect their feet from the rocks and terrain.

A few years later, all of the athletes were wearing some form of flexible footwear while they competed. The days of bare feet were over.

Great Britain

During the early 1800s, inventors in Great Britain noticed that individuals were running as a form of leisurely exercise. As a result, the inventors decided to create a shoe to accommodate those runners. They began to make the first running shoes out of leather, although they later noticed that the material was not able to keep up with the athletes. Leather stretches when it comes in contact with moisture, which meant one rain shower or puddle would spoil the shoe's potential.

To fix this, they needed to create something that was durable and long lasting.

United States

A few years later, in the United States, Wait Webster patented a process that made it possible to attach rubber soles to the bottom of leather boots. At the same time, back in Great Britain, John Boyd Dunlop from Liverpool Rubber Company was exploring bonding canvas to rubber, launching the very first plimsolls. (What are thoooose?) The original plimsolls are markings on the hull of a ship that signify the ship's load, a measurement introduced by Samuel Plimsoll. The footwear plimsolls took that name because the Brits thought the rubber in shoes resembled the hull of a ship.

Both Dunlop and Plimsoll created a pivotal development in the history of sneakers. However, they used their inventions for footwear intended for the beach. These early versions of rubber shoes were therefore known as "sand shoes."

By 1839, the American chemist Charles Goodyear arrived at a remarkable discovery: rubber became pliable if heated up and mixed with sulfur, a process known as vulcanization. (Now you know what "VULCANIZED" means on the outsole of the Converse x Off-White Chuck Taylor.) Vulcanization could extend the lifespan of shoes—the soles would not get too hot in the summer or too cold in the winter. Waterproof and durable, the shoes would also withstand snow, sleet, and rain.

Great Britain

We hop back over the pond in 1865 for the arrival of the modern-day sneaker. Bolton, a British company that goes by Reebok today, added spikes to the bottom of plimsolls to help athletes run and exercise with more traction. They unknowingly invented the world's first sneaker—durable, pliable, and comfortable, aiding in all athletic endeavors.

In case you're wondering how sneakers got their name, there are two theories: sneakers have soles that make less noise than their leather counterpart, which makes it easier to sneak around; or, since rubber shoes were popular among the poorer classes in the United States, the word sneaks, which can mean thieves, was adopted to describe the shoe.

United States

In 1892, Goodyear released a sneaker called Keds, which combined canvas and rubber at a time when such a process was uncommon. Funnily enough, most sneakers were produced by tire companies at this time, not actual shoemakers.

Everything changed when Converse was founded in 1908. The company began to manufacture sneakers in 1917, releasing its iconic silhouette, the All Star. It was intended to be an indoor gym sneaker, but once basketball players tried the sneaker out on the court, it was a wrap.

Chuck Taylor, a well-known basketball player, was hired by Converse to go around the country and promote the sneaker in 1921. This is how the sneaker's name transformed into the Chuck Taylor All Star, and as a result, Chuck Taylor is remembered more today for his contributions to sneakers than basketball. The All Star rose in popularity and was labeled as the official sneaker of the US basketball team during the Berlin Olympics. This was the first time the rest of the world got a glimpse of what was happening in American sneaker manufacturing—naturally, they all wanted a pair.

Germany

At the same time as Converse's success, two German brothers named Adolf and Rudolf Dassler launched a rubber sneaker company out of their mother's laundry room. They made designs based on running distance, which made their product particularly popular among serious sprinters and long-distance runners. The most famous athlete at the time to wear their sneakers was Jesse Owens, an American track and field runner who won four gold medals at the Berlin Olympics.

However, there was trouble in paradise for the brothers, and they broke up in 1948 due to disagreements following World War II. Rudolph ended up founding Puma, while his brother founded adidas, based on his nickname—Adi.

Japan

During the same year, Kihachiro Onitsuka founded Onitsuka Tiger/ASICS in Japan, hoping to help children and families following the war. The company was designed to help provide kids a better future through the development of their athletic abilities.

Boston

In 1962, the American sneaker company New Balance decided to integrate science into its products. New Balance, which had been founded in Boston in 1906, became the first company to launch scientifically tested sneakers, designed to improve support and performance.

Two years later, Nike was founded by Phil Knight, a University of Oregon business major, and his track coach, Bill Bowerman. Nike was originally a distributor of Onitsuka Tiger sneakers in the United States. Eight years later, the two started to make their own sneakers after Bowerman had an inspiration one day while making breakfast with his waffle iron. What if he made a sole by pouring rubber into the iron? Waffle soles were born, and they decided to stick with the name Nike, named after the Greek goddess of victory.

For a mere $35, a student at the University of Oregon designed the "swoosh" logo for them. This turned out to be a wise investment by Nike (and probably one of the biggest come ups of all time). If only *Sneaker Law* had existed back then; this designer would have had all the intellectual property knowledge she needed to protect herself (more on this in chapters 2, 7, and 8).

In 1978, Nike collaborated with a former NASA engineer to create a hollowed-out sole filled with dense gas. The goal was to provide extreme support and cushioning for runners and athletes. The sneaker was labeled the Nike Tailwind and sold in stores that same year.

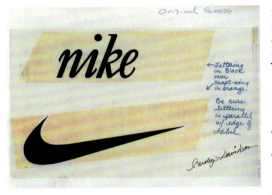

Source: Nike

Source: Nike

In 1984, Nike introduced a new concept: partnering with famous athletes to promote its sneakers. The brand collaborated and teamed up with Michael Jordan that same year, creating the Air Jordan I, one of the most classic sneakers of all time, which is still worn and re-released continuously on a global scale to this day. The collaboration, which later transformed into the Jordan Brand, turned out to be one of the most iconic partnerships and sneaker collections in the history of sneakers.

Two years later, Nike released the Air Max I, an air-cushioned sneaker that went on to solidify the company as an international sensation. By the 1990s, sneakers had finally become mainstream, due in large part to Nike's efforts to develop and market sneakers as cool and relevant. Additionally, thanks to their depiction in music videos and movies, sneakers became synonymous with street cred and hip-hop culture.

Nike then went on to introduce NikeiD, which enabled customers to customize certain sneakers by choosing materials, colors, patterns, laces, and even personalized stitching for their favorite kicks.

By the 2000s, luxury collaborations had become something of the norm, with celebrities and athletes all clamoring to create their own limited-edition sneaker. Today, sneakers are cooler, more sought after, and more fashionable than ever before.

Influential Sneaker Companies to Know Today

We've already name-dropped some of the biggest sneaker producers in the world in our timeline. Now, it is time to look further into the top sneaker companies, including the companies' founding and rise to prominence, as each have forayed into influencing the future of footwear.

Reebok

Reebok was founded in England in 1958 by brothers Joe and Jeff Foster. The two intended to carry on their family's legacy of athletic footwear, heralded by their grandfather, Joseph William Foster, who, under the J. W. Foster brand, designed some of the earliest spiked running sneakers used in track and field events.

The Fosters initially considered naming their company Mercury, but it proved too difficult to trademark. Instead, they turned to the Afrikaans word for the Grey Rhebok, a species of African antelope. Reebok was born and began witnessing great success in England. One can trace the company's geographic origins by the Union Jack flag used in Reebok's early branding.

Source: Stadium Goods

In 1979, the sneaker company came to the United States for a trade show, when Paul Fireman, an American wholesaler, spotted the company and asked for its exclusive licensing and distribution rights in North America.

By 1981, Reebok was worth around $1.5 million, and that number was only going to increase. A few years later, in 1984, Fireman acquired the parent company, Bolton, becoming its sole owner. One year later, Fireman brought Bolton public on the New York Stock Exchange. In 1986, Reebok was the leading athletic footwear brand in North America, capitalizing on the potential of sneaker style and fashion.

Source: JPstock / Shutterstock.com

Source: Reebok

Also in 1986, Reebok received major pop culture clout for securing a placement on the main character of the movie *Aliens*.

By 1987, the company's sales totaled $1.4 billion, one thousand times what Reebok was worth in 1981. Just one year later, Reebok claimed $1.8 billion, or 26.7 percent of the sneaker market, which outshined Nike at $1.2 billion.

In 1988, through a partnership with industrial design firm Design Continuum, Reebok began developing the world's first inflatable sneaker. Less than one year later, it dropped the Reebok Pump, which featured inflatable chambers to offer a custom fit that could be expanded and contracted with a rubber pump built into the sneaker's tongue. The sneaker exploded on the scene after NBA basketball player Dee Brown stopped to inflate his sneakers on live television moments before winning the 1991 NBA Slam Dunk Contest.

Sticking to its proven basketball formula, in 1996, Reebok added Allen Iverson as a brand ambassador and collaborator, debuting his signature "Question" sneaker, which was soon followed by the Reebok "Answer" series.

With technology in sneakers becoming so important during the 1990s, in 1997, Reebok released the DMX Run, a sneaker that was once hailed as the greatest running shoe of all time. It featured ten bulbous air pods, enabling air flow from one pod to help distribute weight and support throughout the sole of the sneaker.

Despite its many advancements in the sneaker world, by the 2000s, the company was suffering in sales compared to adidas and Nike. In 2005, adidas acquired Reebok in a deal valued at $3.8 billion. Under the new adidas leadership, Reebok pivoted and rebranded during the later 2000s. From collaborations with rap phenom Kendrick Lamar to the futuristic designs of Pyer Moss, Reebok has managed to stand the test of time.

Reebok continued to struggle under its new adidas ownership. In 2016, adidas announced a four-year turnaround plan for the business and began a large-scale operations consolidation in 2017. By 2018, adidas reported that the business restructuring and profitability plan was ahead of schedule and that it expected Reebok to start turning a profit before 2020. As of 2019, it had close to 8,000 current employees working in its worldwide locations. Despite the brand's recent struggles, adidas has stated that it remains committed to continuing its legacy. So expect more exciting kicks from Reebok in the years to come.

Source: Monticello / Shutterstock.com

adidas

adidas has undoubtedly enjoyed a surge of popularity in consumer preferences over the last ten years. What started as a company centered on athletic performance has morphed into so much more, as kids and adults alike seek out "the brand with the three stripes" for school, casual wear, and high fashion.

As we have mentioned, in 1925, within the small German town of Herzogenaurach, Adolf and Rudolf Dassler designed their first pair of sneakers and went on to change the world. When the brothers had a falling out, it was Adolf who founded adidas, after his nickname "ADI" and last name "DASsler."

When Adi Dassler died in 1959, he held over 700 patents related to sports sneakers and other equipment. In 1978, Dassler was inducted into the American Sporting Goods Industry Hall of Fame as a founder of modern sporting goods. Earlier in the same decade, adidas received global notoriety when US boxer Muhammad Ali lost his first fight to Joe Frazier in the "Fight of the Century." Both men wore adidas in the ring. Ali would later switch to Everlast, but Frazier remained in adidas for their next two fights, Super Fight II and the "Thrilla in Manila."

adidas went public in 1995, and today is labeled the number two sneaker company in the world, with over 57,000 employees and offices in over 200 countries. As mentioned, adidas acquired Reebok in 2005. adidas also bought German soccer club FC Bayern München. According to Forbes, as of 2020, adidas had $25 billion in sales, a net profit of $1.5 billion, and a market value of $44.9 billion.

Source: Suriyawut Suriya / Shutterstock.com

Source: Sorbis / Shutterstock.com

Puma

Following the Dassler fallout of the 1940s, Adolf's brother, Rudolf, went on to found Puma, based on his similar knowledge of and passion for sneakers. Officially established in 1948, Puma released its very first soccer sneaker, called the Atom, the same year.

Source: Puma

It was not long until key athletes were wearing Puma sneakers. In 1952, runner Josef Barthel wore Pumas while he won an Olympic Gold Medal in the 1500m. Four years later, Puma trademarked its formstripe.

In 1968, Puma created the cat logo that we all know today. That same year, Tommie Smith won the Olympic Gold 200m in Mexico while wearing Pumas. Going on to make the Black Power salute, with his Pumas right next to his feet in the shot, Smith was banned from the games. Subsequently, there was a less-than-happy sentiment about the Puma company.

Despite this, athletes such as Diego Maradona and Boris Becker continued to sport Pumas during the 1970s and 1980s, and Puma continued to release new sneakers with great success. One of the most iconic Puma styles to ever release is the Puma Clyde, which dropped in 1968 and was designed by Walter "Clyde" Frazier, and is still popular today.

Source: Stadium Goods

Like its major competitors during the 1990s, Puma took a stab at a scientific sneaker model by debuting the Puma Disc. The Disc was a laceless sneaker that could be tightened or loosened by simply twisting a disc located on the sneaker's tongue.

In 1996, Puma released the Cell, which included the first foam-free midsole, another technological breakthrough for sneakers. Since then, Puma has managed to remain a relevant, sought-after sneaker company. As of 2019, the company was worth approximately $4 billion and had 12,894 employees. Some of its most recent and noteworthy collaborations include Jay-Z, Rihanna, Kyle Kuzma, Rhude, Neymar, Alexander McQueen, Va$htie, and J. Cole.

Source: Puma

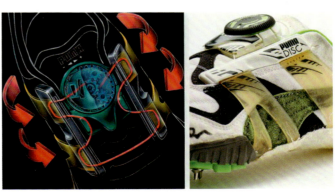
Source: Puma

Nike

We already covered a good deal of Nike's history, so we will keep this section brief. After being established in 1964 as Blue Ribbon Sports, the brand opened its first retail outlet in 1966. In 1971, Blue Ribbon was renamed Nike. The newly branded company launched its first line of sneakers in 1972. Despite its market dominance, this makes Nike a much younger company than all of the aforementioned brands. In 1978, the company went public.

With immediate and monumental success, Nike went on to acquire a variety of brands, including shoe and sneaker companies Cole Haan, Canstar Sports, Inc., Umbro, and Converse, Inc. Nike has worked with many of the world's biggest athletes, and is hailed as the number one sneaker company in the world today.

As of 2020, *Forbes* reported that Nike had $41.3 billion in sales, $4.3 billion in net profits, and a market value of $135.6 billion, blowing all of its competitors out of the water. The company employs approximately 70,000 people across 1,000 retail stores worldwide.

Source: pio3 / Shutterstock.com

New Balance

New Balance was founded by William J. Riley in 1906. As an Irish immigrant living in Boston, Riley wanted to create a product modeled after the chickens strutting around his backyard. Seeing how well they balanced themselves on their three-pronged feet, Riley was inspired to make a sneaker that molded to humans' natural foot arches.

Riley partnered with Arthur Hall, a retired salesman, in 1927, and the two continued to make arch supports for workers whose jobs required an abundance of standing and difficult positions. By 1960, the company made a name for itself as one that helped budding athletes, inspiring Hall's daughter, Eleanor, to design the first New Balance sneaker, the Trackster. Officially launched in 1961, the Trackster claimed the title as the world's first scientifically tested sneaker with a sole made for traction. The company even accommodated different foot widths so athletes could perform at their very best.

Adopted as *the* track and cross-country sneaker company across Massachusetts, New Balance still remained a lean operation without much nationwide success. In 1972, New Balance was purchased by Jim Davis, who was determined to turn the brand into a household name. He was successful. Four years later, New Balance launched the 320, which featured the "N" logo that we all know today. Voted as the number one running sneaker by Runner's World magazine at the time, the rest was history.

Source: New Balance

The company is still headquartered in Boston today and owned by Davis. As of 2019, New Balance had annual sales of over $4 billion and employed approximately 5,000 people around the world.

Source: Savvapanf Photo / Shutterstock.com

Source: Sorbis / Shutterstock.com

Chuck Taylor All Star (by Converse)

Last but not least, we have Converse. Founded in 1908 as a rubber shoe company by Marquis Mills, Converse was the first brand to combine canvas with rubber, introducing what was possible in the world of sneakers. By 1910, the company was in daily production, and in 1917, focusing on the popularity of basketball, it created the All Star basketball sneaker.

Source: Stadium Goods

Partnering with basketball player Chuck Taylor in 1936, Converse made the white high-top Chuck Taylor, designed for the upcoming Olympics and retailed for a whopping $3.95. Naturally, the brand took off. By 1957, Converse held 80 percent of the entire sneaker industry, making the company the biggest in the world at the time.

However, the brand struggled beginning in the late 1970s through the rest of the 1990s due to increased competition from Nike and other brands. In 2001, Converse filed for bankruptcy, and two years later, Nike swooshed in (pun intended) and bought the company for an estimated $305 million. It proved to be one of Nike's greatest investments. Converse has since made a strong comeback; its sales have ballooned from $200 million in 2001 to more than $1.9 billion in 2019. Converse employs approximately 3,000 people across the world today.

Source: emka74 / Shutterstock.com

Source: JHVEPhoto / Shutterstock.com

Major Sneaker Deals

Now that we have explored the history of sneakers and some of the largest sneaker companies in the market, let's look at some of the biggest sneaker deals that have gone down throughout the last century.

Michael Jordan x Nike

Source: Stadium Goods

Source: Stadium Goods

Source: Stadium Goods

The Michael Jordan and Nike sneaker deal is arguably the most famous sneaker endorsement-turned-partnership in the last century. The first Air Jordan sneakers were made exclusively for MJ in 1984, and ever since, the Jordan Brand has been unstoppable.

Structured as a brand of sneakers and athletic wear built around Michael Jordan and his notoriety, over the years, Nike and Jordan have released a total of thirty-five numbered sneaker styles (not including various colorways and variations of each, and other Jordan Brand models), sometimes re-releasing the earlier models more than once.

To get Jordan to join forces with the company, Nike offered him $500,000 per year for five years. Nike has stated that it was not so easy getting the basketball star to agree to the deal. At the time, Jordan was hoping to work with adidas, but since the company was undergoing a leadership change, they were unable to strike a deal. Converse also approached Jordan with a lackluster offer that did not get him excited.

In true competitor fashion, Jordan actually took Nike's offer directly to adidas, hoping the brand could match or come close to it. Again, the deal did not work out, and Jordan reluctantly signed with Nike. Once the partnership was locked in, Jordan began wearing the sneakers on the court, first sporting the Nike Air Ship. Shortly thereafter, he debuted the Air Jordan I, which helped Nike sell more than $70 million worth of sneakers between April and May of 1985. By the end of the year, Jordan made Nike more than $100 million.

Today, it is estimated that Michael Jordan earns roughly $130 million per year from his deal with Nike. As of May 2019, overall Jordan Brand wholesale revenue hit $3.14 billion, up 10 percent from 2018. With recent collaborations from the hottest designers, celebrities, fashion houses, and streetwear brands, including Virgil Abloh, Drake, Travis Scott, Christian Dior, and Supreme, the Jordan Brand shows no signs of slowing.

LeBron James x Nike

Nike has always had a penchant for roping in the best NBA players in partnerships at the right time. In 2002, while Nike was the leading sneaker brand in the NBA after its decades of partnership with Michael Jordan, the company had its eyes set on LeBron James to add to its roster of athletes like Tiger Woods and Venus Williams. At the time, LeBron James had also been approached by Reebok but ended up signing with Nike, fulfilling a childhood dream and following in Michael Jordan's footsteps.

Nike released the Air Zoom Generation with James in 2003, followed by the Zoom LeBron II, III, IV, and V through 2008. The company then released the LeBron VI, VII, 8, all the way through the current model, the LeBron 18.

Newspapers claimed James executed a deal with Nike that was $28 million lower than it would have been with Reebok. However, recent headlines have reported he has re-signed with Nike on a lifetime deal that could end up exceeding $1 billion.

Kanye West x adidas

Source: Stadium Goods

Source: Stadium Goods

Source: Stadium Goods

Kanye West and adidas partnered in 2015 to launch the adidas x YEEZY line. The first co-branded adidas YEEZY sneaker, the YEEZY 750 Boost, retailed for $350, making it one of the most expensive retail sneakers in the game. A celebrity and design endorsement from West, coupled with the unusually high price, limited supply, and astronomical demand began the partnership with a bang. Sneakers have clearly come a long way since the days of $4 Converses.

Since the beginning of the collaboration, adidas and Kanye have already released many different YEEZY sneaker styles (all in multiple colorways and not including multiple boot, slide, and foam runner models): the YEEZY Boost 750, YEEZY Boost 350, YEEZY Boost 350 V2, YEEZY Powerphase, YEEZY 500, YEEZY 500 High, YEEZY Boost 700, YEEZY Boost 700 V2, YEEZY 700 V3, YEEZY Boost 700 MNVN, YEEZY Boost 380, and YZY QNTM.

As of April 2020, it was reported that YEEZYs bring in an estimated $140 million per year for Kanye. With more rumored and leaked releases, expect nothing but more amazing styles and designs from Kanye, adidas, and the YEEZY camp.

Off-White x Nike

Source: Stadium Goods

In November 2017, Nike and Off-White, a high-end luxury and streetwear company led by Virgil Abloh, who is also the Men's Artistic Director at Louis Vuitton, joined forces to release the highly coveted Off-White x Nike "The Ten" series. The collection, featuring reconstructed and refreshing takes on current and past Nike models, took the sneaker industry by storm. Each release sold out instantly, and the present resale value of all of the models combined is enough to cover a down payment on a house!

The collection, which continued to release in different colorways and versions after the initial launch, features iterations of the Air Jordan I, Air Presto, Air Force 1, React Hyperdunk, Zoom Fly, Air Max 90, Air Max 97, Blazer Mid, Air Vapormax, Converse Chuck 70 (remember that Nike owns Converse), and others. Capitalizing off the massive success of the partnership, Nike and Off-White continue to release sneakers and other products to this day.

Sneakers That Changed the Game for Good

It goes without saying that YEEZYs, Chuck Taylors, and Air Maxes changed the game of sneaker adoration for good. But there were also other sneakers that exploded onto the scene and changed public perception of sneakers and sneaker culture forever.

Let's look at some of the most iconic sneakers of all time.

Stan Smith (by adidas)

The Stan Smith is still the most popular sneaker that adidas has ever released. Named for American tennis legend Stan Smith, the sneaker features a sleek and elegant design originally developed for the French tennis star Robert Haillet. When Stan Smith began to wear the sneaker toward the end of the 1970s, a touch of green was added to the heel, solidifying the classic adidas kicks that we all know today. As of 2016, adidas had sold over 50 million pairs of Stan Smiths. For more than forty years, this sneaker has managed to stand the test of time.

Source: Stadium Goods

Air Jordan XI (by Nike and Jordan)

As unmistakable as it gets, the Air Jordan XI features a shiny, patent-leather upper—so shiny that Michael Jordan received a $5,000 fine in each game he wore the Concord XIs. It's also a perfect sneaker to wear off the court (and down the wedding aisle). Michael Jordan's affinity for the XI made it one of Nike's biggest selling products of all time.

Air Force 1 (by Nike)

The Nike Air Force 1 is arguably the most important sneaker in the history of hip-hop. Since its release in 1983, the sneaker has been regarded as Airs, Uptowns, or Forces depending on where you live in the United States. Although available in countless colors, any sneakerhead will tell you that nothing compares to a fresh pair of white Air Force 1s. (As Nelly would say, "Give me two pairs. I need two pairs.") To give you a sense of just how major this shoe is, Nike still sells a staggering 10 million pairs every year.

Chuck Taylor All Star (by Converse)

Now over a hundred years old, there is something to be said about the Converse Chuck Taylor All Star. The classic, high-top Converse style is still sought after by sneakerheads and non-sneakerheads alike. It is reported that Converse sells about 270,000 pairs of Chucks per day. Yes, we said per day.

Suede (by Puma)

Walt "Clyde" Frazier launched the Suede by Puma in the 1960s, right before he became an icon at the 1968 Olympics. To date, the likes of Jay-Z and Nipsey Hussle have sported the sneaker, which was closely linked to the birth of hip-hop in the 1970s and 1980s.

Source: Stadium Goods

The Pump (by Reebok)

Made popular by the 1980s commercials "pump up, air out," the Pump is still a sneaker bought and celebrated today. With an orange basketball logo that brings our memories back to Dee Brown's iconic slam dunk contest, these sneakers didn't come close to its rival Air Jordan series but left an indelible mark on sneaker history and culture.

990 (by New Balance)

Lovingly referred to as the "original dad shoe," the New Balance 990's bulky style has been a staple in the world of fashion since the 1970s. The company has released countless iterations of the 990, as well as a sibling series, that master the art of plain perfection, with the iconic gray colorway.

If you are a true sneakerhead, you own at least one pair of these game-changing sneakers—perhaps all of them (if not, take the L). Of course, there are dozens of other sneakers that have changed the game, with plenty more to come.

Now that you are well versed in all you need to know about the beginnings and historical influence of the sneaker industry, let's talk business and all you need to know to start one.

2

Starting Your Own Business

"If I had to pick of all the things that I'm involved in, the most important is the Jordan Brand because it is my DNA. It is who I am."

—MICHAEL JORDAN

When it comes to Nike, adidas, Converse, Reebok, New Balance, Puma, and the many other sneaker companies that exist around the world, each one is unique. Each has its own history, strategy, product, designers, manufacturers, licensors, collaborators, employees, and more. Despite all of these differences, every sneaker company shares one strong commonality—each is its own business and brand.

Sneaker businesses are not limited only to the brands that make them. Remember, this is a $90 billion industry! There are resellers, retailers, manufacturers, distributors, designers, licensees, advertisers, media, technology, and consulting firms.

So how does each sneaker business get started? What is the difference between a business and a brand? And how do you build a strong brand?

When starting your own sneaker business, you must first consider which type of entity to form. Will you want to form a sole proprietorship, partnership, limited liability company (LLC), or corporation? What are the differences between each entity? What is required to form each type? Second, you will need a strong business plan. Without this, you cannot steer your company to growth and success.

Once you have a solid business plan, you must think about creating your brand. How will intellectual property help protect your brand and grow your business? What are the differences between copyrights, trademarks, and patents? How do you file a trademark, copyright, and patent? And last, how will you hire employees who can help accomplish all your business goals?

We think that the answers to all of these questions are grails. However, you do not have to go to Stadium Goods to find them—we provide all of the answers in this chapter!

Entity Types & Formation

Forming an entity is one of the first steps to starting your own sneaker business. Entity formation dictates the structure of the business and how it will operate. A business entity is an organization created by one or more people that facilitates specific business activities or to allow its owner(s) to carry on a trade. For example, Nike is a corporation, and its business operates and is structured according to corporate laws and regulations. StockX, on the other hand, is a limited liability company (LLC), and its business operates and is structured according to limited liability laws and regulations.

Before deciding which entity fits your sneaker company, it is important to know the differences between them and what steps are required to form each one.

Sole Proprietorship

Jared, one of the authors of this book, had a sneaker reselling business in college. He would often wake up early in the morning for releases (sometimes after a few too many beers from the night before), secure his pairs, and go back to sleep. The money was good, he was able to work out of his college dorm, and he never had to change out of his PJs. Not a bad gig.

When Jared started reselling sneakers, he instantly became a sole proprietor. Sole proprietorships require no formal action to be created. As long as there is only one individual who owns the business, a sole proprietorship is automatically formed as a result of that individual's business activities. This means, like Jared, you may quite possibly be a sole proprietor as well and not even know it!

Why did Jared decide to operate his reselling business in this way? Well, a sole proprietorship is the simplest and least costly entity to form. There is little or no paperwork involved, and Jared was able to start flipping pairs of kicks right away. Jared could have hired employees to work for the company, but in a sole proprietorship, he must be the only owner. For Jared, since he was working independently out of his college dorm, a sole proprietorship seemed right at that time.

With sole proprietorships, however, there is no legal distinction between the owner of the company and company itself. This means that although Jared solely owned all of the business's assets, he also faced unlimited personal liability for all of the company's debts and obligations. Jared alone would be liable for any injurious acts committed by him or his employees. So if Jared was sued for any business-related reason, as the owner, he could have been held personally liable for all damages, meaning that his personal assets, rather than the company's assets, would have been at stake.

Also, if Jared wanted to grow his business by hiring a manager and potentially obtaining outside investments, he would not have been able to do so under a sole proprietorship. A sole proprietor enjoys the benefit of having complete control of the management of the company, but because there can be only one owner in a sole proprietorship, this type of business entity is not a viable means for achieving significant growth. Sole proprietors are limited in their ability to hire individuals to manage and operate the company. A sole proprietor may also only use his or her own financial resources to fund the company and has no ability to raise capital or garner investors to help the company grow.

Jared ran a successful business for some time and, luckily, did not face any personal liabilities or other negative consequences. In hindsight, however, Jared may have been better off forming another type of entity for his sneaker reselling business. We will explore these other entities in the sections to come.

Taxation

Unlike other entities, sole proprietorships are not taxed separately from the owner. As a result, the business income is considered to be personal income of the person running it. Thus, when Jared filed his taxes, he included his reselling revenue and expenses on his personal tax return. Sole proprietorships are advantageous from a tax perspective because there is no double taxation. When filing a tax return, a sole proprietor will report any income, losses, and expenses on their individual Schedule C and the standard Form 1040.

How to Form a Sole Proprietorship

As mentioned, a sole proprietorship has no formal requirement for its formation or operation. The sole proprietorship is not considered an official legal entity, and due to this, there is no legal distinction between the owner and business. There may still be licenses and permits that need to be obtained and statutory requirements that must be adhered to; these vary by the industry, state, and locality of the business.

For example, in New York, there is a statutory requirement that sole proprietorships must file a "doing business as" (d/b/a) certificate. When opening and operating a sole proprietorship, it is always recommended to check and comply with any state and local laws.

Partnership

General Partnership

Let's take Jared's reselling business a step further. Say he is now making some decent money as a sole proprietor for his reselling business but is tired of selling out of his college dorm. He wants to open a physical store in Brooklyn, but to do that, he needs a partner. If Jared, as a sole proprietor, decides to go into business with other individuals or entities as owners, his company's sole proprietorship status will no longer be valid. Therefore, he must consider whether he would like to form a different type of entity.

Jared calls Kenneth, and the two decide to open a sneaker consignment store called Legal Sneakers. They agree to each contribute $50,000 to the business (called a capital contribution) and split everything fifty-fifty. Whether they know it or not, Jared and Kenneth have just formed a general partnership. A general partnership is when two or more people, individuals, corporations, or other entities, referred to as partners, agree to carry on a business for profit as co-owners. Each partner has the right to make business decisions, legally bind the company in contracts, and otherwise fully participate in the partnership's management.

By opening the business together, both Jared and Kenneth are agents of the general partnership and authorized to act on its behalf. Jared and Kenneth must both be involved in the day-to-day business affairs. Jared agrees to take care of sales and inventory, while Kenneth handles store operations. The store opens with much success, and they now have a decent inventory of purchased and consigned kicks. Everything should go pretty well as long as they can flip those pairs.

What about the downside? A general partnership, like a sole proprietorship, is not considered a separate legal entity from its partners. Under a general partnership, Jared and Kenneth would face unlimited personal liability for the partnership's debts, liabilities, and obligations. Any acts committed by either partner in the ordinary course of business may affect them both. Say (hypothetically, since this would never happen), Jared purchased a pair of Nike Air Yeezy 2 Pure Platinums for $2,000, knowing he could flip them for $5,000 or more through Legal Sneakers. On his way back to the store, Jared runs into Yeezy Busta, who conducts a legit check on the sneakers and breaks some bad news to Jared—the Yeezys are "Feezys" (fakes) and not worth more than $50 (again, this would NEVER happen to Jared). As a general partner, Kenneth would be equally responsible for that loss of $1,950. All general partners share in the Ls!

Jared and Kenneth have recovered from the Feezy fiasco and business is boomin' (just like Benjamin Kickz). They want to open a store in London (where some call sneakers "trainers"), but they will need to raise money to do it. Unlike a sole proprietorship, where the growth of the business (outside of the money that the business makes) is limited by the owner's financial resources, a general partnership can increase its assets in two ways: it can either require the existing partners to contribute additional capital, or add new partners who are required to contribute their own assets. Most of the capital Legal Sneakers holds is tied up in inventory at the moment, so Jared and Kenneth decide to ask their friend, Harvard law school professor and fellow lawyer Nana, if she would like to become a partner. Nana already owns a shop in London that Legal Sneakers can use and she has agreed to help run the store. In exchange, Jared and Kenneth only require Nana to make a capital contribution of $10,000. There are now three general partners in Legal Sneakers who all share equally in the profits and losses.

A partner (referred to as an assignor in this context) can assign their interest in the partnership to someone else (an assignee). However, the assignee of the partnership interest does not become a partner unless the other partners give their consent. Say Nana, the assignor, is willing to transfer her interest in Legal Sneakers to Kenneth's wife, Safia, the assignee. Safia is only entitled to receive Nana's share of the profits of the partnership and Nana's interest once the partnership dissolves. Additionally, Safia has no ability to participate in the management of the partnership unless she is formally made into a partner. If a partnership wants to prohibit assignments of interest, it could do so in a written partnership agreement signed by all general partners.

In the event that there is a change of ownership in a partnership, one of the partners dies, or a partner becomes bankrupt, the partnership automatically dissolves unless a partnership agreement exists that specifically states the partnership will continue to exist.

Limited Partnership

A limited partnership is similar to a general partnership in that it exists when two or more people, individuals, corporations, or other entities, referred to as partners, agree to carry on a business for profit as co-owners. Unlike general partnerships, limited partnerships usually have one or more general partners and one or more limited partners.

Legal Sneakers continues to grow, and Jared, Kenneth, and Safia need additional capital to expand further. Rather than add another general partner to the mix, they decide to raise money for the business by asking Jake, Rylan, and Daphne to join as limited partners. The three will participate as "silent partners," solely to invest in the business. As limited partners, Jake, Rylan, and Daphne do not participate in the management of the business and, therefore, are not liable for its debts and obligations. Limited partners are only liable for debts and obligations up to the amount of their actual financial contribution to the partnership.

By adding limited partners, Legal Sneakers will have more opportunity to garner investments. Investors like Jake, Rylan, and Daphne can invest money into the partnership in exchange for equity. Limited partners do not face unlimited liability as they would with general partnerships. As long as there are no prohibitions set forth in a partnership agreement, a limited partner can also assign their partnership interests. Different from a general partnership, upon a limited partner's death, the partnership will not dissolve. Instead, the limited partner's estate is assigned the limited partner's rights in the partnership.

Taxation of Partnerships

Both general and limited partnerships enjoy the same tax benefits as sole proprietorships: partnerships are not taxed separately from the partners, meaning there is no double taxation. This is called pass-through taxation. For partnerships and sole proprietorships, an informational tax return must be filed, which decides how much in taxes each individual owner of the business pays.

How to Form a Partnership

Like sole proprietorships, partnerships have no formal formation requirements. In fact, it does not even matter whether the individuals, corporations, or other entities intend to create a partnership. All that is needed for a partnership to be formed is two or more people, corporations, or other entities, acting together to run a business as co-owners with a profit-sharing arrangement. With this in mind, one may think of the many sneaker collabs (which we will discuss in chapter 5) and wonder whether all would be considered partnerships in the legal sense. The answer is yes. However, if individuals, corporations, or other entities involved in the business do not want to create a partnership, they can overcome this presumption by showing evidence that the parties had no intention to share the profits of the business. This is commonly done by stating in the agreement between the parties that their relationship is that of independent contractors and that there is no assumption of a partnership or some other unintended structure.

Despite there being no formal requirements or federal laws that govern partnership formation and operation, there are state laws, and they vary. Furthermore, every state except for Louisiana has adopted either the Revised Uniform Partnership Act or the Uniform Partnership Act. These acts provide various rules on partnership formation and operation, which should be followed.

Typically, a partnership must be registered within the state where it does business. For both general and limited partnerships, a business certificate must be filed with the local county or state authorities. The state(s) that the partnership operates in will dictate which counties and/or states the partnership must register in. We recommend checking your state and local laws to determine what requirements are applicable to your partnership.

Although not required, all partners can enter into and execute a partnership agreement. These are beneficial because they outline the different partnership terms, including the governing laws, the partnership's purpose, capital contributions, management and voting requirements, ownership interest, withdrawals and additions of partners, profit and loss distribution, dissolution procedures, and more.

Limited Liability Company

Jared, Kenneth, Jake, and Safia decide that they want to take their business to the next level, but Rylan and Daphne hold differing opinions on the future of the company. As a result, Rylan and Daphne decide to leave Legal Sneakers and receive their investments back. Jared's wife, Rosalind, loves the vision and wants to be a part of the business. They make the decision to form a limited liability company (LLC) together called Legal Sneakers LLC, due to the many benefits associated with this type of entity.

An LLC is a business entity where one or more people, known as members, have limited liability with respect to liabilities and contractual obligations for the business that the company engages in. Limited liability is one of the main benefits of LLCs: members are not personally liable for the company's debts or liabilities. Instead, the liability of an LLC is limited to the debts and liabilities of the company itself. This is unlike sole proprietorships, general partnerships, and for general partners in limited partnerships, where owners and partners can be held personally liable for the company's debts and liabilities. Thus, under Legal Sneakers LLC, its members—Jared, Kenneth, Jake, Safia, and Rosalind—will have limited liability in connection with the business. By creating an LLC, Legal Sneakers would join many other sneaker companies—LLCs are one of the most popular business entities in the sneaker industry for small to large nonpublic companies. Businesses such as Stadium Goods, Kith, StockX, Flight Club, and many others operate as LLCs.

Although LLC members enjoy limited liability, they can still be held personally liable under a legal theory known as piercing the corporate veil. If an LLC or corporation (which we will discuss in the next section) is sued, courts will examine how the entity is run to determine whether to pierce the corporate veil and find its members personally liable.

Courts generally look for the following factors:

01 When there is no distinct separation between the company and its members. This can happen if the members of the LLC (or in the case of corporations, shareholders or directors) mix up their personal finances with those of the company—for example, if Jake uses the Legal Sneakers company credit card and bank accounts to fund his personal kick collection or for other purposes unrelated to the business.

02 When members (in an LLC) or shareholders or directors (in a corporation) engage in fraudulent or wrongful behavior—if Kenneth and Jared convince a distribution company to commit to a deal by turning over fraudulent and inflated financial reports for Legal Sneakers.

03 When the LLC or corporation is undercapitalized and does not have sufficient funds to operate—if Legal Sneakers does not have enough money to run its business.

04 When there is a lack of corporate formalities required for operating as such an entity—if Legal Sneakers does not file its articles of organization or articles of incorporation correctly, or does not have an operating agreement or corporate bylaws in place.

If any of the aforementioned factors are present in connection with the actions of an LLC or corporation, courts may find a piercing of the corporate veil, which would leave the members, shareholders, or directors personally liable for those actions of the respective entity.

As an LLC, Legal Sneakers can allow all its members to own a portion of the company, partake in the management of the company, and still enjoy limited liability. This is unlike partnerships, where the general partners could be held personally liable for the debts and obligations of the business, and where the partners' participation in the management of the business could affect their liability.

Another benefit for Legal Sneakers as an LLC is the potential for growth. LLCs are flexible when it comes to investments and profit sharing. Investments by the members do not need to match up to the ownership percentage in the business that they will receive. In fact, it is possible to be a member without investing any money at all.

Additionally, LLCs can receive investments without having to give an ownership interest in the company to the investor. Moreover, LLC members can generally assign their interest in the company at any time, and new members can be added as well. These attributes can attract passive investors for the company.

When it comes to profit sharing, LLCs distribute proceeds to its members according to each member's ownership percentage in the LLC, or according to a different distribution percentage if mutually agreed upon by the members.

Taxation

A major benefit for LLCs is that members can choose to be taxed as a partnership and, as a result, receive pass-through taxation. This is unlike corporations, where shareholders can be subject to double taxation. However, if the LLC wishes to do so, it can be taxed like a corporation and be subject to double taxation. There are scenarios where this type of taxation can be advantageous. When it comes to taxes, it is always important to consult with a tax professional to see what is best for you and your business.

How to Form an LLC

For Legal Sneakers to structure its business as an LLC, it first would need to file articles of organization with the secretary of state in the state where it wishes to operate. The articles of organization outline the basic information about the company. This generally includes the LLC's name, address, member information, management structure (LLCs can be member managed or manager managed), purpose of the business, and registered agent, which is another person or entity authorized to receive legal notices, documents, and correspondence on the company's behalf. Each state has specific requirements, so it is important to visit your state's website to ensure that your LLC is compliant with all stipulations. Many states have forms with all of the required information.

For Legal Sneakers, it will be important for its members to execute an operating agreement. Operating agreements establish all of the guidelines, rules, limitations, financial information, functions, and all other terms for the LLC. Some states require operating agreements, whereas others do not. Regardless of the state you are in, it is truly important to have an operating agreement in place. Besides the fact that the operating agreement is the blueprint for the LLC's business (speaking of the blueprint, Jay-Z's Roc-A-Fella Records is an LLC—s/o to Hova!), it also creates legal separation between the members of the LLC and the LLC itself, which is needed to secure limited liability for its members.

Important terms to include in an operating agreement include definitions of major terms, name of the LLC, purpose for which the LLC was formed, date that the LLC was formed, term of the LLC, principal office and address, name and address of registered agent for service of process (if you have one), names and addresses of each member, whether the LLC is member managed or manager managed, capital contribution of each member and nature of that contribution (which could be cash, personal property, real property, intellectual property, services, etc.), other funding procedures (such as loans and capital calls), procedures for adding and accepting new members, procedures for removing members, limited liability of members and managers, management structure, meetings, dissolution and termination, and miscellaneous provisions (such as governing law, amending of the operating agreement, mediation and arbitration, notice, and severability).

We know that this may all sound like a lot, but it is important—and the reason why consulting with an attorney is crucial when it comes to drafting an effective operating agreement.

> Sidebar: If Kenneth and Jared wanted to start their own sneaker law firm, they might opt for a professional limited liability company (PLLC). Anand & Goldstein PLLC has a nice ring to it, don't you think? In many states, PLLCs are used by licensed professionals such as lawyers, doctors, accountants, and others. With the exception of the requirement that members of PLLCs must be one of the required licensed professionals, for the most part, PLLCs and LLCs are the same. However, with PLLCs, members can be held personally liable for claims of malpractice. Objection!

Corporation

Legal Sneakers LLC has really taken off. In addition to its original members, Jared, Kenneth, Jake, Safia, and Rosalind, the business now has over 1,000 employees and fifteen different locations. The company wants to expand, attract top talent, acquire other businesses, and gain market exposure and brand equity. One way to accomplish this is to offer shares of its stock to employees and investors. Transferring ownership and shares to many different individuals and entities can be difficult with an LLC, so Legal Sneakers decides to pay a visit to its trusted advisors at the off-white shoe (or sneaker) law firm Bellizio + Igel PLLC. After a very long, billable meeting, the firm suggests that Legal Sneakers convert their LLC into a corporation. Let us explain why this would be advantageous.

A corporation, sometimes called a C corporation (or C corp), is a legal entity that's separate from its owners. Like an LLC, a corporation can invoke its "corporate veil," which you now know will protect its owners from personal liability. Corporations have an additional and distinct advantage over LLCs when it comes to raising capital because they can do so through the sale of stock, which is a benefit in attracting investors and employees, something that Legal Sneakers certainly wants to do.

It costs more money to form a corporation than other entities, and corporate record-keeping, operational processes, and reporting are more complex. Also, unlike the entities we previously discussed, with corporations, there can be double taxation. Corporations must pay income tax on their profits, and in some instances, those profits are taxed twice—first, when the company makes a profit and then again when dividends are paid to shareholders on their personal tax returns.

In some cases, another type of corporation, called an S corporation (S corp), can be utilized to avoid the downside of double taxation. S corps allow profits, and some losses, to be passed through directly to owners' personal income without ever being subject to corporate tax rates. However, S corps cannot have more than one hundred shareholders, and all shareholders must be citizens of the United States. Taxation of corporations can be pretty involved, so it is best to consult with a tax professional when deciding which corporate entity is right for you.

Articles of Incorporation & Bylaws

Just as an LLC must file articles of organization with the state government, a corporation must file articles of incorporation. This should be filed in whichever state you intend to incorporate, using the applicable form that is provided on the state's division of corporations website. By filing articles of incorporation, you will obtain approval from the state to conduct business.

The information required on the articles of incorporation generally includes:

01 The corporation's name and main address

02 The corporation's general purpose

03 The duration of the corporation, if you do not intend for it to exist indefinitely

04 The name and address of the corporation's registered agent and registered office

05 The number and type of shares of stock that the corporation is authorized to issue

06 The names and addresses of the incorporators or person(s) who sign the articles of incorporation and ensure that they get filed. This can be anyone and does not necessarily have to be an officer, director, or shareholder of the corporation

In addition to the articles of incorporation, every corporation must have a set of bylaws. Similar to partnership and operating agreements, these internal documents govern the way the corporation will be run and operate; they are usually not filed with the state.

An effective set of bylaws will typically include the following:

01 The time, place, and protocol for holding regular meetings of officers, directors, and shareholders

02 Number of directors and corporate officers authorized to act on behalf of the corporation (and in some cases their compensation)

03 The fiscal year of the corporation

04 Procedures for amending the articles of incorporation and bylaws

05 Any rules on the approval of contracts, loans, checks, and stock certificates

06 Procedures for keeping corporate records

You can find several templates for corporate bylaws online, but these are fairly detailed documents, so we recommend consulting an attorney or other business professional if you have questions about corporate governance and how best to tailor bylaws to your business.

Writing a Business Plan

Running a business without a business plan is like taking a road trip without GPS, or rocking a pair of Nikes with adidas socks—you might not end up where you thought you would, or you may get roasted by your friends! The essential process of writing a business plan forces you to consider what exactly your business intends to do, how it will get there, and lets you do it all in style.

Kenneth, the other author of this book, recently decided after many years of practicing law to go back to school for his Executive MBA (Masters of Business Administration). As a part of the course's Capstone project, he was required to create a business plan for a business of his choosing. He and Jared were busy planning how to write *Sneaker Law*, so Kenneth used the opportunity to create a business plan for this book.

Does a book really need a business plan? Yes. Writing a business plan forced Kenneth to consider how the book would be written, how much it would cost to make (or print), to whom it would be marketed, how many copies it would need to sell so Kenneth and Jared can (at least) break even, and how they will plan for future releases, products, and ideas so that *Sneaker Law* can become much more than just a book.

SNEAKER LAW

BUSINESS PLAN

TABLE OF CONTENTS

TABLE OF CONTENTS	2
EXECUTIVE SUMMARY	3
BUSINESS DESCRIPTION	4
MANAGEMENT SUMMARY	5
ORGANIZATIONAL STRUCTURE & MANAGEMENT	5
THE MANAGEMENT TEAM AND AUTHORS	5
ADVISORY BOARD MEMBERS	6
OTHER STAFF	6
SKILLS CONCERNS	6
INDUSTRY BACKGROUND	7
COMPETITIVE ANALYSIS	10
MARKET ANALYSIS	12
MARKETING PLAN	14
UNIQUE SELLING PROPOSITION	14
PRICING & POSITIONING STRATEGY	14
DISTRIBUTION	14
PROMOTIONAL STRATEGY	14
OPERATIONS PLAN	15
LOCATION	15
INVENTORY AND SUPPLIES	15
EMPLOYEES	15
APPENDIX A: SOURCES	16

With the right planning, even a book can turn into a successful business and brand (we hope). In this section, we will walk you through the process of creating a business plan for your sneaker business.

Every business plan is unique, but there are certain sections that you will want to highlight. We have included these below in the general order in which they should appear. Follow this guide and you will be on your way to writing your own effective sneaker business plan.

01 Executive Summary

This is a short but compelling summary of the entire business plan and what you would like your business to accomplish. Every business plan begins with an executive summary. It gives the readers an overview of the business: products, services, management, market, competition, financial summary, and capital requirements. You'll provide further information about all of these in the rest of the plan.

02 Business Description

This is the second part of every business plan. Here, you would typically provide the company mission statement, vision, marketplace in which you want to position the business, price point of your products or services, and how your business will be different from others. This section can also outline your goals and how you plan to achieve them.

03 Management Summary

In this section, you will provide an overview of the team that will be involved in setting up the business. This includes the company founders, any advisory board members, and key hires that you intend to make in the early stages of the company's growth. People reading your business plan will want to know why you and your team are qualified to run and develop your business. Highlighting each person's work experience and contributions to the business will be helpful. If there are any areas where the team is lacking experience and will need to find outside help, that should also be noted in the management summary.

04 Industry Background

Here, you will provide a background of the industry in which your business sits. For example, if you are talking about sneakers, you will want to highlight that it is a $90 billion industry. But don't stop there. You may need to do some research on how your sneaker product fits within the industry or a certain subsection of it. Find out how big the industry is in terms of size, consumer reach, future growth, and whether there are any barriers to entry. Understanding your market is critical to positioning your business in the best way.

05 Competitive Analysis

Here, you should go into detail about any potential competition for your product or service. For example, if you are creating a revolutionary comfort sneaker, you may want to discuss brands such as Allbirds, Vans, HOKA ONE ONE, New Balance, adidas, and Nike and how your comfort technology will be better or stand apart. A useful tool for this section is to include a SWOT (Strength, Weakness, Opportunities, and Threats) analysis for each competitor so that you have a clear sense of how to distinguish your product or service. Even if you are a first mover (meaning your business is the first of its kind and you have no competition in the marketplace), it is important to examine other companies that have executed different products in a similar fashion, and why yours will be just as good or better. For example, *Sneaker Law* is the first book that teaches you all you need to know about the sneaker business, but there are plenty of wonderful books about sneakers, business, and law. By examining these separately, we were able to feel fairly confident that there was a real need and market demand for this book. We hope you agree!

06 Marketing Plan

A good marketing plan will identify your product or service's unique selling proposition (USP), which is the one thing that makes you stand out from your competition. Think of the USP as your one-line elevator pitch or the thing you might say if you were going on an episode of *Shark Tank*. Here's the USP for *Sneaker Law*: "the first book that will teach you all you need to know about the sneaker business." Catchy, right? We think so. The marketing plan should also contain information about the pricing and positioning strategy of your product or service. For example, if you plan to sell LED shoelaces, you should include what it will cost to produce them and how much you will sell them for. Also included in the marketing plan is how you will distribute and promote the product. Would you try to sell LED laces to people age fifty and older? Unless you are an OG, probably not! The more specifics and details, the better!

07 Operations Plan

In the operations plan, you should discuss where the business will be located, where and how it will produce its products or offer its services, and what employees (other than executives or key management) will be necessary to operate the business. Will you need a physical office or store? Where will that be located? Will you make your products there or at a third-party facility? How many people will you need to run the company and what will their roles be?

08 Financial Plan

Finally, no business plan would be complete without a financial plan. If you are not comfortable with financial plans, including creating income statements, cash flow statements, and balance sheets, you may want to consult a financial professional to assist you with this. It will be worth your time to do some solid budgeting and forecasting. This way, you will know how much working capital you will need to launch the business, what your overhead or operating costs will be, how much you plan to sell, what you need to do to break even, and when. After all, you probably want the business to make some money, right?

Again, we recognize that this sounds like a lot. But business plans are critical in any industry—the sneaker industry is no exception. Following this outline will provide a solid roadmap for your business and specifically define each of its components. This can help ensure success and growth for whatever sneaker business you choose to launch. Good luck

Branding

Now that we have taken you through the various entity types and you have a better understanding of how to start your business, it is time to discuss how you can start building your brand. What is the difference between a business and a brand?

A business is the company or organization that produces a product or offers specific services. A brand is the image or identity that a business projects and the way consumers perceive the business.

When you think of Jordan Brand, what comes to your mind? Is it the Jumpman or wings logo? Specific pairs of Jordans? MJ's iconic moments on the court? The commercials with Mars Blackmon? What about the many famous slogans like "It's gotta be the shoes," "Inspired by the greatest player of all time," or "Be legendary"? Well, all of these are in fact a part of the brand's identity. In chapter 6 of this book, we will explain how to market your brand, but when starting a sneaker business, it is vital to know how to create and protect your brand. To do this, you need to know the fundamentals of intellectual property and how its laws can help and affect your business. Accordingly, in this section we will explore the essentials of intellectual property when it comes to branding, which include copyrights and trademarks.

Intellectual Property Essentials

We now know that every business can create a brand, which is its image or identity. A brand can be refined over time using elements such as logos, slogans, photos, advertisements, videos, and more. All of this material, or "brand content," is intellectual property that can be protected. For a full rundown of intellectual property and how all of its components impact the world of sneakers, check out chapters 7 and 8. For purposes of this chapter, though, we will look at two kinds of intellectual property essential to branding: copyright and trademark. After a brief description of the two, we will explain how you can apply for a copyright and trademark. After reading, you can be well on your way to building and protecting a brand of your own!

Copyrights versus Trademarks

Copyrights and trademarks are vital to any brand, and they are used for many types of works. But what is the difference between a copyright and trademark, and what works do each protect?

Copyright protects original works of authorship, which include, but are not limited to, musical, architectural, graphic, literary, dramatic, photographic, audiovisual, and artistic works. One of the main goals of copyright law is to allow the creator of the work to reap the benefits of their creativity, time, and effort.

Correspondingly, the owner of a copyright has the exclusive right to distribute, reproduce, display, publicly perform, prepare derivatives, and license the work. In order to obtain a copyright, the work must be fixed in a tangible form. Therefore, ideas cannot be copyrighted.

When it comes to sneaker companies, there are various assets that can be copyrightable. These can include, but are not limited to, images, logos, websites, videos, literature, audio, and potentially the sneakers themselves.

Trademarks, on the other hand, typically protect words, phrases, designs, symbols, or a combination that identifies and distinguishes the source of the goods or services from others. For sneaker companies, trademarks are used for brand names, logos, symbols, phrases, product lines, and possibly for elements of sneakers themselves.

How to File a Copyright

In the United States, it is not necessary to obtain a copyright registration to protect a work. A work is protected by copyright at the time it is created in a fixed and tangible form. However, there are distinct advantages to holding a copyright registration. Should your copyright be infringed upon, a copyright registration will be necessary to bring an infringement action. Furthermore, by registering a copyright, the owner has a presumption of validity and the right to recover certain damages and attorneys' fees in the event of infringement.

When filing a copyright application, you will need to submit an application form with the US Copyright Office and provide a copy or copies of the work. Begin by creating an online account at www.copyright.gov. Click on "Register a Copyright" and go through the steps by logging into the Electronic Copyright Office (eCo) Registration System. Here, you can find the appropriate application, whether your work is literary, a performing art, visual art, photograph, motion picture, or other digital content.

The eCo Registration System will walk you through the steps and is fairly straightforward. Should you have any questions, there are helpful tutorials and other resources online you can use. If you register the copyright online, you can typically submit an electronic copy of the work, which is quite simple. In some cases, however, the US Copyright Office may request a physical copy.

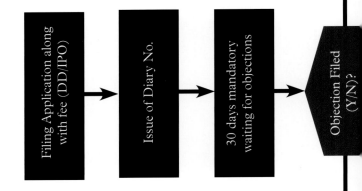

The fees for a copyright registration vary depending on whether the application is done online ($45 for a single application with one author, work, claimant, and not a work made for hire; $65 for all other standard filings), on paper ($125), a renewal registration ($100–$125), group registration ($35–$500), supplementary registration ($100–$150), preregistration ($200), or other types of registrations ($100–$500). There could be additional fees (e.g., special handling and appeals) depending on the nuances of each copyright registration.

The Copyright Office generally only reviews copyright applications for basic requirements and with a low level of scrutiny. If no refusals are issued by the Copyright Office, registration takes about a year from filing the application but can be expedited for special circumstances.

STARTING YOUR OWN BUSINESS

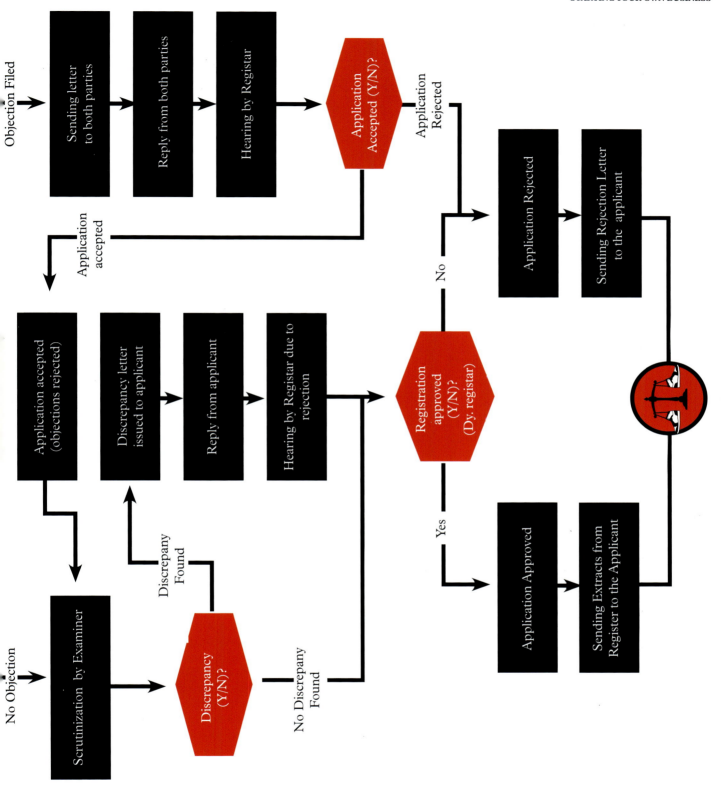

How to File a Trademark

There are five steps to filing a trademark:

01
Choose Your Trademark and Conduct a Trademark Search

Without a name, logo, or slogan, you cannot have a trademark. Therefore, the first step in the trademark filing process is to choose the name, logo, or slogan for the trademark that you wish to register. As soon as you have that, you can focus on the application process.

In the United States, trademark applications are filed with the US Patent and Trademark Office (USPTO), which is located at www.uspto.gov. Prior to choosing a trademark, it is recommended that you conduct a trademark search (referred to as a knockout search) to ensure that your trademark is not already being used by someone else. You would not want to create a brand and then find out that someone else has prior rights in the trademark.

Having to rebrand or potentially face a lawsuit is more expensive and aggravating than renaming and clearing a trademark at the outset. Choosing whether to search the mark in just the United States or in other countries as well will depend on your plans for your business and your budget. If you are a US company, you should, at a minimum, clear the name in the United States before proceeding with a trademark.

An easy way to conduct a knockout search is by using the TESS platform on the USPTO website. In the search engine, you can type in the key words for your trademark. Then select "live and dead" to incorporate registered marks that are active and not currently active, and select "plural and singular" to view the entire range of potential marks that may be similar to one you would like to register. Even if a registered trademark is dead or abandoned, you may run into issues in securing the trademark due to those marks potentially having common law protection. Common law protection is offered when a mark is still used in commerce but not federally registered.

You should also conduct a general Google search to see if there are any trademarks similar to the one you would like to register. If you find a similar mark, even if that mark is not registered with the USPTO, it may have common law protection, which could affect your ability to secure the rights to your prospective trademark. There are also detailed search engines that some trademark attorneys use to ensure that no potential conflicting trademarks exist. Bottom line: do some digging and be sure you have a mark that no one else does!

02
Choose the Classes

Once you have conducted adequate searches and believe that there are no conflicting trademarks, you also need to choose the correct class(es). There are forty-five classes of goods and services to choose from. Classes 1–34 cover goods, and Classes 35–45 cover services. When deciding which to include in your application, you should research each class. You can do so by searching through the USPTO Trademark ID Manual. For example, sneakers and apparel fall under Class 25 and retail stores are covered under Class 35. However, for your sneaker company, there may be other classes under which you want to register. Searching through each class can be confusing, but if you are able to narrow down to the essential classes for your brand, you will save time and money.

After choosing which class(es) you will file your trademark in, you must choose the identifications/descriptions for the trademark in each applicable class. These can be found in the ID manual. If the identifications that you are looking for are not listed, you must create your own identification entry, which should specifically, concisely, and clearly describe your goods or services. For example, the YEEZY trademark was filed in Class 25 and described as "Clothing, namely, footwear, shoes, sneakers."

 *(Use the "Back" button of the Internet Browser to return to TESS)*

YEEZY

Word Mark	YEEZY
Goods and Services	IC 025. US 022 039. G & S: Clothing, namely, footwear, shoes, sneakers. FIRST USE: 20150200. FIRST USE IN COMMERCE: 20150200
Standard Characters Claimed	
Mark Drawing Code	(4) STANDARD CHARACTER MARK
Serial Number	86981009
Filing Date	August 6, 2013
Current Basis	1A
Original Filing Basis	1B
Published for Opposition	June 24, 2014
Registration Number	5125895
Registration Date	January 17, 2017
Owner	(REGISTRANT) Mascotte Holdings, Inc. CORPORATION CALIFORNIA c/o Pryor Cashman LLP, 7 Times Square New York NEW YORK 100366569
Attorney of Record	Brad D. Rose
Type of Mark	TRADEMARK
Register	PRINCIPAL
Other Data	The name(s), portrait(s), and/or signature(s) shown in the mark identifies the nickname/pseudonym/stage name of Kanye West, a living individual, whose consent(s) to register is made of record.
Live/Dead Indicator	LIVE

03
Select the Filing Basis

After selecting the applicable classes and corresponding identifications for your trademark, you need to choose a filing basis. The application can be based on use, an intent to use, or a foreign registration. The difference? Either you are currently using the mark (select Section 1[a]), in which case you would file a use-based application, or you plan to use it sometime in the future (select Section 1[b]), in which case you would file an intent-to-use application. For example, if you are in the process of creating your own sneaker brand and are not selling the sneakers yet, you can file an intent-to-use application, under Section 1[b], which will allow you to fully register the trademark for your brand once you begin to actually sell sneakers and use your brand in commerce. The Lanham Act (which we discuss in greater detail in chapter 7) defines commerce as "all commerce which may lawfully be regulated by Congress" and most commonly means interstate commerce.

When filing an intent-to-use application, the applicant will declare that it has a "bona fide intention" to use the mark on all of the goods listed in the application in the near future. Unlike use-based applications, you do not need to provide a specimen or a date of first use because you have not started using the mark yet. However, the trademark will not register until you are actually using the mark in commerce, and as we will discuss later, you have only six months (or more if you file an extension) to begin using the trademark in commerce following the date that the intent-to-use application is allowed.

For applications based on a foreign registration, you will not need to prove use of the mark in connection with the trademark filing and can instead rely on the foreign registration. However, you will need to show use of the mark in connection with all of the goods between the fifth and sixth year after registration to maintain the trademark registration.

For use-based applications, all of the goods listed in the trademark application must be used in commerce at the time of the application. Sales that are only obtained outside of the United States will not qualify as use in commerce in the United States. Therefore, if you sell your sneakers in the European Union but not in the United States and want to file a trademark application here, you would need to file your trademark based on an intent-to-use basis (or based on a foreign registration). When filing a use-based application, you will also need to state the date of your first use in each class and submit a specimen showing proof of the mark's use.

04
Submit the Specimen

For each class that you register your trademark in, you must submit a specimen that shows that the trademark is being used in commerce for that specific class. A specimen is an example of your trademark in use. So, for example, if you are applying for a trademark for your sneaker company's name in Class 25 for the use of the mark in connection with sneakers, an acceptable specimen would be to submit a photo of your of sneakers with the brand's name in the insole, which is what YEEZY submitted for its specimen:

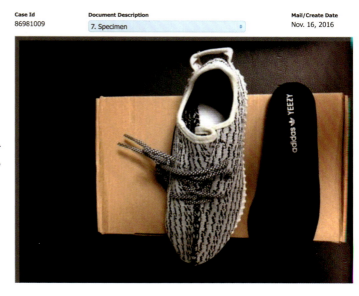

05
Finalize the Application, Pay the Fees, and Submit

Once steps 1–4 are complete, you will have to fill out some remaining information, pay the fees, and then, at last, submit the application! It costs $225 per each class of goods/services for the TEAS Plus application and $275 per each class of goods/services for the TEAS Standard application. The TEAS Plus application was designed to be easier for the applicant and USPTO. Applicants who use it can choose only identifications for their goods/services that are already included in the ID manual. For the TEAS Standard application, applicants can input their own identifications without selecting the predefined identifications that are included in the ID manual. Once you have checked all of your answers and ensured that everything looks correct, you can submit the application. Congratulations! What happens next, though? How long does it take for the USPTO to approve of your application? What if they find issues with your application? How do you protect your trademark if it is accepted? Do you have to renew the trademark after time passes? We will answer all of these questions in chapter 7.

Hiring Contractors & Employees

By now, you know how to start a business, formulate a business plan for success, and apply for intellectual property protections, but no business can truly grow without help. At some point, there will be too many tasks for you, or you and your founders, to do alone; you will need to start hiring. If you followed the steps in "Writing a Business Plan," you have a general idea of who you need to hire and what their tasks will be.

There are two ways you can bring in outside help: (1) by engaging independent contractors who will do discrete tasks on a project-by-project basis or (2) by hiring employees, who will work either part time or full time for your business in a specific role. If you are not clear on what the difference is between the two, head over to chapter 7, where we discuss independent contractors, employees, and the issues that can arise with worker misclassification.

Independent Contractors

The Internal Revenue Service (IRS) defines independent contractors as people who are in an independent trade, business, or profession in which they offer their services to the general public. These are self-employed individuals and can include lawyers, accountants, and freelancers such as designers, writers, photographers, information technology specialists, and others. Independent contractors can be found almost anywhere. There are freelance websites where you can find amazing writers, designers, artists, web gurus, and more, all who are willing to help you with your sneaker business. Lawyers and accountants have professional organizations that can refer you to the right kind of person for your business needs, hopefully one who is also a sneakerhead! Personal referrals are the best way to find good contractors, so be sure to ask your business friends who they have used before.

Independent contractors pay their own taxes. This means that when you hire an independent contractor, you are only responsible for paying their fees, and it is their responsibility to report that income to the federal and state government. Any independent contractor you hire should typically receive a 1099 tax form at the end of the year, which reflects the amount you paid that contractor for their services. You will need to know the contractor's taxpayer identification number and mailing address to fill out the Form 1099, so it is recommended that each independent contractor provide you with a Form W-9 on which this information is recorded.

When hiring these individuals, you will want to have a contract that defines the following:

01 The scope of the services that they are providing

02 The length of the project

03 How much the independent contractor will be paid and when

04 Who will own any intellectual property created under the contract (see "Work for Hire" in chapter 7)

05 How either party may terminate the relationship

Employees

An employee is anyone who performs services for you, provided that you control the work and how it will be done. This aspect of control is what differentiates an employee from an independent contractor. Generally speaking, if you, as an employer, wish to have someone work for your sneaker business on a consistent basis, set their hours of work, dictate their job duties, tell them to come into the office, and provide them with the tools to do the job, you are dealing with an employee.

Hiring an employee is slightly more involved than hiring independent contractors. Employers are responsible for paying certain taxes and filling out specific forms. Here is a step-by-step guide on how to hire your first employee:

01 The Interview Process

You will most likely want to meet and interview the person you plan to hire. When conducting the interview, it is helpful to get an idea of whether they have the proper credentials for the job. Request a résumé, ask about their work experience, and what makes them qualified for the position. There are, however, more personal questions that are off limits. It is unlawful to ask about an applicant's age, sexual orientation, marital status, religious affiliation, or race. Questions pertaining to the nature of a physical, emotional, or mental handicap can only be asked if an applicant will need special accommodations for performing a specific job. For example, if you are hiring someone to work in the stockroom of your sneaker shop, it is fine to ask if they have any physical limitations that would prevent them from doing the job, and if so, what accommodations they might need. It is not okay to ask if they are pregnant or plan to get pregnant soon. There are many great online resources on how to conduct job interviews. It is considered an art form that takes time, so it is perfectly fine to seek help with this process. Both you and the interviewee will feel more comfortable if you are well prepared!

02 Reference Checks

If you like the candidate and plan to hire them, it might be wise to ask for references from past employers or if none, their trusted sources. Ask the candidate if they can provide you with two or three names of people whom they have worked for or with. Call or email those individuals and ask them what kind of employee and person the candidate is, whether they enjoyed working together, and if there is any reason why you should not hire the candidate. You will usually get decent feedback that can aid you in making a hiring decision.

03 Negotiate a Salary and Position

If you have decided you want to hire the candidate, he or she will need to know the most important part: how much will he or she get paid? If you have not discussed pay or salary during the interview, now would be the time to lay that out. Let the employee know if they will be hourly or salaried. Perhaps you want to give the employee a formal offer letter or contract. (See more on wages, hours, offer letters, and employment contracts in chapter 7.)

04 Record Keeping and Reporting

The candidate agrees to the job, signs the offer letter or contract (if applicable), and is ready to roll. Your work is done, right? Not yet! There are additional steps to formalizing the employee's hiring. This is sometimes referred to as onboarding. Part of the onboarding process will be filling out the appropriate paperwork. Mandatory filings include:

01 Notice of Pay Rate

Most states require that you provide each hourly nonexempt employee with a notice explaining their wages, including rate of pay (including overtime); how the employee is paid: by the hour, shift, day, week, commission, and so on; your regular payday; the employer's official name and any other names used for business; the address and phone number of the employer's main office or principal location; and any allowances taken as part of the minimum wage (tips, meal, and lodging deductions). Sample forms can usually be found on your state's Department of Labor website.

02 W-4 Form

This form should be filled out by the employee and contains all of their necessary federal tax withholding information. Downloadable at irs.gov.

03 I-9 Eligibility Form

This verifies the identity and employment authorization of individuals hired for employment in the United States. All US employers must properly complete Form I-9 for each individual they hire for employment in the United States. Downloadable at uscis.gov.

04 W-2 Form

This will be filled out by you or your accountant and reports the actual amount of wages and tax withholdings for each employee in a given year. The W-2 can be sent in either paper or digital form and must be received by employees no later than January 31 of the following year. Downloadable at irs.gov.

05 Proof of Workers' Compensation Insurance

This is insurance to protect from any on-the-job injuries. Consult with an insurance provider about what coverage is needed for your business and how it can be obtained.

There are many third-party employee payment and record-keeping services that can simplify the process of hiring and onboarding employees. These include ADP, Paychex, Quickbooks, Surepayroll, Gusto, Onpay, Square, Paylocity, and others. Do your research and find the best provider for your business and to help with your employee record-keeping and payroll requirements.

As this chapter has shown, knowing how to create a sneaker business and build a brand is essential to be successful and effectively operate in the sneaker industry. For example, imagine wanting to create a sneaker without knowing anything about entity formation, copyrights, trademarks, or hiring contractors and employees; the business would not fare well! Fortunately, you are now armed with all of the tools necessary to create your own sneaker business and build a brand. We can now move on to one of the dopest parts of sneaker creation: **design!**

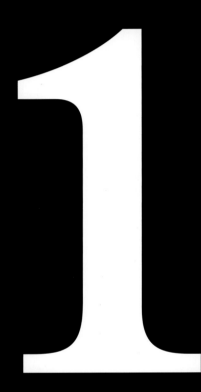

Design

"A basic design is always functional, but a great design will say something."

—*TINKER HATFIELD*

Design is the very foundation of the sneaker; it is the most critical step in the creation process. Before your favorite sneaker drops, and if you are lucky, winds up in your closet, it needs to be designed. A design is usually a plan or drawing produced to demonstrate the look, function, and workings of a product before it is made.

As you can imagine, many steps go into designing the perfect sneaker. The process typically begins with research, inspiration, ideation, and material acquisition. Some sneakers are purely functional, designed for comfort or performance, whereas others are truly works of art. Some have the perfect balance of both performance and aesthetics.

How does one identify a good sneaker design? What does a sneaker designer do? How does one become a sneaker designer, and who are some of the most influential sneaker designers in the world? Fortunately, we have answers to all these questions and more. So let's get into it!

What Makes a Good Sneaker Design?

Whether it's a simple, timeless sneaker design like the Nike Air Jordan 1, the adidas Stan Smith, the Converse Chuck Taylor, or something more obscure like the adidas Jeremy Scott Wings, the Louis Vuitton Archlight, or the Balenciaga Track, design can make or break a sneaker.

Good sneaker design plays to the shape, strength, and structure of the sneaker, not against it. Good sneaker design balances the right colorway and the perfect silhouette, while drawing on inspiration from a variety of current, futuristic, or historical references. Whatever it is, good sneaker design takes everything into account, before the sneaker is even made, to ensure one smooth, symbiotic experience and presentation when all is said and done.

Without a solid design, a sneaker is nothing.

What Does a Sneaker Designer Do?

Sneaker designers sit at the intersection of sneaker production and creativity. As you can imagine, designers do more than sketch ideas on pieces of paper. From the ideation stage all the way through the production of the sneaker, design is an in-depth process that involves a multitude of tasks. Some, but certainly not all, are below.

Knowing Styles and Trends versus Making Your Own Waves

Knowing the current landscape of the sneaker industry can play a huge part in the execution of a successful design. Some sneaker designs set the stage for a new era. However, it would be impossible to know what "setting the stage" means if the designer does not know current market demands and expectations. Sneaker designers need to be well acquainted with sneaker presentation and overall fashion styles and trends. This certainly does not mean that following trends will translate into a successful design. In fact, breaking away from the norm and creating new and innovative designs differentiates classic designs from average ones. Let's look at the dad shoe era. YEEZY and adidas rebirthed the dad shoe by creating the YEEZY Boost 700 Wave Runner. Following the creation of this revolutionary design, designers and brands took note and followed suit. Shortly after the Wave Runner dropped, the Balenciaga Triple S, Gucci Apollo, Fila Disruptor (for the basic ones out there), and many others followed. Even the Nike Monarch, an old dad shoe that originally released in the early 2000s, made a resurgence after the Wave Runner released. As you can see, coming up with the right design, at the right time, can be truly game changing.

Rough Design Drawings

In the early stages of sneaker design, designers usually translate their ideas into drawings and sketches. These drawings are generally rough and involve many drafts. In addition to drawing designs on paper, many designers use digital design programs to create elaborate 2D and 3D models. These programs enable designers to refine their sketches with ease.

Research and Development

Research and development, or R&D, is an essential part of the sneaker design process. The sneaker design needs to be thoroughly thought out, which is impossible without meticulous research and testing. R&D is important for performance, aesthetic, comfort, and even injury protection. Adequate functionality and design of a sneaker are in part the result of good R&D. It helps designers get their creative juices flowing. Part of the R&D process involves testing different samples of the sneaker. By doing this, designers and brands can improve its performance and functionality.

Sample Sneakers

The sample is another vital component of the sneaker design process. Samples, or prototypes, are early versions of sneakers and usually differ from the final product in terms of design, materials, and general construction. Samples are crucial for the overall production and creation of a sneaker—they help with performance, structure, fit, materials, design, and marketability. Generally, it takes several samples of a sneaker before the final version is achieved. After the final sample is complete, the sneaker can move to production, with all production pairs of the sneaker mimicking the features of the sample. Very few sneaker samples end up making it to production; most never end up releasing. As a result, some unreleased samples are highly coveted by sneakerheads and collectors and sell for incredibly high amounts on the secondary market. An unreleased colorway of Kanye West and Nike's Air Yeezy 1 that Ye wore during a Grammy performance in 2008 is said to have sold for $100,000.

Quality Control and Assurance

After all these steps have been taken, the sneaker undergoes quality control and assurance procedures. This final step in the design process ensures that the product accurately reflects the final design specifications. Quality control and assurance procedures also guarantee that the materials being used for the sneaker meet the designer and sneaker company's standards and prevent defects in the sneaker. Quality control is discussed in further detail in the "Manufacturing" section, but we raise it here because a good designer will stay involved in the entire sneaker manufacturing process to ensure that their vision is carried out from concept to product.

As a whole, to be an effective sneaker designer, an individual must have an eye for color, texture, and patterns, knowledge of foot anatomy, good drawing ability, skills with digital design programs, excellent communication skills, and a passion for fashion, styles, and trends.

Sneaker designers can be found in many places. Outside of the obvious, such as fashion houses, footwear brands that supply big chain stores, and catalog companies that specialize in sportswear, sneaker designers can come from anywhere. Tinker Hatfield went to the University of Oregon School of Architecture and was formally trained in design. Kanye West, the famous college dropout, on the other hand, never graduated from Chicago State and is not formally trained in design. Despite this, Tinker and Kanye are arguably equally successful in sneaker design. As long as one works hard at their craft and puts their mind to it, anyone can become a successful sneaker designer. In the next section, we will give you some suggestions on how you can achieve that goal.

How to Become a Sneaker Designer

If you have an interest in designing sneakers, know that the path is not easy, but with determination and hustle, it can be very rewarding. Sneaker companies are always looking for talented individuals with a passion for design and sneakers to create their next best pair of kicks. Although there is no formal blueprint for becoming a sneaker designer, there are many things you can start doing now to prepare yourself for a lucrative career in the sneaker business. No matter where you are located or what kind of style you love, if you start with the resources and information we provide here, we hope you too can one day create the next hottest sneaker design.

Attend a Notable Design School

Although some designers have taken less traditional routes, if you do not have a significant amount of experience or contacts, obtaining the credibility of a diploma in the field of art and design from a solid academic program is a wise idea. The right school and program can teach you the fundamentals of design and sneaker making. It can also help you land a coveted internship or postgraduate job at a sneaker or fashion brand.

If you decide you want a formal education in design, you will be pleased to know there are at least 200 art and design schools around the world. Each school has bachelor and advanced degree offerings, and although we cannot possibly cover all of them, in this section, we have listed, in alphabetical order, a selection of schools that have been consistently recognized on an international level and offer programs in sneaker or footwear design. Again, there is no one guaranteed path, so we list the schools only as a suggestion of how you can enhance your working knowledge of design through specific academic programs.

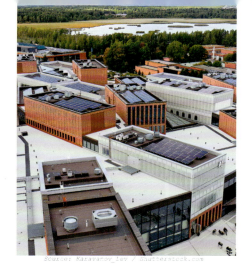

Aalto University (Finland)

Aalto University, based in Espoo, Finland and founded in 2010, is a relatively new multidisciplinary science and art school. The university has a school of arts, design, and architecture and offers a master's program in fashion, clothing, and textile design. The program prides itself on teaching students on a high artistic and professional level. Students can develop skills and a knowledge base that are useful in a career in fashion and sneaker design.

Central Saint Martins (United Kingdom)

Based in London and a constituent college of the University of Arts, London, Central Saint Martins is an internationally known arts and design school. Offering an assortment of courses in design, art, and performance, Central Saint Martins has a program dedicated to accessories, footwear, and jewelry. With respect to footwear, the school has several courses covering a range of topics, including shoe pattern cutting, shoe design, trend forecasting, production techniques, creative direction, drawing and rendering techniques, and much more.

Fashion Institute of Technology (United States)

The Fashion Institute of Technology (FIT), located in New York City, is a world-renowned college that specializes in fashion, design, art, business, and communications. FIT has an assortment of courses for students in the associate and graduate degree programs, and individuals exploring continuing and professional studies. FIT offers a program where students can obtain Associate in Applied Science (AAS) and Bachelor of Fine Arts (BFA) degrees in Footwear and Accessories Design. With nearly forty courses in the FIT program in total, ten focus solely on footwear. FIT also recently partnered with Complex on an online Sneakers Essentials program that covers topics such as manufacturing and production, distribution and retail, media, brand strategy, and marketing. Overall, FIT is an incredible place to learn about sneaker design and other areas of the sneaker business.

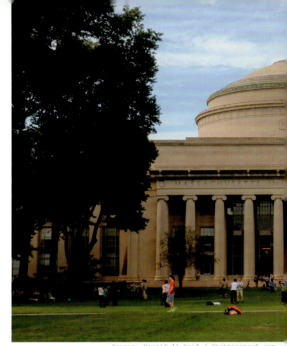
Source: Yousif Al Saif / Shutterstock.com

Source: eXpose / Shutterstock.com

The Hong Kong Polytechnic University (Hong Kong)

The Hong Kong Polytechnic University specializes in world-class research across many disciplines. The fashion design program boasts an exceptional curriculum in metallic textile design and development, integration of fashion design and wearable technology, interactive photonic textile design and development, ergonomics in design, high-performance sportswear, and most importantly, aesthetic and functional footwear.

DESIGN

Massachusetts Institute of Technology (United States)

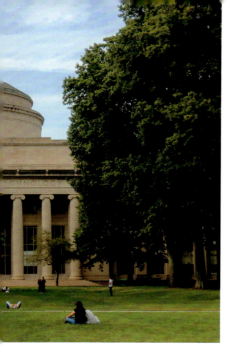

For those proficient enough to be accepted to the Massachusetts Institute of Technology (MIT), this prestigious institution will provide you with the best in academics. Known for its intense programs in science, engineering, and technology, MIT allows students to elect to take their program in art, culture, and technology, which offers undergraduate classes in public installation and media arts, and has a prominent master's program. Students can also cross-register and earn credits for visual arts classes at other well-known Boston-area institutions such as Harvard University, the Massachusetts College of Art and Design, and Wellesley College. MIT students can also access the Center for Art, Science, & Technology facilities, which make it incredibly easy to collaborate with other students and staff. In 2018, MIT partnered with Puma to perform extensive research in the field of biodesign, or using living materials such as algae or bacteria to create products. With this partnership, the two created biodegradable breathing sneakers that provide ventilation as the product organically decays over time, and deep learning insoles that improve an athlete's performance through real-time biofeedback. Science meets sneakers at the highest level!

Source: DW labs Incorporated / Shutterstock.com

Parsons (New School) School of Design (United States)

Located in New York City, the Parsons School of Design is considered by some as the best school in the world for art and design. Among its wide array of degree offerings is a robust fashion program with seven different focuses. Parsons offers several courses related to footwear and also has a shoemaking studio, where students can work on sneaker design and creation.

Source: Pensole

Source: DW labs Incorporated / Shutterstock.com

Pensole Academy (United States)

Pensole is a design academy based in Portland, Oregon and founded by Dr. D'Wayne Edwards, a longtime Nike and Jordan executive with more than thirty years of sneaker design experience. Specializing in sneakers and footwear, Pensole also focuses on functional apparel and accessories, concept making, color theory, prototyping, materials, and much more. Many sneaker designers learned the ins and outs of sneaker design at Pensole. Between 2010 and the publication of this book, Pensole helped secure close to 500 students with jobs at leading sneaker brands, including Nike, Jordan, adidas, YEEZY, Converse, Puma, Under Armour, and others. Pensole offers high school, college, and master-level courses. Overall, Pensole's highly specific and specialized training in sneakers makes it a distinguished school for learning how to design sneakers.

Politecnico di Milano (Italy)

Founded in 1863, the Politecnico di Milano is known worldwide for its engineering, architectural, and industrial design programs. In case you do not know, the Italian footwear industry is one of the pillars of the fashion system. Politecnico has campuses across Italy, an annual enrollment (at the time of this book's publication) of over 46,000 students, and boasts a 94 percent postgraduate employment rate. Many programs and courses are offered in English, making it a wonderful international school that welcomes talented students from all over the world. The school has recently partnered with SciLED (Science Led Shoe) to develop and teach new skills for the design of drastically improved comfort, sustainable, fashion-oriented, and scientifically led footwear products. The project aims to equip the footwear sector with updated high-level skills to create sustainable products, while making job openings more attractive for young people with modern curricula and innovative learning methods.

Pratt Institute (United States)

Located in Brooklyn, New York, Pratt Institute has a robust fashion and industrial design program that is known for placing designers in some of the world's leading fashion and sneaker brands including Nike. Pratt offers twenty-seven majors across four schools that cover art, design, architecture, and arts and sciences. Because of Pratt's proximity to many fashion houses, its students often receive coveted internships and gain critical hands-on experience at top brands before they graduate. The school has a studio class on footwear design, which teaches students how to design and construct a variety of footwear. Students who take this course learn the concepts of footwear design, develop skills for working with a last, and learn pattern making, sewing, construction, and techniques for creating closed shoes.

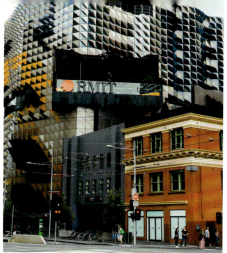

Rhode Island School of Design (United States)

Rhode Island School of Design (RISD) is one of the most famous art schools in the United States. RISD has concentrations in apparel and industrial design, sculpture, and just about any other visual medium that one can think of. In addition, students may cross-register for classes just over the hill at Brown University at no extra cost. As a result, RISD students have access to just about any art and art-related class of interest, which is probably why nearly 97 percent of graduates are employed within one year of graduation. Two relevant design classes offered by RISD are "Handcraft Your Own Sneakers," a two-day workshop offered through the continuing education department, and "Introduction to Basic Shoemaking," a studio offered by the school's apparel design and industrial design departments.

RMIT University (Australia)

Located in Melbourne, RMIT University (formerly known as Royal Melbourne Institute of Technology and Melbourne Technical College) specializes in technology and design and is Australia's largest higher learning institution. RMIT's fashion program features several courses that cover merchandising, marketing, textile development, and more. The school offers a certificate in custom-made footwear, which is the only certificate devoted to footwear in Australia. The certificate provides students with technical and practical skills that are needed to create custom footwear.

Royal College of Art (United Kingdom)

Based in London, the Royal College of Art is the world's only wholly postgraduate university for both art and design. The school offers a range of degree programs spanning art and design principles. Within the fashion degree program, you can specialize in footwear, accessories, and millinery (hat making). These specialties have dedicated workshops, where students can study traditional craftsmanship and work on designing their own products. In fact, the specialism works with adidas and several other leading fashion brands. This affords students with the opportunity to study the construction, aesthetic, and design of sneakers in depth. Additionally, students learn about and help develop new materials and techniques related to the design of sneakers. The Royal College of Art welcomes students from around the world to learn about all forms of art and design.

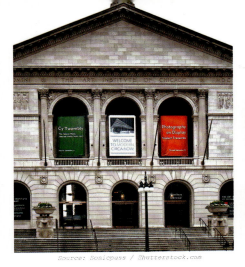
Source: Sonicpuss / Shutterstock.com

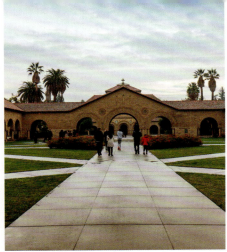
Source: Pnnchen / Shutterstock.com

Source: pxl.store / Shutterstock.com

School of the Art Institute of Chicago (United States)

The School of the Art Institute of Chicago is known for its superb curriculum in art and design. The Department of Fashion Design offers a bachelor's degree in fine arts in design pathways, a master's degree in fashion, body, and garment, and a post-baccalaureate certificate in fashion, body, and garment. Within the design program, the school offers courses in footwear design, where students can learn about footwear history, lifestyle, materials, processes, pattern making, experimental construction, samples, design illustrations, and more. Fun fact: Kanye got an honorary degree from the School of Art Institute of Chicago.

Stanford University (United States)

The Stanford Arts Institute, which opened in 2006 in sunny California, is a relatively new addition to the well-known Stanford University, founded in 1891 and (at the time of this book's publication) boasts 6,994 undergraduate and 9,390 graduate students. Stanford, unlike many typical American universities, prides itself on putting arts at the forefront of its academic offerings. The Hasso Plattner Institute of Design, dubbed the "d.school," is a rich, diverse, and collaborative program where virtually any idea can be brought to life in one of its many makerspaces across the campus. The d.school believes that a good design education starts with certain core abilities, including how to navigate ambiguity, learn from others, synthesize information, and experiment rapidly. Definitely a school and program worth checking out.

University of the Arts, London (UAL)

According to the QS World University Rankings, the University of the Arts, London is one of the top two universities in the world for art and design. The university offers thousands of courses in art and design and has its own college of fashion. Within this college, students can earn an MA in footwear. This master's-level program teaches students about the intricacies of footwear design. In particular, students are taught footwear creation, technical innovations, technical analysis and development, and much more. The UAL is a great starting point for a career in sneaker design.

University of Oregon (United States)

Just a short distance from both Nike and adidas's HQs, the University of Oregon offers a unique master of science program in sports product design. This program aims to prepare students to be chief members and leaders of multidisciplinary development teams within more than 800 sports product companies in Oregon and elsewhere. Additionally, the program educates students on different methodologies behind innovation, athletic performance, sports product marketing and branding, and sustainability. Students take a number of required studio product design courses coupled with strategic management electives to school them on the sportswear industry as a whole. Private corporate partners that have helped fund the program include Nike, adidas, Under Armour, Columbia Sportswear, Intel, Logitech Modo, Sigma Design, and others, making this program both enriching and practical.

Other Options

Now that you know some of the best schools where you can obtain an education geared toward sneaker design, what are some additional options for obtaining design experience and getting exposure as a designer?

Learn the Tools of the Trade

If you have not attended a design school or started learning how to design on your own, you need to become familiar with the tools that sneaker designers use to put their ideas on paper (or screen). Great design can start with just about anything, but if you want a brand to take you seriously and consider your designs for their next release, you will need certain tools to help you create, hone your craft, and put your best design foot forward.

The tools designers use vary widely. Some designers are old school and still prefer a pencil and a sketch pad, but today's sneaker artists who want to stand out employ new technologies that make the design process more efficient and effective. Designers can now sketch digitally, on their computer, tablet, or even phone, by using illustration programs and digital pencils. The gold standard for over thirty-five years now has been the Adobe suite, which includes Illustrator, Photoshop, InDesign, and other useful applications. The CorelDRAW Graphics Suite is another amazing program for digital creation and has just as many bells and whistles as Adobe. But both are costly and certainly not the only design programs on the block. If you are new to design and looking for cheaper options, there are many free or more inexpensive design software programs available to get you started. With a solid digital illustration program, you can easily bring intricate ideas to life, create multiple colorways or design variations with a click of a button, and be well on your way to building a professional portfolio.

If you want to really step up your design game and prepare your designs for ultimate sample creation (or prototyping), you will want to get proficient with 3D modeling programs as well. Even if you do not want to 3D print your design, understanding 3D modeling and creating a 3D rendering of your idea can be a massive timesaver when it comes to the design and manufacturing process. Many of today's top designers and design assistants turn to 3D computer-aided design (CAD) programs such as Adobe Dimension, Adobe Fuse, Blender, Autodesk Maya & 3d max, Sculpteo, Shoemaster, or ICad3D+ to create lifelike renders of the shoes that may one day make it to the assembly line. If this all seems like a lot, do not be discouraged; there are many wonderful tutorials, user-made videos, and other online resources available to get you started and become proficient with the 2D or 3D design software of your choosing.

Get an Internship

After you have gained a bit of design knowledge and started to independently hone your craft, you need to get on-the-job experience. Obtaining the right training and finding good career mentors can start with an internship (preferably a paid one, but even if it is unpaid, it can be worth it). Landing a decent design internship at a sneaker company can be difficult, especially if you do not have many connections in the business. However, solid design experience can be acquired through many other businesses, too. Many of the famous designers that we will discuss later in this chapter got their start designing things other than sneakers, such as cars, clothes, and houses, and working in other mediums such as music, metals, and plastics. Do not be discouraged if your first practical experience is not obtained by working on sneakers. Design is everywhere! An internship with any kind of product designers or other creative individuals may help you develop a unique perspective that you can bring to the world of sneakers. If you do not know much about the opportunity you might be applying for, look into things such as how big the studio is and their quality of work. Do everything you can to be useful once you are in the door. Be a sponge and soak up as much information as possible. When the internship is over, find a way to combine what you have learned and the background you have attained in life and apply those to your love for sneakers.

Network

When it comes to getting any design experience, whether a mentorship, internship, freelance, or full-time position, networking is key. We cannot stress this enough. Many designers were able to get their start in sneakers because they knew someone influential in the game who was willing to give them a shot or introduce them to someone else willing to do the same. Find these people, make connections, and figure out how you can be helpful to them. You can start by getting on their radar and just letting them know that you are interested in learning more about them. Informational interviews can be a great and nonthreatening way to connect with someone you admire without making them feel uncomfortable or that you only want a job. Sometimes relationships can take years to cultivate, and you may find yourself trying to chase down a contact who never seems to want to help you out at all. Do not be discouraged. Keep pushing and find other ways to break that door down. Get noticed by standing out in other ways, which we will cover in the following section.

Here is an example of networking, although not directly applicable to sneaker design, you may find useful. The authors of this book, Kenneth and Jared, met as a result of one reaching out to the other on LinkedIn. At the time, Jared was a legal intern at Complex, writing unique articles about legal issues in the sneaker industry. Kenneth, then a partner at a New York City law firm, was researching legal issues in the sneaker industry, saw Jared's articles, and was excited to learn that someone else in the legal field shared his passion for sneakers. Kenneth looked on LinkedIn and discovered that Jared was also living in New York City, attending Brooklyn Law School, the same law school Kenneth attended. Kenneth messaged Jared to see if he wanted to link up one day. The two met for coffee and started concepting a way to bring their knowledge and love for sneakers to people who wanted to learn more about the business. A few months later, the idea for *Sneaker Law* was born. The two would talk and text every day, whether it was an idea for the book or a new sneaker release (many kicks were copped and Ls were taken as well). Over time, Kenneth and Jared became very close friends, worked tirelessly to finish writing this book, and are now co-authors of *Sneaker Law*. Long story short, without networking, this book (and a great friendship) would not exist, so get out there and start networking today!

NOV 15, 2016

Kenneth Anand · 1:12 PM

Hey Jared - read your Complex articles. Nice to see you reporting on the legal aspects of footwear design/protection. Just reaching out as a BLS alum/lawyer/sneakerhead. I've represented a number of footwear designers. Let's link up sometime.

- Kenneth

Jared Goldstein, Esq. · 1:17 PM

Hey Kenneth,

Thanks for reaching out. It's always great to meet a fellow legal sneakerhead! I would love to link - are you free this Thursday for lunch or coffee? I have a meeting at 3:00 and free any time before then.

-Jared

Build Your Portfolio

One of the most effective ways to get noticed is to build your portfolio. It is never too early or too late to build your design portfolio. This is something accomplished designers still do, even late into their careers. A good portfolio is like a designer's résumé or business card. The primary way a potential employer or contractor can evaluate and hire you is based on your experience and portfolio, so it is important to show what you have worked on, even if it is independent work and you did not make any money from it. Show your passion to the world and start getting recognition for it today.

You can build your portfolio the traditional way, by printing your designs and making a book that you can showcase when interviewing for potential jobs. But with today's competition in a booming sneaker industry, getting your work seen in person by the right people can be challenging. Sneaker job opportunities are highly competitive as well, so you will need to find other ways to reach your targets. One great way to get exposure is to start a social media page highlighting your design work. Several designers have been discovered on Instagram, for example. They built a network and found real design work in the industry just by posting their unique designs, colorway concepts of existing kicks, design inspiration ideas, and other images relevant to sneaker design. These ambitious and creative individuals built a virtual mood board to attract a community of like-minded people and other excited followers who love and appreciate their work. Some have done it overnight with the right and timely concept, hashtag, or other viral content. Other designers have beautiful, engaging websites, blogs, or vlogs where you can see and explore their design work. In short, there is no right way to build or showcase your portfolio, reach your audience, and get noticed by decision makers in the sneaker business. Whatever you do, start doing it now!

Famous Sneaker Designers You Should Know

Now that we've learned the steps to becoming a successful designer, let's take a look at some of the most influential designers in the sneaker game. As you will see, each designer took their own unique path; there is no single, clear-cut way to becoming a sneaker designer. But with the right practice, hustle, drive, and networking, you can make it.

We fully acknowledge the challenge of creating a comprehensive list of sneaker designers, given just how many individuals have donated their time, energy, and creative vision to the culture of sneakers over the past few decades. With that being said, there are several designers that we believe every up-and-coming sneaker designer should know. We have them listed here in alphabetical order.

Virgil Abloh
(Off-White, Nike, Louis Vuitton)

"VIRGIL," arguably one of the hottest designers in the decade from 2010–2020, is the founder and creative director of Off-White and the artistic director for Louis Vuitton menswear. Born in Chicago, Virgil had a knack for design at a young age. In 2002, he graduated from the University of Wisconsin–Madison, where he received an undergraduate degree in civil engineering. Instead of taking in graduation day like students typically do, Virgil attended a meeting with John Monopoly, Kanye West's then-manager. This proved to be a pivotal choice in his life. Shortly after, Virgil began working with Kanye, and an unbreakable friendship and insurmountable working relationship was born.

In 2006, Virgil continued his design education by obtaining a master's degree in architecture from the Illinois Institute of Technology. A few years later, Virgil and Kanye interned together at Fendi in Rome. Yes, you heard that right: Ye and Virgil were interns together. That is how seriously they took design and how badly they wanted to become successful in fashion and sneakers. In 2010, Virgil became the creative director at Donda, Kanye's creative agency. A couple of years later, Virgil created Pyrex Vision, a streetwear brand, which was his first fashion company. In 2013, he launched his own brand, Off-White. To this day, Off-White is popping and one of the most famous luxury fashion brands in the world. After Virgil showed the world his unique design talents, Louis Vuitton took notice and named him the artistic director of Louis Vuitton menswear in 2018. This was a monumental moment: Virgil was the first African American designer at Louis Vuitton, one of the most historical luxury brands in the world.

In his roles at Off-White and Louis Vuitton, Virgil has designed an assortment of sneakers for both brands. However, it was Virgil and Off-White's celebrated collaborations with Nike that cemented Virgil's place on the Mount Rushmore of sneaker designers. In 2017, Virgil and Nike unveiled their collaboration, dubbed The Ten. As mentioned in chapter 1, The Ten featured a collection of ten classic Nike, Jordan, and Converse sneakers with Virgil's deconstruction and redesign of the silhouettes. The sneakers in the collection include the Air Jordan 1, Air Force 1, Air Max 90, Air Max 97, Presto, Blazer, and Converse Chuck Taylor. Virgil and Nike went on to release many different colorways of The Ten and additional sneakers outside the collection. As Virgil and Nike continue to collaborate, sneakerheads remain on the edge of their seats in anticipation.

Source: Nike

Source: FashionStock.com / Shutterstock.com

Yoon Ahn/Ambush
(Reebok, Nike, Converse, Dior)

Yoon Ahn is a Korean-born designer who was raised in Seattle, graduated from Boston University, and moved to Tokyo in 2003. Ahn got her start designing jewelry, such as chains and rings, for her rapper husband, Verbal. In 2007, Yoon and Verbal launched their own fashion brand, Ambush, creating clothing and jewelry worn by countless musicians, celebrities, and other fashion influencers. In 2012, Ambush and Reebok teamed up on an ultra shiny silver and, in 2013, a blue-and-red version of the Pump Fury HLS.

In 2019, Ambush was busy in the world of sneakers. Ahn and Verbal's brand collaborated with Nike on an Air Max 180 and with Converse for a futuristic take on the Chuck 70 and Pro Leather silhouettes. The next year was no different, as Ambush collaborated again with Converse on a duck boot and Nike on a Dunk High. Sticking to her roots, Ahn is currently heading up jewelry design at Dior Homme ("that's Dior Homme, not Dior Homie"), but if the last two years are any indication of what is to come for Ahn and Ambush in the world of sneakers, we should expect many more exciting collabs.

Tiffany Beers
(Nike)

Known as Nike's "mad scientist," Beers got her start in plastics engineering, earning her bachelor of science from Penn State. She first worked at Rubbermaid, designing, developing, and testing consumer products. In 2004, Beers brought her talent and knowledge to Oregon, where she joined Nike and, over the next two years, helped develop the company's famous air-cushioning systems. In 2005, Beers moved to Nike's Innovation Kitchen (aptly named after the place where, in 1971, Nike co-founder Bill Bowerman created a revolutionary rubber outsole by pouring urethane into his waffle iron). In the Innovation Kitchen and its offshoot, the Pantry, Beers helped with the prototyping and full-cycle development of many famous Nike shoes, including Tinker Hatfield's Air Mag, Kanye West's Air Yeezy, Tom Sachs's collection, and the Kobe 6. In 2012, Beers was promoted to senior innovator and innovation director, becoming Hatfield's chosen director and developer for all his designs. In this five-year stint, Beers developed many more shoes, including the 2016 iteration of the Air Mag and the Hyperadapt 1.0 auto-lace sneaker. Over her fifteen-year career at Nike, Beers has earned over forty patents for footwear innovations, a truly remarkable feat and testament to her genius in footwear. She now works in San Francisco and is head of gaming innovation and audio engineering for Logitech and Astro Gaming.

Source: Tiffany Beers

Source: Stadium Goods

Salehe Bembury
(Cole Haan, Greats, YEEZY, Versace, New Balance, Anta)

Like many New York designers, Salehe Bembury grew up infatuated with sneakers. But from his earliest sneaker sketches at age ten, it was clear that he was more than just a consumer. Salehe majored in industrial design at Syracuse University and got his first job at Payless, which he credits for giving him a broad perspective into a variety of shoe designs. He got his first major break designing for Cole Haan, a traditional menswear company that made waves when it started bringing comfort and sneaker technology to its traditional formal shoe line. From there, he moved to designing footwear for the function-meets-fashion startup Greats. Not long after, Salehe's passion and drive landed him a role as a men's footwear designer at YEEZY in the midst of Kanye's season 3 and 4 fashion shows. From there, he became Versace's head of footwear design, and in 2018, Salehe designed the Chain Reaction: a chunky-yet-sleek ultra-luxe silhouette that proudly displays the Versace brand heritage with some of the most impressive patterns and colorways ever seen on a sneaker. Salehe's arsenal of design collabs also include sneakers with New Balance and Anta. Anyone who has studied Salehe's work and rapid impact on the game can see that the best is surely yet to come from this talented young designer.

Don C
(Nike, Converse, Louis Vuitton)

Chicago-born Don Crawley, better known as Don C, is more than a sneaker designer, he is a fashion icon and founder of the luxury clothing brand, Just Don. Don was the manager and DJ for Kanye West who, in 2011, began sporting Don's custom made, python s k i n brim snapbacks that immediately went viral. Ever since, Don started channeling his love for fashion and sneakers into a lucrative career. Don has created some incredible sneaker designs over the years, most notably the Just Don x Air Jordan 2, an upscale rendition of the retro sneaker that was first produced by Nike in Italy back in 1986. Although the Jordan 2 would rerelease several times, it would not reach its newfound level of popularity until Don put his attention to detail and luxury stamp on the sneaker. In addition to collaborating on sneakers with Converse and Louis Vuitton, Don designed his own signature sneaker with Jordan Brand—the Just Don x Jordan Legacy 312, named after Don's Chicago hometown area code.

Source: Nike

Source: Stadium Goods

Nike Doernbecher Designs by Children (Nike, Jordan)

Every year since 2003, Nike has partnered with the Oregon Health & Science University (OHSU) Doernbecher Children's Hospital in choosing children to design select Nike and Jordan sneakers. The program, called Doernbecher Freestyle, gives children the ability to use their imaginations and incorporate their own colorways, themes, and features into their chosen Nike sneaker. All proceeds from the sneakers are donated to the children's hospital, and through this program, Nike has raised approximately $24 million. Each year, sneakerheads wait with excitement to see what the kids cooked up. The children never disappoint—some of the most coveted Nike and Jordan sneakers are Doernbecher editions. This partnership benefits sneakerheads, children, and a truly amazing cause alike.

Source: Nike

Source: Stadium Goods

Dr. D'wayne Edwards (Jordan)

Dr. D'wayne Edwards has over thirty years of experience in sneaker design, but he never went to college or design school. As a child, Edwards constantly drew sneakers. He entered a Reebok design competition at the age of seventeen. He won but was not old enough to be hired. Edwards stayed on his grind and—fast forward six years later—became the head designer at LA Gear. Years later, Edwards became design director at Jordan Brand, where he became one of six designers to ever design an Air Jordan. (He designed the Air Jordan 21 and 22.) In 2010, Edwards left the Jordan Brand and pivoted to another side of the sneaker industry. Edwards's nontraditional path propelled him to create Pensole, the sneaker design academy, where he and his team do incredible work educating the sneaker designers of tomorrow.

Source: Pensole & Dr. D'Wayne Edwards

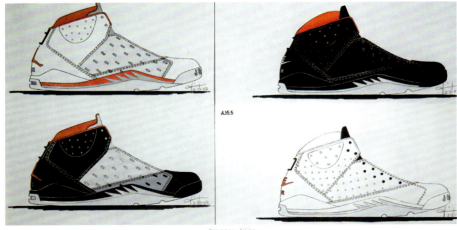

Source: Nike

Ronnie Fieg
(adidas, Nike, Converse, ASICS, New Balance, Vans, Diadora, BAPE, Puma, Filling Pieces, Buscemi, Del Toro, Versace)

The title says it all: Ronnie Fieg is an OG in the sneaker game and has designed with pretty much every major brand. Growing up, Fieg was always a sneakerhead. When he was thirteen, he worked at his second cousin's sneaker store, where he learned the ropes of the sneaker business, becoming head buyer when he was twenty-five. In 2006, a short time after, ASICS reached out to Fieg and the two collaborated on the Gel Lyte III. Today, Fieg has collaborated with ASICS over fifty times. Whew. One of Fieg's biggest accomplishments is founding KITH in 2011. KITH, one of the flyest retail establishments in the world, is its own multifunctional lifestyle brand for men, women, and kids and offers sneakers, clothing, and other creative products, even delicious cereal treats! On the sneaker front, Fieg and KITH have collab'ed and designed a myriad of sneakers for adidas, Nike, Converse, ASICS, New Balance, Vans, Diadora, BAPE, Puma, Filling Pieces, Buscemi, Del Toro, and Versace. We hope we didn't miss any!

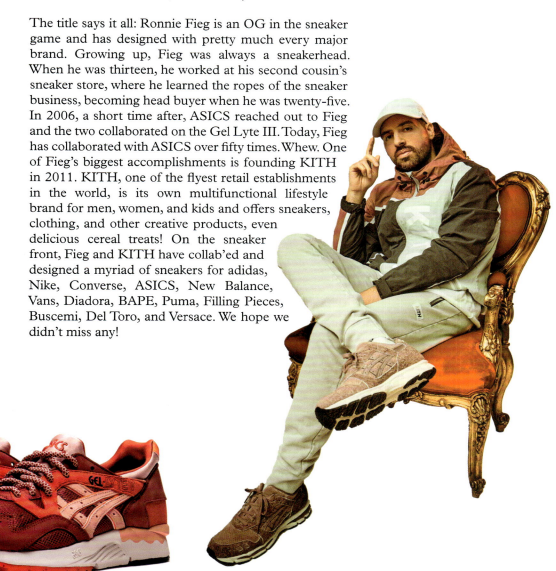

Source: Stadium Goods

Source: Andrew Boyle

Source: Stadium Goods

Hiroshi Fujiwara
(Fragment, Nike, Louis Vuitton, Converse, Visvim)

Commonly referred to as the godfather of streetwear, a moniker not handed out to just anyone, Hiroshi Fujiwara has been transforming fashion and design for over thirty years. He is a true OG and legend in the sneaker space or just space in general. Fujiwara laid down the blueprint for people like Kanye West and Pharrell on how to master multiple creative and commercially successful disciplines, including music, contemporary fashion, design, and pretty much anything else he touches. One could write an entire book (and people have) on the history of Fujiwara, including his roots in the 1980s Japanese hip-hop scene; literally birthing the Harajuku fashion district and movement; mentor to Nigo (BAPE, Human Made); early Takashi Murakami collaborator; design partner with Nike design guru Tinker Hatfield and CEO Mark Parker...His accomplishments go on and on. In the sneaker world, Fujiwara is perhaps best known for his brand Fragment Design and the highly coveted collaborations it has done over the years with Nike (Air Jordan, Air Force, Air Max, Nike Lab, Nike Clot Tennis, Running, etc.), Converse, Visvim, and Moncler, just to name a few.

Source: Nike

Tinker Hatfield
(Nike, Jordan)

One of the greatest sneaker designers of all time, Tinker Hatfield has designed countless legendary sneakers for Nike and Jordan, including every Air Jordan from the III to the XV, the Air Max 1, Air Max 90, and the Mag. In 1977, Tinker graduated from the University of Oregon School of Architecture with a bachelor's degree in architecture. In 1981, Tinker joined Nike to design retail, offices, and apparel showrooms. In 1985, he changed departments and began his career in sneaker design. In 1987, he designed the iconic Air Max 1.

A few years later, Tinker began designing for Air Jordan and went on to create the legendary Air Jordan III. From there, he designed an assortment of illustrious sneakers that shifted the paradigm for sneaker culture. His notable silhouettes include the Air Max 90, Air Jordan V, Air Jordan VI, Air Jordan XI, Air Jordan XIII, Mag, and many others. Currently, Tinker continues to design sneakers for Nike and the Jordan Brand, and the sneaker community still gets hyped every time a new Tinker sneaker drops.

Source: Nike

Source: Nike

Source: Nike

Stephanie Howard
(Nike, New Balance, Reebok, Converse, Vans)

Stephanie has over twenty-five years of experience including as a Design Director at Nike and Lead Designer at New Balance. Stephanie has designed over one hundred products that have been in the market, has multiple design and utility patents, and has worked with brands including Nike, New Balance, Reebok, Bauer, Converse, The North Face, Vans, Timberland, Titleist, Tracksmith, Smartwool, and Xtratuf. In the sneaker world, she's best known as the designer of the New Balance 850, which originally launched in 1996 and was re-released in 2019. At Nike, she led the first women-specific running footwear design initiative in the early 2000s. Stephanie currently is the founder of HOW AND WHY, an award-winning consulting studio, working on visual brand language, product design, and innovation strategy for leading brands and startups.

Source: Stephanie Howard

Source: New Balance

Jerry Lorenzo
(Fear of God, Nike)

Jerry Lorenzo is the founder of Fear of God, a luxury streetwear brand that launched in 2013. Lorenzo received his undergraduate degree at Florida A&M University and later obtained an MBA from Loyola Marymount. Although Lorenzo did not have a formal background or education in fashion or design, he was eager to learn and wanted to find a way to enter into the industry. He reached out to Jon Buscemi, a luxury sneaker designer and friend. Buscemi connected Lorenzo with a developer in Italy, who taught him how to design. After a year and a half of learning, Lorenzo released a sneaker he designed himself.

Since then, Lorenzo has released many different sneakers with Fear of God and had many notable collaborations. These include collabs with Nike, Vans, and Converse. Lorenzo's collaboration with Nike is arguably his most popular. The Nike x Fear of God line includes the Air Fear of God 1 (his signature sneaker), Air Raid, Moccasin, and Air Skylon II.

Lorenzo's talents and design aesthetic have garnered notice and admiration from the likes of Kanye West and Virgil Abloh (both of whom Lorenzo has worked with), Alessandro Michelle, and many others.

Source: Jerry Lorenzo

Source: Stadium Goods

Sergio Lozano
(Nike)

Lozano, who started with Nike in the early 1990s, is best known for his design work on the Air Max 95, one of the most iconic running sneakers of all time. Before his disruptive and brand minimalistic design won the hearts of fashion and running enthusiasts alike, Lozano worked on Nike's All Conditions Gear (ACG) line. During his tenure at Nike, Lozano had the good fortune of working alongside Tinker Hatfield, and Lozano often credits Hatfield as a mentor and influencer. Hatfield challenged Lozano to think about his personal journey and incorporate those unique sentiments into his designs. Since its release in 1995, the Air Max 95 has been retro'ed countless times and reproduced in scores of colorways, proving it remains a timeless athletic and fashion staple. Since its creation, other notable brands and designers have brought their own creative take on Lozano's design, including Supreme, Riccardo Tisci, Commes des Garçons, Joshua Franklin aka Stash, Atmos, and Piet Parra.

Source: Stadium Goods

Source: Nike

Cynthia Lu
(Cactus Plant, Nike)

Cynthia Lu is the founder of Cactus Plant Flea Market (CPFM), the innovative and world-famous streetwear brand. Lu started her career in fashion as an intern at Complex. Subsequently, Lu worked with Pharrell at Billionaire Girls Club and, later on, at i am OTHER. Lu went on to become Pharrell's personal assistant and close friend. Lu and CPFM are known for a DIY and avant-garde design and have collaborated with some of the biggest stars and brands in the game, including Pharrell, Kid Cudi, Kanye West, Lil Wayne, Human Made, Comme des Garçons, and Stüssy. CPFM even collab'ed with The Rolling Stones—how cool is that? Notably, Lu and CPFM collaborated with Nike on several highly anticipated collections of clothing and sneakers. Sneakers that came out of these collections include the Vapormax, Air Force 1, and Blazer. It is always exciting to see what Lu and CPFM cook up next.

Source: Nike

Source: Nike

Source: Nike

Aleali May
(Jordan)

Aleali May is a stylist, model, influencer, and sneaker designer. May always had a propensity to work in the fashion industry. In 2010, she worked part time at a Louis Vuitton store in Chicago. Later on, she worked at RSVP Gallery, the conceptual retail store and brainchild of Don C and Virgil Abloh. As time went on, May acquired an enormous following on social media, and people recognized her eclectic taste and influence in fashion and style. In fact, in 2016, May caught the attention of Franke Cooke, a former designer for Jordan Brand. This led to several meetings at Nike HQ in Portland, where Jordan Brand subsequently signed May to a sneaker deal. The deal made May the second woman to ever design for Jordan Brand and, later on, the first woman designer to ever design a unisex Jordan sneaker (the Jordan 1 Aleali May Shadow). Currently, May has collaborated with Jordan Brand on three fire sneakers, two Jordan 1s and one Jordan 6. It looks like May is just getting started, and we are sure sneakerheads cannot wait for her next sneaker to drop.

Source: Nike

Source: Stadium Goods

Mark Miner
(adidas, Salomon, YEEZY, Nike)

Mark Miner, former senior designer at Nike and current vice president and creative director at adidas, boasts an impressive design résumé. At Nike, Miner was credited with designing many of the brand's high-performance running sneakers, including the Nike Free Run. Miner, who studied fine art at Parsons School of Design, is most known for making high-tech performance sneakers that mimic the feel, structure, and contour of the bare foot. We discuss Mark in depth in chapter 7, as he and two colleagues made headlines when Nike sued them and their new employer, adidas, for allegedly breaching certain restrictive covenants and "poaching" the talented designers. The controversy makes clear that Miner is highly sought after and has made a real impact on the world of sneaker design.

Nigo
(BAPE, BBC, Ice Cream, adidas)

Tomoaki Nagao, nicknamed Nigo by the famous Japanese artist and godfather of streetwear Hiroshi Fujiwara, is best known for starting the fashion brand A Bathing Ape (BAPE). Like several other accomplished sneaker designers on our list, Nigo has a background in music production and was a DJ for the Japanese rap group Teriyaki Boyz. Nigo and BAPE have a long and rich history in sneakers. Although BAPE was founded in 1993, it did not release its first sneaker, the Bapesta, until 2002. The Bapesta was an instant hit and collector's item among sneakerheads everywhere, with its Nike Air Force 1-like silhouette, bright colorways, and lightning bolt-turned-star logo emblazoned on the side. Nigo was also a significant creative influence on musician Pharrell; the two partnered on the Billionaire Boys Club and Ice Cream brands and designed many more unique and coveted sneakers together. Created in 2014, Nigo currently runs the fashion label Human Made, where he has collaborated with adidas on several sneakers. Additionally, Nigo has collaborated and designed with many others including Kanye West, Ronnie Fieg, adidas, Daft Punk, Marvel Comics, and even SpongeBob SquarePants.

Source: Everett Collection / Shutterstock.com

Source: Stadium Goods

Rick Owens
(Rick Owens, adidas)

Rick Owens, best known for his gothic style of design, is the founder of his eponymous high-end fashion company. Owens attended the Otis College of Art and Design but dropped out before graduating. Shortly thereafter, he took a pattern-cutting course at the Los Angeles Trade Technical College. Before entering into sneaker design, Owens gained a wealth of fashion design experience by working with his own label in addition to other fashion brands. In 2006, Owens released the Dustulator Dunk, which was his first sneaker. Owens released many different silhouettes thereafter, but a fan favorite is the Geobasket, which launched in 2008. In 2013, Owens and adidas unveiled the first of many sneaker collaborations together. Overall, Owens has left his mark on sneaker culture, and his silhouettes are highly regarded and influential.

Jason Petrie
(Lebron, Nike)

Jason Petrie has an impressive résumé designing sneakers for Nike, specifically the LeBron James signature line. Petrie took a unique path to becoming a designer. While attending North Carolina State, Petrie interned at Converse. After working on his design skills at Converse, he began sketching sneakers on his own time. He would post his work on NikeTalk, the OG online sneaker forum (the real ones know about #NikeTalkDenim), and garnered a lot of attention. In fact, Petrie got so much love that Fila reached out and hired him to design sneakers in Italy for two years. Shortly thereafter, Petrie left Fila for Nike, where he designed many sneakers for Nike Basketball. In 2009, Petrie took over LeBron James's signature line as head designer, a title that he holds as of the publication date of this book. As a result, Petrie has designed every signature LeBron model from the LeBron 7 on.

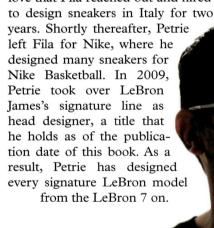

Source: Nike

Source: Nike

Raf Simons
(ASICS, adidas Originals, Raf Simons)

Please don't step on my Rafs! Raf Simons has been in the fashion game since 1995, when he created his own eponymous and critically acclaimed clothing label. As the decades of his career and label progressed, he also began designing for storied fashion brands such as Jil Sander, Dior, and Calvin Klein. In 2009, Raf collaborated with ASICS on the Technical Trainer. In 2013, he made sneaker waves when he redesigned the iconic adidas Stan Smith, paying homage to its classic silhouette but adding signature elements that made the sneaker literally fly off shelves upon release. His relationship with adidas blossomed, and the two released some iconic kicks, including the Ozweego, Stan Smith Strap, Micropacer Stan Smith, Response Trail, and Detroit Runner.

Source: FashionStock.com / Shutterstock.com

Source: Stadium Goods

Steven Smith
(New Balance, Reebok, Nike, YEEZY, etc.)

Known by many as the Godfather of the Dad Shoe or simply STVNSMTH, Smith has been designing some of the most fire chunky kicks since the 1980s. Nike, adidas, New Balance, and Reebok are just some of the companies that you will find on Smith's impressive kick design résumé. His notable sneaker creations include the Nike Air Streak Spectrum Plus, Reebok Instapump Fury, and the New Balance 1500, 574, and 997 models. Smith credits his creative process to a hybrid of engineering and artistic sensibilities, carefully balancing the opposites of logic and art. These days, Smith is enjoying a welcomed revival of the dad shoe trend. He works in Calabasas and Wyoming alongside Christian genius billionaire Kanye West. With West, Smith has contributed to many of the YEEZY brand's latest and most groundbreaking sneaker designs, including the 700 Wave Runner, 500, and eco-friendly Foam Runner. Knowing his work ethic and design process, one can only imagine the countless wild sneaker sketches and samples Smith has created for YEEZY that will never release, while we anxiously await the ones that will.

Source: Steven Smith

Source: Reebok

Source: Stadium Goods

Christian Tresser
(Nike, Reebok, adidas/YEEZY)

Christian Tresser has designed many classic sneakers for Nike, adidas, and Reebok. Tresser attended the Academy of Arts in San Francisco, where he developed his skills in design. His first big design gig was with Reebok, where he designed the Aztrek and DMX Daytona Runner. Shortly thereafter, Tresser joined the design team at Nike and designed the iconic Air Max 97. Most recently, he teamed up with YEEZY and adidas, where he helped design the 700 MNVN. We can't wait to see what Tresser cooks up next.

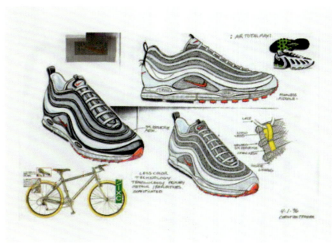

Kanye West (YEEZY, adidas, Nike, Louis Vuitton, BAPE)

Kanye West is more than a fashion and culture icon, producer, rapper, and devout Christian. He is a sneaker god. Aside from his influence on modern-day fashion and his lucrative hip-hop discography, which includes twenty-one GRAMMY Awards, in recent years, Kanye has transformed his passion for design into a billion-dollar empire with his YEEZY x adidas collaboration.

Nothing Kanye does is ever conventional, so it is no surprise that his path to design success followed that credo. Way before his global YEEZY partnership was solidified, Kanye was making fashion and sneaker waves with the individualistic style he brought to each musical project, beginning in 2004 with The College Dropout. In 2007, shortly after his second album, Late Registration, dropped, Kanye collaborated with Japanese streetwear brand BAPE and Nigo to release the College Dropout Bapesta. That same year, as mentioned, he took an internship at Fendi with his longtime friend and creative partner, Virgil Abloh. According to Kanye, the two didn't do much there: "We interned at Fendi, but we ain't do sh*t. We ain't get to do nothing. We were just happy to have a key card." Notwithstanding, we are pretty sure Kanye and Virgil soaked up some serious vibes.

Source: DKSStyle / Shutterstock.com

Source: Nike

After the infamous internship, Kanye worked with Balmain and Giuseppe Zanotti, where, according to him, he designed, but never received credit for, two of their popular high-top sneaker styles. In 2008, Kanye began working with Louis Vuitton, where he created the Jasper, Don, and Mr. Hudson styles (released in 2009).

During the same period, Kanye collaborated with Nike, and in April 2009, Nike released the famous Kanye-designed Air Yeezy. The Air Yeezy 2 would drop in 2011, after which Kanye tried to renegotiate his deal with Nike. In an interview, he said he ultimately left Nike because they were unwilling to pay him royalties for the sale of his own sneaker. Today, Kanye is the owner and creative director of YEEZY, collaborating exclusively with adidas for the YEEZY sneaker, boot, slide, and foam runner releases. The marriage between Kanye and adidas began in 2013 and was further solidified in 2016 in what adidas publicly called "the most significant partnership between a nonathlete and a sports brand." According to a Forbes article, as of 2019, the YEEZY brand had generated $1.5 billion in sales and was expected to keep growing. Less than one year later, in an interview with GQ, Kanye stated that YEEZY was worth $4 billion.

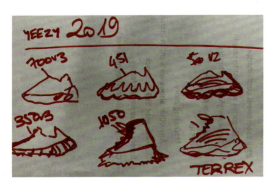

Source: Kanye West Twitter

Pharrell Williams (BAPE, BBC, Ice Cream, adidas, Nike, Chanel)

Very few contemporary designers can hold a candle to the creative résumé of Pharrell Williams. Pharrell is without a doubt an artistic savant, or as he likes to say, he is "OTHER." Pharrell has publicly discussed synesthesia, or his ability to "see sounds," as a creative influence in his design work, which is a mind-blowing ability. We could go on at length about Pharrell's impressive collaborative fashion design work across the apparel and accessories categories, not to mention his music production, songwriting, singing, rapping, and other live performance achievements. Speaking sneakers only, Pharrell for sure ranks up there with the top designers of the world and has more than paid his dues.

Many do not realize that Pharrell has been heavy in the sneaker game since the early 2000s. Long before Pharrell teamed up with adidas for his worldly and colorful Human Ultimatum (Hu) line (NMD, Trail, Solar Glide, Tennis, and Crazy BYW), Pharrell was heavily influenced by Japanese fashion and culture. During his early travels with his hip-hop band N.E.R.D., Pharrell became friends with Nigo. Pharrell brought back a lot of the style and influence he experienced on his travels with Nigo, including his Japanese brand, BAPE. Pharrell teamed up with Nigo and BAPE on several sneaker collabs before ultimately opening their own immediately successful streetwear brands, Billionaire Boys Club (BBC) and Ice Cream. Both carried a variety of colorful branded kicks and collabs. Pharrell continued to bubble in the fashion subculture over the years, and in 2011, he partnered with Jay-Z to grow the distribution and licensing arm of the BBC label, but it would not be until 2014, when Pharrell donned the famous Vivienne Westwood Mountain Hat during the Fifty-Sixth Grammy Awards, that he would be internationally recognized as a fashion force. Shortly after, Pharrell partnered with adidas on the aforementioned Hu line, and the rest is and will be sneaker history.

Source: Stadium Goods

Source: Parisa Michelle / Shutterstock.com

Sean Wotherspoon
(Nike, adidas, ASICS)

Sean Wotherspoon is most famously known for designing the Nike Air Max 1/97 "Sean Wotherspoon." He got the opportunity to design the silhouette after winning Nike's 2017 Vote Forward competition with his multicolored corduroy design. His work on the silhouette was celebrated across the sneaker community, and the sneaker instantly became a classic. Before designing the Air Max 1/97, Wotherspoon did not have a history in sneaker design. Instead, he was a sneaker collector and one of the founders of Round Two, a sneaker and fashion resale store with multiple locations across the United States. Wotherspoon is now partnering with adidas and ASICS, designing sneakers for each brand. You can usually catch Sean at Round Two LA, his streetwear and sneaker resale shop, where he excitedly awaits the sneakers customers bring in to sell.

Source: Nike

Source: Stadium Goods

Giuseppe Zanotti

Born in 1957, Italian designer Giuseppe Zanotti began doing freelance design work for fashion houses in his early twenties. He would later branch out on his own and launch a footwear collection. One of his best career moves was buying a small shoe factory in San Mauro Pascoli, where he grew up. He redesigned the factory and started producing women's heels, which brought him immediate success with US wholesalers such as Neiman Marcus, Saks, and Barney's (RIP). In 2000, Zanotti opened his own boutique in Milan and has since expanded his monobrand stores worldwide. In 2010, he brought his ornate designs to the world of sneakers, creating a line of luxury kicks that made an immediate impact. Over ten years later, Zanotti is still manufacturing and distributing sneakers on a massive scale, combining sportswear inspirations with glam-rock style. His sneaker creations have been worn by hundreds of celebrities, including Kanye West, who collaborated with Zanotti on several shoe designs. Another notable Zanotti celeb-inspired collaboration was with artist Kid Cudi; the all-red, puffy Kid Cudi x Giuseppe Zanotti high-top sneaker was launched as part of Zanotti's 2015 spring/summer collection. Kids See ~~Ghosts~~ Zanotti!

We have just gone over the intricacies of sneaker design and many of the industry's famous designers. If design is your goal, you should now have the information you need to break into the sneaker biz. But we can't stop here. Next, we need to explore how a sneaker is manufactured and ultimately distributed to the consumer.

12

4

Manufacturing & Distribution

> "I think it's a couple thousand people that touch each shoe by the time it's made."

—TIFFANY BEERS

Once a sneaker is designed, the product must be manufactured, or made on a large scale using machinery. How does the design get transformed into something tangible? How will the sneaker get manufactured from concept to product? We'll explain! The manufacturing process involves sampling, creation of the last, wear and performance testing, and quality control. Then the sneaker will be produced in varying quantities. When all these steps are completed, the sneaker will be ready to hit the market.

After a sneaker is manufactured, it needs to be distributed to consumers and sneakerheads alike. Distribution, in the general sense, means the action of sharing something out among a number of recipients. When referring to product sales, distribution involves selling and delivering products and services from the manufacturer to the consumer. In this chapter, we discuss the essentials of manufacturing and distribution to give you a full overview of how kicks are made and finally delivered to your feet. Let's go!

Manufacturing

How and where a sneaker is produced is vital, and there are various considerations involved. This section explores the components of a sneaker, materials used when making a sneaker, factories where sneakers are typically produced, prototypes, production quantity, size runs, and more. An Air Jordan 1, for example, undergoes many steps in the manufacturing process to turn it into the classic silhouette that it is. First, the sole, midsole, insole, upper, toebox, and other components of the sneaker have to be produced. Next, the mold/last of the sneaker must be created. After that, the parts are combined to create a prototype of the sneaker. Then even more steps are required to get it ready to ship to a happy sneakerhead. Let's take a look at each one.

Sneaker Components & Materials

Creating an effective sneaker takes more than design. It must be functional and, in some cases, perform at extremely high levels in demanding conditions. Therefore, a design must take into account how the sneaker will be constructed and the materials that will be used. In this section, we examine how sneakers are constructed, first by looking at the sneaker's main components and core materials. Each component must be carefully designed, researched, developed, and manufactured, then stitched, glued, or somehow fused to make the full sneaker.

Depending on the design, there can be many components of a sneaker, but all are generally divided into two parts: the sole and the upper. Let's take a look, moving from the bottom up.

The Sole

The sole is the bottom part of the sneaker and can be separated into three subparts: the outsole, the midsole, and the inner sole, or insole. The outsole is the bottommost part of the sneaker that touches the ground. Many different types and blends of materials can be used for an outsole, but typically, a durable but flexible synthetic rubber or polyurethane is chosen to withstand shock and provide traction. Depending on the sport or intended use, the outsole tread can be smooth, grooved, spiky, or some combination. For example, the sole and tread composition of a basketball sneaker is very different from that of a tennis, running, or trail sneaker, because they are used on different surfaces and in different conditions.

Directly above the outsole lies the midsole. The midsole is placed between the upper and the outsole and is where the cushioning and stability lies. Most sneaker midsoles are made of a foam called ethyl vinyl acetate (EVA) or polyurethane. Within the midsole, the sneaker will usually have some additional cushioning system. This can take many forms and is usually the most marketed part of the sneaker, supposedly providing comfort, balance, and in some cases, spring in the wearer's step. Famous and heavily marketed examples of midsoles over the years include the Hexalite from Reebok; Gel and FlyteFoam from ASICS; Boost from adidas; Air, Air Max, Zoom, Lunarlon, and React from Nike; Ignite from Puma; Hovr from Under Armour; Abzorb and RevLite from New Balance; and many others. It's gotta be the shoes!

Above the midsole, inside the shoe, is the inner sole or insole. This is the footbed, the part of the shoe that makes contact with the underside of your foot. The insole is often made of foam and is removable or lightly glued to the midsole, in the event you want to replace or substitute it for your own insole or orthotic. Real sneakerheads know that you should cover up or swap out your insoles so your foot doesn't rub off the branding or other insole details. Depending on the shoe, the insole may come with additional foam or firm plastic support for your arch, which is the middle inner part of your foot that generally supports your body weight when you stand and move.

Now that we've covered the three main parts of the sole and have our sneaker base, let's move north, to the upper.

The Upper

The upper refers to the part of the sneaker that covers the toes, the top of the foot, the sides of the foot, and the back of the heel. The upper is composed of several distinct subparts, each of which varies depending on the design of the sneaker. These are the toebox, vamp, tongue, eyestays, laces, midpanel, and heel.

Beginning with the front of the sneaker, we have the toebox (sometimes referred to as the toecap). The toebox protects the toes and is made of varying materials, depending on the type of sneaker. Common materials are leather, canvas, mesh, knitted polyester, and other breathable polymers. A good toebox is wide enough to accommodate most foot sizes and to allow for proper movement as the sneaker is utilized. Some toeboxes have ventilation to allow heat to escape, because people tend to sweat in the front of their sneaker. For comfort and performance, finding the right toebox fit is essential. For collectors and sneakerheads, however, the toebox signifies the part of the sneaker that we stress about the most, making sure we do not crease or scuff this part where damage is most visible to onlookers. The best example of this kind of sneaker paranoia is the man or woman who removes his or her sneaker before a marriage proposal, just so he or she does not crease their kicks while on a bended knee. Sentimental, yet practical!

Next we have the vamp, which extends upward from the toebox to cover the front and center part of the foot. The vamp can vary in size and length, depending on the style of sneaker, and is usually made of the same materials as the toebox and rest of the upper. Connected to the vamp, often separately, is the tongue, above which the laces are tied to help fasten and seal the sneaker around the foot. Traditional laced sneakers have holes in the vamp called eyestays (or eyelets), through which the laces are fed. The side part of the sneaker, connecting the vamp to the heel, is called the mid-panel or quarter. Finally, in the very rear of the sneaker is the heel. Besides keeping the entire foot snugly in place from front to back, the heel is usually where you can find the sneaker manufacturer's logo and some other interesting accessory or branding. For example, the Air Jordan 3 has a plastic heel tab, whereas the YEEZY 350 Boost often has a heel pull, both of which are helpful to hold on to while slipping your sneakers on and off. Who unties their shoelaces anymore?

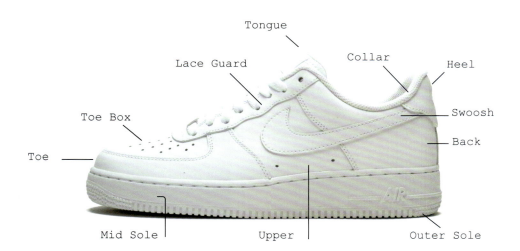

Again, although these are the main components, each sneaker is slightly different. Some sneakers have no tongue, woven uppers, nylon toeboxes, detachable logos, stretchable neoprene tongues, zippers instead of laces, Velcro pockets, plastic ornamental designs, rigid soles, and a wide array of advanced cushioning systems. This is the beauty in sneaker design and manufacturing—the possibilities are endless. So now that we know the components, how do we make the sneaker?

The Sneaker Manufacturing Process

A designer can have the freshest design, but if he or she is unable to go through the proper manufacturing process, the sneaker will never come to fruition. Choosing the right manufacturer and properly going through the necessary manufacturing steps is a critical part of sneaker creation.

The Last

When you have passed the point of design and selecting materials, a last (sometimes referred to as a mold) must be created. It is the framework and core for creating all future pairs of that sneaker. The last is a three-dimensional form used to set the overall look, shape, fit, and construction of a sneaker. Typically made out of wood or plastic, the last includes specific dimensions for the heel, instep, toebox, and forefoot. It is of the utmost importance that the last accurately depicts every detail and facet of the sneaker to ensure that all pairs of the sneaker are properly manufactured. If the last is off by even a small detail, the sneaker's look, fit, and shape could be off.

The last is composed of over thirty measurements that dictate how the sneaker will look and function. The central measurements in the last include the toebox, flare, tread, forefoot, throat opening, heel-to-ball, and girth measurements, which include the waist, ball, heel, and instep. Once these measurements are in place, the sole and upper should form around the last, which in turn, completes the last. When creating a last, it is important to use a reputable manufacturer and/or professional to ensure that it is faultless and accomplishes what is necessary in order to successfully manufacture the sneaker.

Source: Akimov Igor / Shutterstock.com

The Prototype

Before you can mass produce your sneaker, you must first develop a prototype, or sample, to ensure that you have a working, aesthetically pleasing, and functional sneaker. This will show you how the sneaker actually looks so you can confirm that it matches up with your vision. You must work with a reputable and knowledgeable manufacturer to create this prototype from which all of your sneakers will be produced. The process often takes time, and you may need to go through a few rounds of prototypes before you have something ready for market. Depending on the complexity of the sneaker design, you may need to consult manufacturers that specialize in particular things. For example, if you intend to create a custom outsole, you will need a manufacturer that can create a mold for the outsole. The upper design may require additional expertise, material sourcing, and development of the last. Once sufficient research and consultation are complete, the manufacturer will work from your design, technical drawings, and as detailed-as-possible specifications to make the prototype.

A prototype can be expensive. The prototyping phase is estimated to cost between $1,000 and $3,000 per style but can be more depending on the complexity and uniqueness of the design. Prototyping can also be time consuming, with development typically taking anywhere from one year to eighteen months. But that is changing. Emerging technologies, such as 3D printing and photorealistic 3D modeling, have cut prototyping time and costs significantly. Over the next decade, we can expect further technological advances in sampling and production, allowing more flexibility and power to all brands, big and small, looking to rush a unique sneaker to market.

Quantity/Size Run

Another important element of the manufacturing process is determining the number of pairs of the sneaker that will be produced. The quantity must be specified. General releases equate to a large quantity of pairs that can be in constant production all year round. For example, the New Balance 574, a sneaker that has been around since 1988, is typically always available for sale in certain colorways and, therefore, is manufactured all of the time.

Conversely (pun intended), sneakers that are limited releases call for a much lower production quantity. The UNDFTD x Air Jordan 4, which dropped in 2005, was limited to a scant seventy-two pairs.

On the other hand, the Nike Air Yeezy 2 in the Solar Red and Pure Platinum colorways, which released in 2012, was rumored to be limited to 3,000 to 5,000 pairs (sneaker quantities are typically not disclosed to the public), which is more typical of a limited release. No matter what the quantity, whether the sneaker is a general release (GR) or quickstrike, the manufacturer must be aligned on this before the sneaker goes into production.

The size run of a sneaker is another essential component of the process. When placing sneaker orders with a manufacturer, it is important to distinguish whether the sneaker will come in men's or women's sizing, or both. If the sizing will be unisex, the men and women's sizing must be displayed on the sneaker size tag and box. GR sneakers are often available for toddlers, kids, and adults in all different sizes. When a sneaker is limited, it usually releases in only adult sizing, and all sizes are not always available. (The big-foot sneakerheads are usually out of luck.) Regardless of whether the sneaker is limited or not, when ordering with a manufacturer, you must convey the quantity of each size. Typically, larger quantities in the more popular sizes (sizes 8–12) are manufactured than in bigger sizes (size 13+).

Source: Stadium Goods

Variations in Size

If you have studied sneaker releases, you know that size runs vary. There are usually marketing reasons behind this decision. A basketball sneaker is more likely to have larger size runs than a running sneaker, because of the difference in demographics. Some sneakers are limited releases and drop in only full sizes (as opposed to half sizes). Some are exclusively available in infant and grade school (GS) sizes; some are not available in sizes other than adult at all. Some are available only in women's sizes. For example, in 2019, Nike did a collaboration with Cactus Plant Flea Market on a Vapormax sneaker that was released in only women's sizes. The sneaker was so popular with men, however, that the larger sizes sold out immediately and are reselling at a premium to this day. Knowing what sizes will sell the most to your consumer base is clearly important to the successful sale of a sneaker.

Source: Stadium Goods

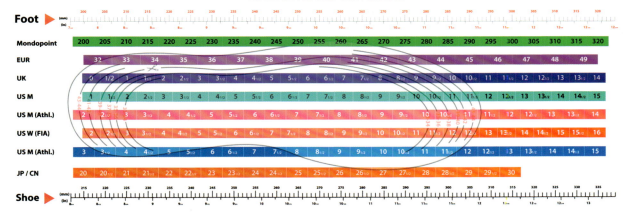

Example: A child's foot that is 185 milimetres (7.3 in) long requires a shoe that is about 15 milimetres (0.59) longer. The inner length of 200 milimetres (7.9 in) is EU shoe size 30 or UK size 11.5

Other Manufacturing Concerns

Quality Checks

Once a sneaker is manufactured, quality checks (also known as inspections) ensure that there are no defects. The naked eye can usually detect them, and if present, they must be corrected. Defects can include excess glue, wax, or other materials, weak cementing, degumming, abrasions, incorrect dimensions, incorrect sizing, and others. It is important to conduct quality checks before the sneaker is shipped from the factory.

Sometimes flaws make it past the manufacturing quality check. When this happens, wholesalers and retailers can detect them by conducting their own checks. They want no issues with consumers who purchase the product. Buyers who detect flaws can contact the retailer or sneaker brand in an effort to resolve the issues.

The manufacturing process is not perfect, and it is common for sneakers to have minor defects. These are commonly referred to as factory flaws and can include a small amount of excess glue, faulty stitching, small abrasions, and other trivial flaws. Although sneakerheads hate to see factory flaws when they cop a new pair of kicks, they are not significant enough for the sneaker to be recalled or replaced. In fact, the authors of this book have factory flaws on some of our grails. Although we are not happy about it, it is unfortunately just a part of the game. However, there is a fine line between factory flaws that are significant but not consequential enough to be sent back to the sneaker brand and those that are unacceptable. These pairs are called B-grade sneakers. B-grades generally end up at outlet and discount stores and often feature a B stamp on the box or tongue of the sneaker.

Packaging

Another essential step in the manufacturing process is the packaging. This may seem inconsequential, but it's not. Packaging not only protects and stores the sneaker, but it also serves as brand marketing and contributes to the overall allure of the sneaker. Packaging used to consist of only a cardboard box with branding on the outside, packing paper, and inserts for inside the sneaker. Think of the OG Air Jordan 1 box from 1985—as iconic as it is, the packaging was simple.

Source: Dylan Ratner

As sneaker culture progressed, packaging materials have also advanced. Nowadays, although the majority of sneaker packaging still comprises the basics, more materials and creativity are often incorporated. This includes plastic film covers, protective wraps, creative packing paper, hangtags, stickers, and other elements. Some sneakers even come with truly exceptional packaging. The Air Jordan 17, which was released in 2002, came in a metal briefcase with a CD.

Here are some more dope packaging examples:

Source: Stadium Goods

Source: Stadium Goods

Source: Stadium Goods

Source: Stadium Goods

Some packaging materials are produced by the manufacturer that creates the sneaker, whereas in other cases, the packaging materials are made by a separate manufacturer in a different location and facility. Some manufacturers use robotic systems to pack the sneakers automatically, while others are packed manually.

Further examples of iconic sneaker packaging include:

Shipment

The final step in the process is shipping the sneakers. Generally, the manufacturer ships the sneakers to the sneaker brand, and the brand houses the sneakers in its warehouse before distributing them to retailers, wholesalers, and consumers. On some occasions, the factory will ship the sneakers directly to the retailers and wholesalers at the brand's direction. Shipment to wholesalers and retailers is typically in bulk. When the brand sells the sneaker directly to a consumer, the sneaker is of course shipped directly to the buyer. We cover all of this later in this chapter.

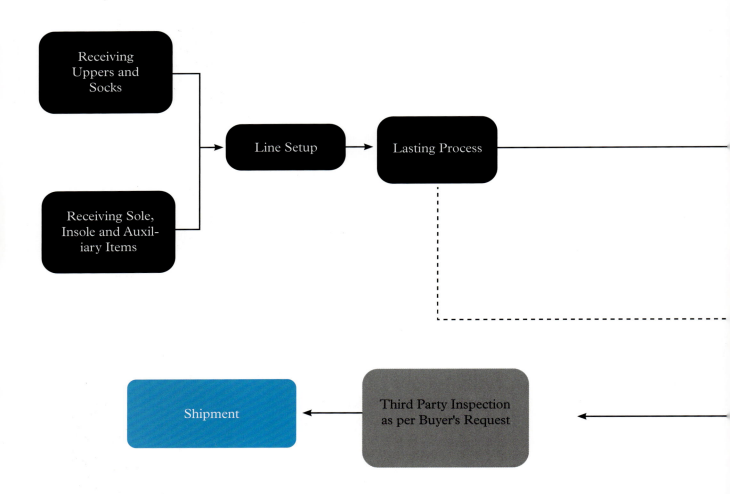

MANUFACTURING & DISTRIBUTION

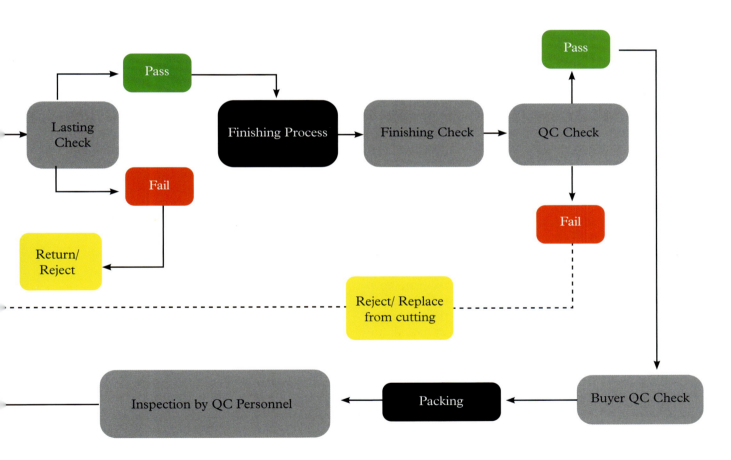

Sustainable Manufacturing

The concept of sustainability is understood and interpreted in many ways. At its simplest level, sustainability is the quality of not being harmful to the environment or depleting natural resources, and thereby supporting long-term ecological balance. With the protection of the planet and environment being a top priority for people all around the world, there has been a call for the fashion industry to adopt sustainable practices throughout the supply chain. The industry has been one of the largest contributors to world pollution. It is the second largest consumer of water, accounts for approximately 8–10 percent of global carbon emissions, and pollutes oceans, rivers, and streams.

There is no debate that as the industry continues to explode, the widespread manufacturing and disposal of sneakers is also hurting our environment. The components of a sneaker are often manufactured using chemicals that are harmful to factory workers and the environment. After they are discarded (but hopefully no one is throwing away their grails), sneakers often end up in landfills where they decay at an alarmingly slow pace while polluting the environment, causing health problems for people and our ecosystem. More than 300 million pairs of sneakers are thrown away each year, and when discarded in a landfill, it can take up to forty years for a pair of sneakers to break down and fully decompose.

As a result, educated consumers are questioning how companies manufacture their goods and reconsidering what brands they will purchase based on their commitment to sustainability. This has forced many brands to create their products in an environmentally friendly way.

Sneaker companies are responding to demands for sustainability in various ways. These include using eco-friendly, raw, and recyclable materials when manufacturing sneakers, avoiding materials that could harm the environment, using new and innovative technologies and materials that are good for the environment, utilizing leftover products and materials that would otherwise be discarded, using fewer materials when creating sneakers, not destroying or throwing away sneakers that do not end up being sold or released, and launching initiatives to reduce their corporate carbon footprint and decrease the chemical waste that goes back into our environment.

For example, in 2018, adidas teamed up with Parley's Ocean School and created the Run for the Oceans program to raise money to educate and empower youth and their families who are living in coastal areas affected by plastic pollution. Parley has estimated that 8 million metric tons of plastic trash end up in our oceans every year. Through the first-year initiative, adidas created more than 5 million pairs of sneakers using materials from collected and recycled ocean plastic waste. In 2019, adidas increased its efforts and manufactured more than double the first-year amount. As part of the Parley initiative, adidas has stated that by 2024, it will only use polyester that is 100 percent recycled. Another great example of adidas taking major steps toward sustainable practices is its collaboration with Allbirds. The two companies announced that they are partnering to create a sneaker with the lowest carbon footprint ever. It is uncommon to see two major sneaker brands join forces, so we are hyped to see what kind of sustainable kicks come out of this incredible collab!

Source: Stadium Goods

MANUFACTURING & DISTRIBUTION

Source: Nike

Nike also has taken significant steps to use recycled and upcycled materials in its sneaker manufacturing. The brand has been recognized year after year for its responsible use of recycled polyester, commonly found in the Nike Flyknit upper material and elsewhere. Between 2010 and 2018, Nike has transformed more than 6.4 billion recycled plastic water bottles into sneakers and apparel. In 2020, Nike released its Space Hippie line, which has the lowest carbon footprint of any Nike sneakers ever. The Space Hippie collection is made from Space Waste Yarn, a 100-percent recycled material made up of plastic bottles, yarn scraps, and T-shirts. The midsole cushion system is made from old Nike Zoom scraps, and the outsole is made of 15 percent recycled rubber.

In 2018, Reebok launched its Cotton x Corn sneaker line, which was designed to use only materials that grow, rather than synthetic materials. These sneakers have uppers made from organic cotton, insoles from castor bean oil, and soles from a corn-based rubber replacer.

Source: Reebok

Many sneaker companies large and small have taken major steps toward sustainable practices, including Veja, Allbirds, Toms, Reebok, Tread by Everlane, Oliver Cabell, Flamingos Life, Nothing New, Clae, Greats, Mercer Amsterdam, Pine, and many others.

Are these initiatives pure marketing hype, or are they really making a difference? We are optimistic that the industry is (pardon another pun) getting off on the right foot. But as we become more eco-conscious, we should demand that more brands be responsible and implement impactful sustainable changes to their production process. We salute all of the sneaker companies that are employing sustainable practices and every brand doing their part for the environment and world.

Best Countries for Sneaker Manufacturing

Many countries have factories that specialize in aspects of the manufacturing process. Sneaker companies use different factories in different areas to manufacture the parts of a sneaker and other factories in distinct locations to create the finished sneaker. Nike's finished products are made in forty-one countries by 533 factories, whereas the materials used for Nike's products are made in eleven countries by seventy-eight facilities.

Sneaker factories are often situated in developing countries. The cost to manufacture goods there is much cheaper because of reduced costs in labor, rent, technology, energy, and transportation. Many sneaker brands have faced issues as a result of poor working conditions, low pay, long working hours, and other hardships for workers. We speak about these issues later on in chapter 7. Popular hubs for sneaker manufacturing include China, Indonesia, Vietnam, Brazil, India, Thailand, Pakistan, Mexico, and Turkey. When it comes to luxury high-end sneakers, Italy leads the way. In the United States, about 99 percent of footwear sold is imported from other countries. Because of this, many people are lobbying for sneaker manufacturing to come back to the States. Most recently, YEEZY has vowed to have their sneakers manufactured in the States by 2021. As a first step, Kanye built a facility in Cody, Wyoming, where YEEZY has already begun producing pairs of its revolutionary Croc-like FOAM RNNR. Other companies that manufacture some of their sneakers in the United States include New Balance, Vans, and adidas. Another potential opportunity for US manufacturers is a result of the trade war between the United States and China. Because of tariffs being placed on sneakers made in China, the cost of producing there is rising, which may drive some sneaker companies to divert manufacturing business from China, and US manufacturing could start to be a more attractive option.

Navigating Factories

Once you have decided where you want to manufacture your sneakers, you will need to engage a factory to handle production. It may not be the same factory that develops your prototype, as some factories are better at the latter than the former. Wherever you decide to mass produce, it is important that you develop a working relationship with the factory, have open lines of communication about the manufacturing process, and stay on top of how your production is going. This can be challenging, for example, if you live in the States and your manufacturer is in Italy or China. In many countries, you can hire a factory sourcing agent to help you navigate this process. But beware, many of these entities can be corrupt and take advantage of new businesses with little knowledge of the manufacturing process and whose leaders don't speak the native language. Challenges can also arise when you contract directly with the factory: there can be language barriers, communication delays due to time differences, and other geographic difficulties. However you plan to engage a factory, make sure you do your research, find others who have used the factory previously, and make sure you have complete control over your product so that if anything happens, you can take back your designs, materials, and your lasts and find a better option.

Third-Party Production Companies

There are companies that specialize in manufacturing sneakers so you don't have to worry about it. Some work well as brokers in the design-to-manufacturing process. These companies enable you to design a sneaker on their website, click submit, and sit back while they have the sneaker produced. They are supposed to oversee the manufacturing process at their respective facilities and deliver a prototype to you when all is said and done.

Most of these businesses will charge a hefty monthly fee or percentage of the profits for their efforts and assistance. Using a third-party company could be a good idea if you do not know a lot about manufacturing and want to get started quickly in the business. Be careful, however, as you will relinquish a lot of personal control over the manufacturing process and may not obtain the product you want in the end.

Distribution

Now that we have laid down the foundation for how the sneaker is made, we need to examine how the sneaker is distributed, or delivered to consumers. Distribution can either be direct, meaning the product will be sold from the manufacturer straight to the consumer, or it can be indirect, with one or more intermediaries used to help pass the product along to its eventual buyer. The chart on the next page illustrates the four main channels of distribution: (1) direct to consumer, (2) retailer to consumer, (3) wholesaler to retailer to consumer, and (4) wholesale agents or brokers, who are used, in some cases, as an additional intermediary between manufacturer and wholesaler.

Each distribution channel has its pros and cons, and companies often employ multiple channels at the same time to maximize sales. In this section, we will explain the various distribution channels so that you have a full understanding of how your favorite sneaker goes from factory to foot.

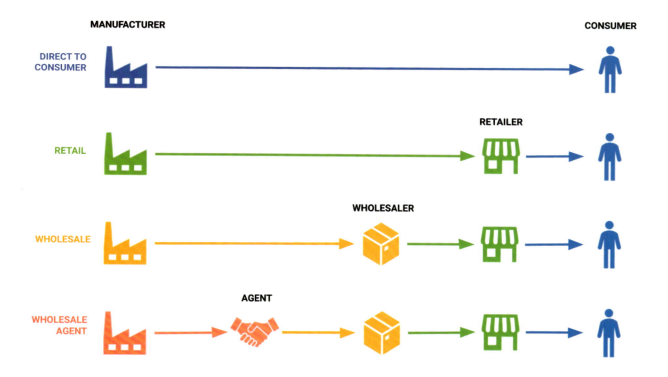

Direct to Consumer (D2C)

D2C distribution allows a company to sell a product straight to the consumer without any intermediaries. Typically, when a company utilizes D2C distribution, it is responsible for the sale, transportation, and shipping of the product to the consumer. Therefore, with D2C, there are no middlemen, and the consumer shopping experience is generally seamless.

From the General Store to Online Shopping

Long ago, if a customer wanted to purchase an item, they would visit a general store, today referred to as a retail store. The options were fairly limited to the one or two brands and various product categories that the store had access to or wanted to carry. Around the turn of the twentieth century, as the economy began to expand and middle-class consumers grew in numbers, general stores evolved into larger department stores, and dedicated retail stores began to emerge. The department stores offered many more product categories (divided into departments) than general stores, and dedicated retail stores had a wider assortment of products within a certain category. Stores of all kinds began popping up everywhere, and in no time, people in urban and suburban areas could shop for just about anything they needed within a short distance of their homes.

Then came the internet, and everything changed. A new D2C distribution channel began to emerge. Because of the internet's unlimited reach, brands that once relied on department stores or their own retail channels (described later in this chapter) could now offer their customers the same product without any intermediary, in a far more personalized way. Brands could access their customers immediately, whenever they wanted, have full control over pricing and product assortments, with less overhead and no intermediary markup.

E-commerce

Today, we refer to this online shopping experience as e-commerce, and it is now the leader in D2C distribution. Sneaker companies thrive off D2C because it allows the company to communicate directly with its customer, build a relationship, and control brand messaging and identity. As a result, many sneaker companies have created engaging e-commerce experiences. For example, in 2015, Nike launched the SNKRS app, which features creative content, personalization, and most importantly, the ability to purchase sneakers, apparel, and other Nike products. We will speak more about the SNKRS app, along with other innovative sneaker e-commerce initiatives, later in this chapter.

Source: Nike

Category	Traditional	Digital (D2C)
Reach	Finite	Unlimited
Personalization	Mass Market	Personalized
Loyalty	Basic	Advanced
Access to Customer	Limited, periodic	Comprehensive
Pricing	Partial Control	Full Control
Speed to Market	Slow	Fast
Merchandising	Limited Control	Full Control
Assortment	Limited	Full

D2C e-commerce distribution also allows sneaker companies to collect customer relationship management (CRM) data from their online consumers. CRM data typically includes shopping behaviors, interactions, interests, and tendencies. Whether you know it or not, this data is being collected about almost everything you do online. CRM data gives companies the ability to learn about and manage their relationships with consumers. It allows companies to directly connect with and market to consumers, keep them informed and engaged, streamline processes, and promote sales. In turn, this allows them to drive success and profitability. So the next time you visit your favorite sneaker website and you see a pop-up asking you if you agree to their use of cookies, you will know why—and may think twice about what information you are giving out. More on these kinds of marketing tactics in chapter 6.

E-commerce also benefits consumers. It is becoming the preferred method of consumer shopping, as more and more individuals are becoming tech-savvy and increasingly comfortable with online purchasing. E-commerce allows consumers to easily compare products and prices, obtain hard-to-find or out-of-stock items from a variety of sellers, all within the confines of their own home, which can help save time and money. In fact, consumers have embraced e-commerce so much that in 2019, global e-commerce sales were $3.5 trillion and are expected to grow to $4.9 trillion by 2021. Online footwear sales have been metro-booming as well and show no signs of slowing; in the United States alone, the current footwear market size for e-commerce is $15 billion and has an average annual growth of 8.1 percent. The bulk of these sales are through D2C distribution.

Multichannel E-commerce

With the proliferation of the internet, just about every major sneaker brand has its own (or monobrand) website. For many brands, however, a website is not enough. To maximize sales, many sneaker brands employ multiple distribution channels both in the online and physical worlds. For example, you can now shop online for your favorite sneaker brand through dedicated apps, targeted advertisements on other websites and apps, and social media sites such as Instagram, WeChat, and Facebook. You can even shout an order to a chatbot, such as Amazon Alexa, and have her place an order instantly. "Hey, Alexa, cop me a pair of all-white Air Force 1s and throw in a Jason Markk cleaning kit so they stay extra crispy." Not exactly but you get the idea!

Here are three examples of major sneaker brands and their multichannel e-commerce approaches:

adidas

In 2018, after posting a 36-percent increase in sales, adidas CEO Kasper Rorsted stated, "The most important store we have in the world is .com, period." The company is clearly ambitious about making the most out of its e-commerce platform, aiming to create an end-to-end process from product creation to point of sale in an entirely digital sphere. As of the writing of this book, e-commerce sales accounted for 12 percent of adidas's company revenue, and that number is expected to continue to grow. adidas manages a website for the flagship brand, as well as a separate website for YEEZY (www.yeezysupply.com).

When a visitor lands on the adidas website, they are greeted to dynamically relevant pages that ask questions and help curate the website experience around the user. adidas has also integrated chatbots onto its sites, which answer pertinent customer questions much more quickly than people can. This has decreased cart abandonment rates on the site, while creating a more personalized experience for users. At the same time, adidas offers the adidas and Confirmed apps, which enable shoppers to browse, buy goods, and enter into online draws for limited releases directly from their phones. The adidas app goes through new selections recommended options, sale items, and more. Additionally, through the Confirmed app, users can try to cop YEEZY and other popular sneakers.

Nike

Nike also has a substantial online presence. Digital sales represent over 20 percent of Nike's total business. In 2017, Nike launched the Nike Consumer Experience (NCX), which formed its own D2C network and ramped up its digital presence. Within the NCX, Nike amplified its e-commerce approach by focusing on loyalty programs, exclusive product releases and events for its members, personalization, and more. As a result, Nike experienced tremendous growth in sales across its website and digital platforms. Nike offers the Nike app to consumers, which is designed to enhance the digital shopping experience and offer benefits such as the NikePlus Rewards Program. This membership program gives users access to exclusive products and Nike experts, personalized workouts, priority access to events, and a slew of other benefits

Through the app, Nike is able to cultivate and use consumer data to enhance the consumer digital experience and create better products. Over 100 million people have signed on for the NikePlus membership program to date. And if you thought Nike was going to stop there, think again. Nike also has the SNKRS app, which provides consumers with easy mobile shopping options tailored to their likes and dislikes. Over the past few years, Nike has used the SNKRS app as the main D2C channel for limited, exclusive, and hyped sneaker releases. Generally, Nike releases these sneakers by either online draw or first come, first served (FCFS). These releases sell out in seconds, and more often than not, users get the "Sold out" or "Not selected" message (L). If you are extremely lucky, you get the "GOT 'EM" message (W). The app also offers a release calendar and engaging content

New Balance

In 2019, New Balance's net sales from its e-commerce platforms equated to approximately $127.9 million. Over each of the past several years, New Balance's revenues have increased, and the company expects to reach $7 billion in annual sales by 2023. No doubt, New Balance's e-commerce sales have had a huge impact on current revenues and will play a crucial role in the company's future earnings. In addition to New Balance's website, where consumers can shop the brand's latest kicks and products, the company also offers an engaging app that enables shoppers to search for products according to filters and preferences. Users can also track their workouts and sync them to smart watches to track calories burned, time spent working out, and other metrics. Users can apply points earned toward future purchases as part of the myNB Rewards program and keep track of future product releases.

The majority of the other major sneaker companies, such as Converse and Puma, for example, have websites and mobile apps as well. Many sneaker companies are working to implement interactive technology experiences such as augmented reality (AR) and virtual reality (VR), with hopes to create a virtual shopping experience right at home. It will definitely be interesting to see what the future holds for sneaker e-commerce.

As you can see, there are many reasons why sneaker brands have flocked to e-commerce and D2C distribution, and this channel of distribution shows no sign of slowing down. Of course, it is not always so simple, especially for new brands, to just open an online shop and start selling immediately. The one downside to adopting a strict e-commerce distribution model is that unless your consumer knows about the brand, they are unlikely to find your website and buy your product. This is where marketing (discussed in detail in chapter 6) is critical, but also why retail and wholesale distribution channels are still thriving to this day. Let's continue our distribution journey by exploring both of these channels.

Retail

Retail is the sale of goods to consumers in small quantities. When we think about retail, we typically mean a physical store, or retailer, where consumers shop and pay the retailer directly for one or more products. However, as we will discuss, retail can also be online. In the retail distribution channel, the retailer functions as the middleman between producer and consumer. The producer will typically sell products in bulk to the retailer, who then sells them at a markup to their consumers. Retailers can also obtain their products from a wholesaler (discussed below) at a discount from what it will charge consumers for the same product. A retail agreement removes the responsibility of sales and marketing from the producer, as they only need to satisfy their retail client with periodic bulk sales and the retailer does the rest.

Monobrand versus Multibrand Retail

Retail comes in two general forms: monobrand (retailers that carry only one brand) and multibrand (retailers that carry several brands). Monobrand examples in the sneaker world include New Balance's flagship store in Boston, Nike's physical store in Harajuku, or the first Vans store in Anaheim, California, which opened in 1966. (Damn, Daniel, back at it again with the white Vans!) These retail stores carry only one brand, their own. Monobrand sneaker stores are a great way to build brand loyalty, to control the consumer shopping experience, and to sell a variety of single-branded products, such as apparel and accessories, instead of just sneakers. They can be expensive, though, as sneaker brands will need to pay for rent, employees, stock, and any other operational overhead required by the shop.

Multibrand retailers, on the other hand, are not owned by one brand but by one individual or company that offers an assortment of brands in one or more locations. Remember our Legal Sneakers example in chapter 2? Other (actual) examples of multibrand sneaker stores include any Foot Locker in a shopping mall, the Kith boutique in SoHo, Dover Street Market in Ginza, and Sneakersnstuff in London. These retailers offer many sneaker brands and related goods, drawing in sneakerheads from all over to cop general and limited releases. These places are more than just stores; they are destinations and experiences!

Why Is Retail Important?

To this day, retail is a booming industry and essential to building brand exposure and heritage. Consumers crave interaction; they love to get out and shop, and retail stores are often found in destination areas that are designed to attract people with money to spend. Once they get you in the store, retailers offer knowledgeable salespeople whose job it is to promote products to shoppers from brands they already know and new ones they may not. For this reason, retail can be a viable means for emerging brands to gain exposure and credibility. The majority of sneaker brands regularly distribute and sell general releases (GRs) to an assortment of reputable retailers. On the other hand, when it comes to limited releases, a retail drop can be a massive event for sneaker brands. Sneakerheads have been known to line up and camp outside of stores days in advance for certain limited releases. For this reason, sneaker brands are extremely selective about which retailers they distribute and sell limited releases to.

For example, on December 6, 2013, Nike released the late- and all-time great Kobe Bryant's signature sneaker, the Kobe 8 "What the Kobe," in extremely limited quantities. Outside of selling the beautiful silhouette D2C through its website and in its monobrand stores, Nike distributed the sneaker to only a select number of multibrand retailers, such as a few Foot Locker House of Hoops stores.

Source: Stadium Goods

MANUFACTURING & DISTRIBUTION

Who Are Some of the Major Retailers in the Sneaker Game?

There are way too many retailers in the sneaker industry to name them all, but here are some notable players (in alphabetical order):

Source: Photomika-com / Shutterstock.com

01 Bodega

Located in Boston, Massachusetts, Bodega is a retail mecca of sneakers and streetwear that gives it a boutique respect. Playing off Boston's love affair with sneaker culture, Bodega is a melting pot of sneaker options for sneakerheads, making it a great place to consider pitching a new, bespoke sneaker design. Additionally, Bodega is a tier-zero shop, meaning it strictly carries limited products from big-name distributors as well as smaller manufacturers. Bodega also has a location in Los Angeles.

02 Concepts

Founded in 1996, Concepts started as a small retail shop in the back of The Tannery in Cambridge, Massachusetts, selling lifestyle products. More than a decade later, Concepts is known as a top-tier collaborator, as well as for its impressive product spread that reflects the risks they are willing to take when it comes to their partnerships. In addition to Boston, Concepts has locations in New York City, Dubai, and Shanghai.

03 Kith

If you are a sneakerhead, it is impossible to not know about Kith—it is arguably the best retail sneaker shopping experience in the world. With three different stores in New York City alone, Kith has managed to make a name for itself as a sneaker, streetwear-centric retailer, carrying everything from Nike and ASICS to Coca-Cola and Versace. In fact, Kith was the major player behind putting ASICS back on the map in 2010. Kith also has Kith Treats in many of its stores, which are cereal/snack bars that offer specially curated cereals, ice cream, and milkshakes.

(You must try the Bam Bam—shout out to Action Bronson!) Kith also takes its presentation seriously, which is why you can view pillars covered in plaster sculptures of iconic sneakers, such as the Air Jordan 1s, at many of their locations, which include SoHo, Brooklyn, Miami, and Los Angeles. Kith also has pop-up shops in these famous department stores: Bergdorf Goodman, Hirshleifers, and Selfridges.

04 Undefeated

Founded in Los Angeles, spreading down the West Coast and over to Japan, Undefeated has collaborated on Jordans, Air Force 1s, New Balances, and Converses. The brand has also launched a clothing component, ranging from a selection that can be found at Urban Outfitters to StockX. Synonymous with high-quality, rare sneaker shopping in California and beyond, Undefeated prides itself on stocking known, new, and emerging brands. In addition to its five locations in Los Angeles, UNDFTD shops can be found in San Francisco, Las Vegas, Phoenix, Shanghai, Hong Kong, Shenyang, and nineteen spots in Japan!

Other notable retail mentions include Foot Locker/Footaction/Eastbay/Champs Sports, Jimmy Jazz, Finish Line, SSENSE, Farfetch, End, Mr. Porter, Wish, Extra Butter, Xhibition, Packer Shoes, Bait, Dover Street Market, Sneaker Politics, Sneakersnstuff, and Lapstone & Hammer.

Retail E-commerce, or "E-tail"

Sneakers and sneaker-related products are not only found through their monobrand or primary online retail outlets; they can also be spotted on apps and websites that carry a range of brands in one place. This catch-all approach to shopping, otherwise known as e-tail, is preferred by many consumers today due to the convenience of shopping a multitude of sneaker brands and sneaker styles in a seamless experience. For example, Foot Locker, which owns Footaction, Eastbay, and Champs Sports, sells sneakers from practically every major sneaker brand via its website and app, where consumers can make purchases, shop new releases, reserve sneakers prior to release, and search sneaker release dates. Eastbay, Footaction, and Champs Sports also provide similar e-commerce experiences. These companies provide consumers with multiple digital platforms where they can easily shop for sneakers from different brands instead of visiting each brand's own e-commerce mediums.

Finish Line is another company that carries the majority of sneaker products through its website and app, where consumers can purchase and reserve sneakers, participate in its rewards program, and search release dates and information. In addition to GRs, Finish Line also sells many limited releases. (Many sneakerheads have spent countless hours in the waiting room, only to get the "Sold Out" message!) Other notable e-tail companies include Farfetch, SSENSE, Jimmy Jazz, Mr. Porter, HBX, Saks Fifth Avenue, Neiman Marcus, and Bergdorf Goodman.

MANUFACTURING & DISTRIBUTION

How Do You Get a Retailer to Sell Your Product?

For those of you starting sneaker brands, positioning your brand in the right retail store can be critical to gaining exposure. So how do you get a new sneaker or sneaker product on the shelves at your favorite store alongside existing and best-selling products? Here are a few tips:

01 First, you need a plan. Like every great business starts with a business plan (see more on this in chapter 2), it will be much easier to focus your efforts on securing the right retailers to sell your product with a retail plan. Decide which retailers are best for your brand and how you will approach them. Find a way to get to the decision makers at each shop. After all, you can't just roll into a department store and expect the sales clerk to put your product on the shelf. Most sizable and multilocation retail stores will have buyers and distributors with whom you should meet or find a way to contact.

02 Next, you need a pitch. Once you can get through to these retail gatekeepers, you will need to convince them to purchase your product, so prepare a product pitch, which should be short and informative. If done in person, you should bring a sample of the product for the buyer to see and explain why it belongs in their store and aligns with products they already carry. Include any positive press or customer feedback you may have received. If you are unable to meet the buyer in person, prepare a pitch package with the same information in a format that can be sent and easily viewed electronically.

03 Carve out a niche for your brand. What is unique about your product? How is it different from the other products carried by the retailer? How does it complement their current offerings? This is the essence of branding and what makes people gravitate toward your product. Unless you can demonstrate how you have created a niche product, it will be difficult to convince a buyer to place it in their retail stores.

04 Start small and work your way up. Not having any luck getting Foot Locker to carry your sneaker or sneaker product? Don't be discouraged—retailers like Foot Locker are massive, and they carry only products they know will sell or that are made by existing, well-developed brands. Start by finding independently run retailers and "mom and pop" shops that are more willing to take a chance on a new brand like yours. Get some serious sales through these independent stores first. Then you can go back to a larger retailer and say, "I sold 20,000 units through a mixture of online and independent retail. Here's why you should sell my product, too."

05 Find a wholesaler. When all else fails, provided you have enough quantities, you may want to find a wholesaler. Read on!

Wholesale

Wholesalers are businesses that function as intermediaries between a manufacturer and retailers. Wholesalers buy products from manufacturers in bulk and at a lower price, referred to as the wholesale price, than what the product sells for on the retail market. Wholesalers then sell the products to retailers for a higher price than what they paid the manufacturer. Thus, after the manufacturer sells the product to the wholesaler, it is no longer responsible for selling and marketing the product, and the retailer then sells the product to consumers, which is generally at the manufacturer's suggested retail price (MSRP), also known as the list price. Let's say Nike sells an Air Zoom running sneaker to Macy's for $45; Macy's would then sell it to consumers for $125, which is Nike's MSRP.

Source: pio3 / Shutterstock.com

Why Are Wholesalers Important?

There are a number of reasons. First, as we just learned in our retail discussion, getting your product into certain retail stores can be challenging. The right wholesalers have strong relationships with retail buyers and can convince them to carry new products. By working with a reputable wholesaler, the retailer also has assurance that the products purchased will be packaged properly, delivered in a timely fashion, and the overall transaction will go smoothly. Wholesalers also tend to offer better prices to retailers because they buy in bulk from the manufacturer, and some wholesalers will not purchase your product unless you have certain minimum product quantities. For this reason, the wholesale distribution channel is one of the most popular methods for sneaker companies looking to sell in mass quantities.

Say, for example, Under Armour just produced 4 million pairs of the Steph Curry 8. The company plans on selling a substantial number of pairs via D2C and through direct retailers. However, 4 million pairs is a lot, and the company needs another distribution channel to sell the remaining sneakers. The wholesale distribution channel is a viable means of selling the sneakers due to the potential to sell in bulk. Thus, Under Armour finds two major wholesale companies and sells 1 million pairs to each. The wholesalers then break down the goods into smaller quantities and sell to retailers that Under Armour does not already sell to directly. After eight months, Under Armour sells all of the pairs of the sneaker and has to place another order to create more. By working with wholesalers, Under Armour was able to sell all their pairs, reach more retailers, and increase revenues.

Wholesale versus Retail: A Summary

Category	Wholesale	Retail
Primary function	Creates a connection between manufacturer and retailer	Creates a connection between wholesaler and customer
Price	Sneakers sold for a relatively low price	Sneakers sold for a comparatively higher price
Competition	Small range of wholesalers	Wide range of retailers
Product quantity	Sold in big bulk orders	Sold in small merchandise batches
Product categories	A few niche products per wholesaler	Wide variety of products per store
Marketing	Not a concern for wholesale	Constantly a concern for retail to attract customers

Wholesale Agents

The fourth and final distribution channel involves a wholesale agent, an additional intermediary who will step between the manufacturer and the wholesaler and, using their relationships, help broker the wholesale transaction. Unlike regular wholesalers, wholesale agents never actually take possession of the physical goods; they utilize their industry relationships to connect manufacturers with the best wholesalers. Wholesale agents will take a fee or commission for arranging the sale, so it may mean slightly lower margins. However, these agents can be especially useful in situations where the manufacturer does not know how to get its products to the right wholesalers.

In chapters 3 and 4, we explained the entire life cycle of a sneaker from start to finish, including all of the exciting steps of design, manufacturing, and distribution. In chapter 5, we step away from the sneaker supply chain to discuss two concepts that play a major role in how sneakers are created today: licensing and collaborations. Put it this way, Jordan Brand wouldn't exist without Nike licensing Michael Jordan's name and collaborating on his signature brand. Let's take a further look.

2 3 4

15

Licensing & Collaborations

"The whole point of collaboration is that you give and take from each other, and that's how you create things that are totally new."

—*VIRGIL ABLOH*

LICENSING & COLLABORATIONS

Licenses are everywhere. If you are looking to secure a career in the sneaker business, or already have one, you will likely find yourself on one side or the other of a licensing agreement. How did adidas make a sneaker with Chanel and Pharrell? Or how could there be a K-Swiss sneaker named after social media maven, investor, and serial entrepreneur Gary Vaynerchuk? To answer these wild questions, one must understand what a license is and the role it plays in sneakers.

Furthermore, without licenses, there would be no collaborations. We therefore have to discuss how the two are related. If you have paid attention to any noteworthy sneaker releases over the last few decades, you know that in the sneaker world, collaborations are at the foundation of the hottest kicks in the game. In this chapter, we cover why licensing and collaborations are pillars of the sneaker business.

SNEAKER LAW

Licensing

A license, in the general sense of the word, means an official permission or permit to do, use, or own something. In a license arrangement, one party, called the licensor, will grant rights in a property to another party, the licensee, without actually transferring ownership of that property. Licensing can be confusing at first, so let us break it down into sneaker terms.

Typical Licensing Arrangements

In the sneaker business, license arrangements generally include the use of one or more parties' names, likeness, brand, or intellectual property (which can include trademarks, copyrights, and patents) in connection with a sneaker or series of sneakers. For example, sneaker entrepreneur and designer Ronnie Fieg has worked with ASICS on more than fifty sneakers. In each of these creations, ASICS licensed Ronnie's name and likeness, benefiting both Fieg and ASICS alike.

Another type of sneaker license arrangement involves one brand licensing to another company the rights to manufacture, distribute, market, sell, and sometimes even design the brand's sneakers. For example, say the Chinese sneaker company Anta wanted to become more widespread in the United States. To do this, the brand could find a company in the States that would be willing to manufacture, distribute, market, and sell the brand's sneakers. Accordingly, Anta would license to the company the rights to do all of these things, and the license would also include Anta's applicable intellectual property in connection with the sneakers.

To have an effective sneaker license, the parties need to ensure that the agreement includes all of the pertinent legal and business terms. (We will cover in detail all of the essential terms that should be included in a sneaker license agreement and all other major sneaker agreements in chapter 8.) When negotiating, it is always important to have a competent attorney who is knowledgeable about licensing and preferably fashion and sneakers. The license agreement and underlying terms should be negotiated and agreed upon by all of the parties involved in the deal. However, this is not to say that the license deal will be successful. Success in the sneaker industry is never guaranteed.

Benefits of Licensing

When parties engage in a sneaker license, they usually foray into a new venture. By doing this, the parties can expand into new markets, create brand awareness, and reach a new segment of consumers. This can benefit each party involved. For example, in December 2018, adidas entered into a license deal with Sadelle's on the Speedfactory AM4 "Sadelle's" sneaker. Located in SoHo, New York City, Sadelle's is one of the best brunch restaurants in New York (and probably the world). If you haven't been, you must try it—the authors of this book can say with conviction that the bagel tower is one of the best things you will ever eat. If you are not from New York, sneakerhead or not, it is not surprising if you have not heard of the restaurant; if you are a regular at Sadelle's, it is also possible that you do not know much about sneakers. By entering into this license deal, both adidas and Sadelle's were able to create brand awareness; each party expanded into new markets and reached consumers that they would likely not have reached if not for the collaboration. Fun fact: Sadelle's also licensed their restaurant name to Kith on a co-branded apparel capsule.

Second, an effective license deal can garner additional expertise, resources, and funds for the parties involved. The most popular sneaker brands have a wealth of expertise in the sneaker industry, resources to help manufacture, distribute, and sell sneakers, and most importantly, a lot of money. Because of this, you often see designers, athletes, musicians, other celebrities, and nonsneaker companies enter into license deals with sneaker companies. These parties, who do not have the expertise, resources, and money, will rely on the sneaker brand to provide support in these areas. On the flip side, for the sneaker companies, the other parties in the deal provide unique value to the brand, such as name recognition and a large following, which can help with overall sales and exposure.

To take licensing one step further, sneaker companies sometimes license portions of their business to third parties. For example, when a sneaker company enters into a license with a third-party design, manufacturing, marketing, or distribution company, they can benefit from and defer to that party's specific expertise and resources.

Last, effective licensing can save costs and increase profits. When sneaker brands enter into license deals with third parties, they usually do so because these parties are able to offer services that are much cheaper than if the brand attempts to develop the same services in-house. Designers, athletes, musicians, other celebrities, and nonsneaker companies often enter into license deals with sneaker companies to save costs on all of the functions and services that the sneaker brand provides. If successful, all parties involved in the license will make money, whether it is from direct sales or indirect opportunities that can arise as a result of the license's success.

Source: adidas

Risks of Licensing

Not all sneaker licenses are effective (or involve bagels and lox at Sadelle's). Sneaker licenses may be poorly drafted or negotiated, one or more parties involved in the deal may not adequately perform, the deal can simply be unsuccessful, or something else may go wrong.

A potential result of a licensing deal gone wrong is brand dilution. This occurs when a brand loses value from damage done to its reputation, for reasons that could include product misuse, overuse, or unsuccessful brand extension, which is when a brand enters into a different business or product category. Hypothetically, say Reebok enters into a sneaker licensing agreement with a popular video gaming influencer. Reebok creates a special edition of the Question Mid, where the influencer's trademarked logo is featured on the tongue of the sneaker, and the influencer's name and likeness are utilized in the marketing of the sneaker. Additionally, Reebok and the influencer create an in-game Fortnite avatar for the influencer, where he is rocking the sneakers. Shortly after the sneaker releases, the influencer gets caught on camera robbing a bank in his Question Mids and is sent off to jail. As a result, Reebok would likely experience brand dilution due to its product being negatively associated with the influencer. Reebok also might experience unsuccessful brand extension because its normal business is not gaming and the behavior of the influencer portrayed the brand in a negative light.

Second, when entering into a license, the licensor usually gives up some degree of control over the brand and actual creation of the sneakers. Thus, there is always a risk that the licensor will not be happy with how its licensed materials are being used or the quality of the sneakers that are made by the licensee. As we will discuss in chapter 8, when negotiating a sneaker license, it is imperative to carefully consider usage rights and scope, and quality control to ensure that the agreement reflects acceptable standards for the parties involved in the deal.

Last, other major terms that should be included in sneaker license can present risks if those terms are not adequately described in the agreement or are unfavorable to parties involved. These can include risks associated with compensation, intellectual property, design approval, distribution, manufacturing, marketing and promotion, counterfeiting, and others. Remember, you should always retain a competent lawyer when negotiating a licensing deal. More on this in chapter 8!

Collaborations

By definition, collaboration is the action of working with someone to produce or create something. A sneaker collaboration, or "collab" as it's often called by sneakerheads, involves a sneaker brand that decides to break away from its core offering and work on a special sneaker or sneaker product with a person or entity outside its own organization.

In this section, we will explore the origination of collaborations in the sneaker business, the difference between collaborations and licenses, and why they have such a tremendous impact on the sneaker game. We will then take a look at some of the most significant sneaker collaborations from athletes, musicians, fashion brands, nonsneaker brands, and more. By the end of this section, you will know all there is to know about sneaker collabs!

How Did the Term *Collaboration* Get Coined with Sneakers?

Sneaker collabs have existed since long before most of us were born. In 1932, as we have discussed, Converse famously collab'ed with Chuck Taylor on its All Star sneaker, featuring Chuck Taylor's name on the ankle patch of the sneaker, which you can still see at your local sneaker stores to this day. In 1935, Converse collab'ed with Jack Purcell, a Canadian world champion badminton player on the Converse Jack Purcell sneaker. Sneaker collaborations in the world of sports continued to dominate for most of the twentieth century. Nike went on to collab with Michael Jordan in 1985, forming arguably the most famous sneaker collab of all time. Close to one year later, adidas and Run DMC created the first musical sneaker collab ever on an iteration of the classic adidas Superstar sneaker. Still, it was not until many years later, in the early to mid-2000s, that sneaker musical collaborations became more widespread. Nowadays, musical sneaker collabs are just as popular as athletic sneaker collaborations. Additionally, the current state of sneakers features a myriad of collabs with designers, entertainers, nonsneaker companies, and more.

License Deals versus Collaborations

You may be asking yourself, "What is the difference between a license agreement and a collaboration?" The simple answer is, not much. Although the term *collaboration* is used more widely and informally today, behind the scenes and on a business level, at the root of every collaboration is a license.

For example, beginning in 2015, a massive collab was launched between adidas and international producer, rapper, singer, and all-around superstar Pharrell Williams. Through the collaboration, adidas created numerous and highly sought-after sneakers, apparel products, and related accessories co-branded with Pharrell's name and his design endeavors. Underlying this collaboration, often referred simply as the Pharrell x adidas collab, is a license, whereby Pharrell granted adidas rights to use his name and likeness in exchange for adidas's commitment to handle all manufacturing, distribution, and promotion for the massively popular products.

Now, the next time your favorite rapper or designer (or rapper-designer) releases a collab with a sneaker brand, you will understand (a) the business deal that accompanied that collab, (b) that some sort of licensing deal was reached in connection with the collab, and most importantly, (c) that this is all part of the business of sneakers. By the end of chapter 8, you will have an understanding of how those deals are negotiated, so keep going!

What Is the Impact of a Collaboration on the Sneaker Market?

Collabs are both exciting for consumers and successful for sneaker brands for several reasons. First, as mentioned, a collab gives a sneaker brand the opportunity to work with people or companies outside of its organization to create a unique product. In this way, a collab can bring in fresh ideas for the brand that may be much needed, especially with older brands or sneaker models that wish to reinvent themselves to stay relevant with an ever-changing consumer base. For example, in 2015, Chicago designer Don C collab'ed with Nike on a Just Don premium redesign of the Air Jordan II, a notoriously overlooked model in the Jordan lineup. Don brought a level of detail, luxury, and refinement to the table, making consumers excited about subsequent general releases of the Jordan II model, even if they could not get their hands on the Just Don versions.

Second, a collab can drive exposure and awareness, not only to the outside collaborator but to the sneaker brand as well. We already illustrated how this factor was important to the collab between Sadelle's and adidas. Another prime example is JJJJound x New Balance. JJJJound, a relatively small but rapidly growing Montreal-based fashion and design company known for its minimalism and attention to detail, is run by designer Justin Saunders. Justin is the man behind many pivotal brands in fashion and streetwear, including Kanye West's Donda and YEEZY. JJJJound is extremely selective about who it collaborates with and how, always carefully treading the fine line between brand exposure and design authenticity. Certainly, without a platform like New Balance, many mainstream sneaker consumers might not know about JJJJound, so the collab is desirable to increase awareness for the boutique brand. At the same time, however, working with smaller brands like JJJJound is necessary for a massive consumer brand like New Balance to stay relevant, cool, and obtain credibility at the intersection of sneakers and fashion.

Finally, collabs can drive revenue, as both parties typically benefit from co-branded and collaborative products. As we have discussed, no collaboration was or perhaps will be as successful as the one between Michael Jordan and Nike. The Nike x Jordan collab has flourished for over thirty-five years, beginning as a five-year, $500,000-a-year endorsement deal in Jordan's rookie season with the Chicago Bulls. At the time, $500,000 annually for a signature sneaker deal was unheard of and seemed like a massive amount of money to both parties. In the first year, however, Nike sold over $100 million in sneakers, shattering the company's $3 million projections. To date, it is estimated that the Jordan Brand is worth over $10 billion and that Jordan has been paid over $1.3 billion since the collab's inception.

Now that we know why sneaker collaborations have a significant impact on the market, we are going to take a look at some of the most notable ones. From the most famous collabs with athletes, musicians, and fashion brands to others that may not be so obvious, we have compiled a list of some serious kick collabs. Here we go!

LICENSING & COLLABORATIONS

Athlete Collaborations

Historically, athletes have been at the forefront of sneaker collaborations. The Converse Chuck Taylor All Star was the first sneaker collab ever, and spearheaded the movement of athlete sneaker collabs. After the release of the Chuck Taylor, sneaker collabs continued to explode in basketball; from Clyde Frazier to Julius "Dr. J" Erving, Michael Jordan to LeBron James, basketball players have dominated the sneaker collab game. Basketball sneaker collabs paved the way for other sport collabs. Athletes in football, baseball, tennis, and other sports started collab'ing with sneaker brands, and now athlete collabs are prominent today throughout the sports industry. In this section, we will highlight (in alphabetical order) some of the freshest and most influential athlete sneaker collabs of all time.

1. Air Tech Challenge 2
2. Nike Air Force 180 Olympic
3. Nike Air Max 720 OBJ
4. Nike Zoom Kobe 1
5. Reebok Court Victory Pump
6. Under Armour Curry 1
7. Nike Zoom KD 4
8. Converse Pro Leather
9. Nike Zoom Vapor RF x AJ3
10. Puma Clyde
11. Nike Air Griffey Max 1
12. Nike Kyrie 2 Ky-Rispy Kreme
13. Reebok The Answer
14. Nike Air Trainer SC
15. Nike Air Zoom Generation 1
16. Air Jordan 11 Derek Jeter
17. Nike Air Jordan 1 Chicago, Nike Air Jordan 1 Bred
18. adidas Rod Laver
19. New Balance Omn1s

LICENSING & COLLABORATIONS

20. Maya Moore x Aleali May Court Lux Air Jordan 1
21. Air Jordan 5 Retro Low Neymar
22. Reebok Shaq Attaq 1
23. Nike Air Zoom Flight The Glove
24. Air Diamond Turf II
25. adidas Stan Smith
26. Air Jordan 1 Hi OG NRG Nigel Sylvester
27. Converse Chuck Taylor All Star
28. Li-Ning Way of Wade 7
29. Nike Serena Williams x Off-White x Blazer Studio Mid Queen
30. Nike Tiger Woods 71 FastFit
31. Big Baller Brand

1. Andre Agassi x Nike (1990)

World-class tennis player, Andre Agassi, joined Nike when he was only sixteen years old. Agassi, an Olympic gold medalist and eight-time Grand Slam champion, was known for his flamboyant colors, signature mullet, and earring. His collaboration played a big part in transforming tennis sneakers into sneakers for multi-purpose performance use. Overall, Nike and Agassi collab'ed on six signature sneakers. The first and most famous was the Air Tech Challenge II, which was released in 1990.

Source: Stadium Goods

Source: Stadium Goods

3. Odell Beckham Jr. (OBJ) x Nike (2019)

Odell Beckham Jr. is known for his sneaker game almost as much as he is known for his incredible play on the field. After rocking an assortment of Nike player exclusive cleats, OBJ landed his first signature model with Nike—the Air Max 720 OBJ, a lifestyle sneaker that has released in various colorways. If we had to guess, we think that this collab is only getting started, and that there will be many more OBJ x Nike sneakers on the way.

LICENSING & COLLABORATIONS

2. Charles Barkley x Nike (1992)

When you think of this collaboration, the word timeless likely comes to mind. There have been plenty of classic Olympic-based silhouettes, but Charles Barkley's Nike Air Force 180 Olympic sneaker from the Dream Team era, like the team, is undefeated. The sneaker released in 1992, and has been retro'ed multiple times. Sir Charles also has several other iconic Nike models, including the Air Force 180, Air Max 2 CB 94, and Barkley Posite Max. Barkley once said in a Nike commercial that he was not a role model. That infamous statement did not stop kids from rocking his sneakers, on and off the court.

Source: Stadium Goods

Source: Stadium Goods

4. Kobe Bryant x adidas (2000)
Kobe Bryant x Nike (2006)

These collaborations are emotional ones. In 1996, after getting drafted to the NBA straight out of high school, Kobe Bryant, who was 17 at the time, signed a sneaker deal with adidas. In 1998, adidas and Kobe launched the KB8, Kobe's first official signature sneaker, which was an iteration of the adidas Crazy 8. Kobe and adidas went on to release an assortment of signature models and continued their relationship through 2002, when Kobe reportedly paid $8 million to be released from his contract. Shortly after, in 2003, Kobe decided to take his talents to the Swoosh and signed a multi-million dollar deal with Nike.

Kobe and Nike have twelve signature sneakers together, and the collab is arguably one of the most historical sneaker collabs ever, not only due to the sneakers' aesthetic features, but the technological and functional innovations that were introduced to the world of sneakers and basketball. After Kobe and his daughter Gianna's unexpected and heartbreaking deaths, the demand for Kobes skyrocketed. Also, Nike committed to furthering Kobe and Gianna's legacy by donating $1 million to the Mamba and Mambacita Sports Foundation, and to continue to release Kobe sneakers. The ongoing Kobe x Nike collab will surely allow fans all around the world to keep purchasing his models and be inspired by his legacy, on and off the court. Kobe Bryant left an undeniable mark on the world, game of basketball, and sneaker culture. Rest in power, Black Mamba!

175

5. Michael Chang x Reebok (1989)

The Reebok Court Victory Pump, which released in 1989, was a special time for Reebok and most definitely an exciting collab for Michael Chang. Chang, the youngest male Grand Slam champion ever, won at the youthful age of seventeen. Similar to the orange basketball displayed on the tongue of the Reebok Pump Omni Lite, the Reebok Court Victory Pump features a fuzzy, yellow tennis ball on the tongue. The original colorway re-released in 2013. This silhouette is nothing short of a classic.

Source: Stadium Goods

Source: Stadium Goods

7. Kevin Durant x Nike (2007)

In 2007, after getting drafted by the Seattle Supersonics as the number two pick in the NBA Draft, Kevin Durant signed a seven-year deal with Nike. In 2008, Durant and Nike dropped their first signature sneaker together, the Nike Zoom KD I. As of the release date of this book, KD has released twelve additional signature sneakers with Nike, for a total of thirteen signature models. In addition to his signature sneakers, KD has collab'ed on other Nike silhouettes, such as various lifestyle models. KD and Nike's deal will continue through at least 2024, so we can certainly expect more fire kicks from KD and Nike.

LICENSING & COLLABORATIONS

6. Stephen Curry x Under Armour (2015)

In 2013, Stephen Curry signed a sneaker deal with Under Armour after Nike refused to match Under Armour's offer. In 2015, after two years of Chef Curry's incredible work on and off the court, Curry and Under Armour dropped the Curry 1, which was the sharpshooter's first signature sneaker. During that same year, the two extended their deal through 2024. As of the release of this book, Steph has seven signature models with Under Armour. This collab is arguably the biggest in Under Armour's history, and one that hoopers and sneakerheads alike have no choice but to respect.

Source: Stadium Goods

Source: Stadium Goods

8. Julius "Dr. J" Erving x Converse (1976)

In 1976, Converse introduced the Pro Leather model. Immediately after its release, basketball players gravitated towards the sneaker. Julius "Dr. J" Erving was one of the first basketball players to endorse the Pro Leather, and due to his skills, swagger, and charm, the sneaker was nicknamed the Dr. J. At the time, the silhouette employed new technology that made the sneaker more durable and lighter than previously-released sneakers. Although technology in sneakers have greatly advanced through the years, the technology in the Pro Leather, like the sneaker itself, has proven to be timeless.

SNEAKER LAW

9. Roger Federer x Nike (2014)

In 2014, tennis superstar Roger Federer and Jordan brand collaborated on the Nike Zoom Vapor AJ3. This sneaker was inspired by the Air Jordan Retro 3. It was always a dream of Federer's to create his own spin on the classic Jordan silhouette. He did just that. This sneaker was very limited and released in multiple colorways—White Cement, Black Cement, and Fire Red.

Source: Stadium Goods

Source: Stadium Goods

11. Ken Griffey x Nike (1996)

Nike and baseball legend Ken Griffey Jr. teamed up on the Air Diamond Fury Mid in 1995, and it was retro'd twenty years later. In 1996, Nike and Griffey dropped the Air Griffey Max, which is his most famous silhouette. Altogether, Ken Griffey Jr. has seven signature sneakers with Nike, and years later, the line is still popular.

10. Clyde Frazier x Puma (1971)

In 1970, Walter "Clyde" Frazier and Puma teamed up for one of the most classic sneaker collabs of all time. Not only did this collaboration produce the iconic Puma Clyde, it broke ground as the first NBA player sneaker endorsement deal ever. After releasing, the Puma Clyde became an instant fashion statement and the silhouette has stood the test of time; the sneaker has immense significance in old school hip-hop and skating culture, and can be found all around the world in an assortment of colorways.

Source: Stadium Goods

Source: Stadium Goods

12. Kyrie Irving x Nike (2011)

Kyrie Irving signed with Nike in 2011 after being selected as the number one draft pick by the Cleveland Cavaliers. Just three years later, Nike welcomed Kyrie to its family of signature athletes, which is not an easy feat. Nike and Kyrie hit the ground running and released their first signature sneaker together—the Kyrie 1. As of the release date of this book, Nike and Kyrie have a total of seven signature sneakers together and counting. There have been many iterations of the Kyries in a multitude of fly, unique, and playful colorways. In fact, the Kyrie signature Nike line has collab'ed with Krispy Kreme, Concepts, Lucky Charms, his alma mater Duke University, and *SpongeBob SquarePants*, which we discuss later.

13. Allen Iverson x Reebok (1997)

"Practice?" This collaboration between Allen Iverson and Reebok is a monumental one, consisting of the Question and Answer signature models. Iverson's impact on sneaker culture is undeniable; he was one of the first to intertwine his swag and interest in pop culture with the NBA world, and this translated seamlessly to his sneakers. The NBA's dress code was arguably created as a direct result of AI's fashion choices; that should speak for itself! Iverson's deal with Reebok, which was signed in 2001, is rather unique. The agreement was structured to work in favor of AI's future—Reebok agreed to pay Iverson $800,000 a year for life, and set aside $32 million in a trust fund that Iverson could only access in 2030. To date, Allen Iverson has eighteen signature models with Reebok.

Source: Stadium Goods

Source: Stadium Goods

15. LeBron James x Nike (2003)

LeBron James, the "Chosen One," was drafted number one in the 2003 NBA Draft by the Cleveland Cavaliers, straight out of high school. After getting drafted, endorsements immediately came flooding in. After several other major sneaker brands vigorously pursued LeBron, on May 22, 2003, he ended up signing a $93 million contract with Nike. LeBron and Nike first released the Nike Air Zoom Generation 1, starting their signature line. As of the release date of this book, LeBron has eighteen models with Nike, along with other sneakers. In 2015, King James reportedly signed a lifetime deal with Nike worth $1 billion. Like LeBron's on-court performance, his sneakers show zero signs of fatigue.

LICENSING & COLLABORATIONS

14. Bo Jackson x Nike (1988)

"Bo knows." Arguably one of the greatest athletes of all time, Bo Jackson played professional baseball and football and was an All-Star in both sports. In 1988, Nike was searching for the right athlete to collaborate on a versatile cross-training sneaker, and there was no athlete more fit for the job than Bo Jackson. Nike and Bo teamed up on the Nike Air Trainer SC, which was designed to be a multi-purposed sneaker that could be worn while playing several sports. This sneaker is a classic, and you are likely to still see it on shelves at sneaker stores around the world.

Source: Stadium Goods

Source: Stadium Goods

16. Derek Jeter x Air Jordan (2003)

RE2PECT. Jordan Brand and the Captain, Derek Jeter, have a long-standing relationship. In 2002, Jeter became the first baseball player ever to sign with, and get endorsed by, Jordan. Initially, the collaboration surprised many, but it made sense considering how dominant of a player Jeter was. Michael Jordan would often tease Jeter about having one more world championship than him, but at the end of the day, it was all love. Jordan and Jeter created an assortment of iconic cleats and sneakers, and the Captain now has thirteen signature models with the brand.

17. Michael Jordan x Nike (Air Jordan) (1985)

Arguably the most important sneaker collab, with perhaps the greatest basketball player and athlete of all time. Nike and Michael Jordan collaborated on a series of iconic sneakers, later becoming the Jordan Brand and a global phenomenon. The Chicago Air Jordan 1 released on September 16, 1985. The rest is history. Every year since, Jordan Brand and Nike release signature Air Jordan sneakers in a multitude of colorways. As of this book's release, the most recent model is the Air Jordan 35. Retro releases, signature sneakers for other players, and non-signature sneakers would go on to be released. This collab is without a doubt the G.O.A.T.

Source: Stadium Goods

Source: Stadium Goods

18. Rod Laver x adidas (1970)

Rodney "Rod" Laver was one of the most dominant tennis players in the 1960s. Laver spectacularly won a record two hundred tournaments and was ranked number one from 1964 to 1970. In 1970, Laver and adidas joined forces and created the Rod Laver sneaker. Fifty years after its initial release, the adidas Originals Rod Laver returned to the shelves; the sneaker is still highly regarded among sneakerheads and non-sneakerheads alike.

Source: Stadium Goods

Source: Stadium Goods

19. Kawhi Leonard x New Balance (2019)

"Board man gets paid." In 2018, Kawhi Leonard signed a multi-year deal with New Balance after deciding to part ways with Nike and Jordan Brand. If you know the Fun Guy and his personality, this collab seems pretty fitting. In 2020, New Balance and Kawhi dropped the aptly-named Kawhi, which was not only Kawhi's first signature sneaker, but also New Balance's first-ever signature basketball sneaker. Although only one Kawhi x New Balance signature sneaker has dropped as of the release date of this book, there are certainly more on the way.

20. Maya Moore x Air Jordan (2011)

In 2011, after being selected number one in the WNBA Draft by the Minnesota Lynx, Maya Moore signed with Jordan Brand, making her the brand's first female signee. Jordan Brand and Moore have collab'ed on a number of retro Jordan models, including the Air Jordan 1, 7, and 10. A memorable collab for sneakerheads is the Maya Moore x Aleali May x Air Jordan collection, which dropped in 2018 and featured colorful takes on the Court Lux Air Jordan 1 and 10.

Source: Stadium Goods

Source: Stadium Goods

22. Shaquille O'Neal x Reebok (1992)
Shaq Brand x Walmart (2004)

Basketball giant Shaquille O'Neal and Reebok teamed up in 1992 and released Shaq's first signature sneaker—the Reebok Shaq Attaq 1. Shaq and Reebok went on to collab together on three additional signature models. In 2004, after deciding that he wanted to produce and sell more affordable sneakers, Shaq created the Shaq brand. Partnering with Walmart and Payless, Shaq released sneakers that retailed for less than $20, and has since sold over one hundred million pairs.

LICENSING & COLLABORATIONS

21. Neymar x Nike (2011)
Neymar x Air Jordan (2016)
Neymar x Puma (2020)

Brazilian soccer sensation Neymar da Silva Santos Júnior, known simply as Neymar, signed an endorsement deal with Nike in 2011. In 2016, Neymar delighted sneakerheads worldwide when he started wearing Air Jordan inspired soccer cleats, and news hit that a Neymar x Air Jordan collab was happening. The two teamed up to create an all 3M reflective, low top Air Jordan 5. Several other retro-inspired Jordan cleats were seen on Neymar thereafter, and his deal expanded as Nike delivered its Shox running sneaker in several Neymar styles and colorways. In 2020, it was announced to much surprise that Neymar signed a deal with Puma that, at the time, was the biggest individual sports sponsorship in history, valued at roughly $30 million per year.

Source: Stadium Goods

Source: Stadium Goods

23. Gary Payton x Nike (1998)

Gary Payton is arguably the greatest defender in NBA history. Payton's tight-knit and suffocating defense on the court earned him the nickname, "the Glove." Accordingly, Payton's two signature sneaker collabs with Nike have glove-like design elements. In 1998, Nike and Payton released the Air Zoom Flight The Glove, a silhouette with a synthetic zipped wrap surrounding the sneaker. The sneaker, along with the Nike Zoom GP, Payton's other signature model, have released and re-released in an assortment of colorways, and are unquestionably classics.

185

24. Deion Sanders x Nike (1993)

Deion Sanders and Nike have a storied history together. In 1993, Nike kicked off its signature line with Sanders by releasing the Air Diamond Turf, a classic sneaker that Sanders, the two-sport athlete, rocked on the football field and baseball diamond. From 1994 to 1998, Nike and Sanders dropped four additional signature sneakers—the Air Diamond Turf II, Air DT Max '96, Air Diamond Turf IV, and Air Diamond Turf V. Like Deion's nickname, this collab is Prime Time.

Source: Stadium Goods

Source: Stadium Goods

26. Nigel Sylvester x Air Jordan (2018)

This 2018 collaboration between Jordan Brand and BMX legend, Nigel Sylvester, is definitely a cool one. The design is very similar to the distressed concept that was popularized by the Italian high fashion brand, Golden Goose. The Air Jordan 1 Hi OG NRG Nigel Sylvester has scuff marks, is distressed, and has a purposely worn vibe. The design yells that it is okay to wear your sneakers, which is something that many sneakerheads are at odds with.

LICENSING & COLLABORATIONS

25. Stan Smith x adidas (1963)

This collaboration between adidas and Stan Smith is one of the most important collabs in sneaker history. In 1971, Stan Smith was the number one tennis player in the world and adidas rushed to sign him to an endorsement deal. Shortly thereafter, Smith began wearing the Stan Smith, which at the time, was named after French tennis player, Robert Haillet. Years later, in 1978, adidas decided to change the name of the sneaker to the Stan Smith, and in addition to Smith's name, the sneaker featured his face on the tongue. The iconic sneaker is known for its quality leather and clean look. As time went on, the sneaker grew in popularity, and can now be found in a variety of colorways and iterations. The Stan Smith went from performance tennis sneaker to international fashion staple, and shows no sign of slowing down.

Source: Stadium Goods

Source: Stadium Goods

27. Chuck Taylor x Converse (1923)

The Converse Chuck Taylor All Star is the sneaker that started it all. After Converse and basketball player Chuck Taylor teamed up on the sneaker in 1932, the silhouette became world famous. Almost a hundred years later, it is still as relevant as ever. You can find people all around the world rocking Chucks. What began as a basketball sneaker is now a part of everyday fashion, spanning genres and generations.

28. Dwyane Wade x Converse (2003)
Dwyane Wade x Air Jordan (2009)
Dwyane Wade x Li-Ning (2013)

In 2003, at the beginning of NBA superstar Dwyane Wade's career, he signed with Converse. Over a six year span, they collab'ed on four signature sneakers. In 2009, D. Wade decided to part ways with Converse and signed a deal with Jordan Brand. Jordan and Wade teamed up on two signature models—the Jordan Fly Wade 1 and 2. After less than three years with Jordan Brand, in 2012, D. Wade shocked the NBA and sneakerheads all around the world by leaving Jordan and signing with Chinese brand Li-Ning. The deal was valued at $60 million over 10 years and included an equity stake in the company. After finalizing the deal, Wade became the face of Li-Ning. In 2013, Dwyane and Li-Ning dropped their first signature sneaker, the Way of Wade 1. At the time, it was one of the most popular sneakers on the market. After many successful years collaborating with Li-Ning, Wade signed a lifetime deal with the brand. As of the release date of this book, D. Wade has eight signature sneakers with Li-Ning and counting.

Source: StockX

Source: StockX

30. Tiger Woods x Nike (1997)

In 1996, Nike signed Tiger Woods, one of the greatest golfers of all time. Tiger's first signature sneaker was the Nike Air Zoom TW, which released in 1997. To date, Tiger has twelve signature models with Nike. This collab is definitely deserving of a Tiger fist pump!

29. Serena Williams x Nike (2018)

"QUEEN." Serena Williams is arguably one of the greatest female athletes of all time. In 2018, Serena, Nike, and Virgil Abloh/Off-White collab'ed on a multitude of sneakers in celebration of Serena playing in the 2018 U.S. Open. Among these sneakers, the Serena Williams x Off-White x Blazer Studio Mid "Queen" was easily the standout model. This particular sneaker combines a beautiful, yet powerful fluorescent colorway, with the staple Off-White yellow zip tie as the finishing touch.

Source: Stadium Goods

Source: StockX

31. Lonzo, LaMelo, and LiAngelo Ball x Big Baller Brand (2017)

In 2016, LaVar Ball, father of basketball brothers Lonzo, LaMelo, and LiAngelo Ball, launched the Big Baller Brand. In 2017, after being disappointed with potential sneaker deals for Lonzo, LaVar and Lonzo decided to take matters into their own hands and launched the ZO2 signature sneaker, which was available for $495 through preorder. The bold move took the sneaker world by surprise—some loved it, while others hated it. BBB released other models, including signature sneakers for LaMelo, and LiAngelo. Since its launch, the brand has struggled with a myriad of business issues, but you can't knock LaVar's hustle and entrepreneurial spirit; his independent approach was audacious and refreshing.

Musician Collaborations

Since the early days of the sneaker, marketing and promotion were reserved for famous athletes. It makes sense—who better to convince a consumer to buy a sneaker than someone who performs at the highest level and makes a living in sneakers on the court or field? Ballers, tennis aces, baseball sluggers, golf pros, and track stars have all been perfect sneaker advocates. But over the last two decades, sneakers have become increasingly popular for their style, fashion, and comfort. As the sneaker consumer has evolved, so has the way in which sneaker companies market and promote to them. Enter the musician! The perfect combination of influence and style. To sneaker companies, musicians are a rare blend of talent and celebrity who have proven to be successful, reach large audiences, and are often looked to for their trendsetting abilities.

LICENSING & COLLABORATIONS

The following musicians instantly boosted sales for sneaker brands by wearing their signature sneakers during concerts, interviews, on social media, or even for a night out on the town. In looking over this list, ask yourself—why was the collaboration so successful, and what artist should be next up in terms of landing a major sneaker deal?

SNEAKER LAW

1   2   3

7   8   9

13   14   15

LICENSING & COLLABORATIONS

4　　　　　　　　　　　5　　　　　　　　　　　6

10　　　　　　　　　　11　　　　　　　　　　12

1. adidas x Jeremy Scott JS Wings ASAP Rocky Black Flag
2. adidas Supersleek 72 WMNS Beyonce Ivy Park
3. adidas Pro Model Big Sean
4. Air Jordan 8 Retro Drake OVO
5. Nike Air Force One Low The Blueprint 2
6. BAPE Dropout Bear Bapesta
7. Louis Vuitton Don
8. Nike Cortez I Kendrick Lamar Kenny 1
9. Air Jordan 3 Retro DJ Khaled Grateful
10. adidas Kid Cudi Torsion Artillery Hi
11. adidas NMD Hu BBC – Heart and Mind
12. adidas Ozweego Pusha T
13. Fenty x Puma Rihanna Fenty Bow
14. Air Jordan 6 Cactus Jack
15. Converse Golf Le Fleur OX

1. A$AP Rocky x adidas (2013)
A$AP Rocky x Under Armour (2018)

"Fashion is almost like a religion, for me at least." In 2018, rapper and fashion icon, A$AP Rocky signed with Under Armour to release a skate inspired sneaker called the AWGE SRLO. Perhaps the most well-known Rocky collaboration, however, was when he linked up with adidas and Jeremy Scott on the adidas JS Wings ASAP Rocky Black Flag. The collab featured Jeremy Scott's signature wings hanging off the sneaker in an all-black colorway, and was the perfect mashup of the two artists' embellished and rebellious fashion styles.

Source: Stadium Goods

Source: Stadium Goods

3. Big Sean x adidas (2013)
Big Sean x Puma (2018)

"Look, think about it, close your eyes, dream about it. Tell your team about it, go make million-dollar schemes about it." The Detroit-born rapper, Big Sean, signed with adidas in 2012, and the two collaborated on multiple models, including the Pro Model silhouette. In 2017, Big Sean moved on from his deal with adidas and signed with Puma. The two came out with their own collection in Spring 2018 that included the Puma Suede Spectra Big Sean.

LICENSING & COLLABORATIONS

2. Beyoncé (Ivy Park) x adidas (2020)

"Tennis shoes, don't even need to buy a new dress; if you ain't there, ain't nobody else to impress." It doesn't get much bigger than Queen Bey. In 2019, when adidas announced a full footwear and apparel collaboration with Beyoncé's activewear line, Ivy Park, fans went wild with anticipation. It would be the first sneaker deal for the pop and R&B superstar, and when it dropped in 2020, it did not disappoint. The first Ivy Park drop had three distinct adidas sneakers: the Ultraboost, two colorways of the Nite Jogger, and the Super Sleek 72.

Source: Stadium Goods

Source: Stadium Goods

4. Drake x Air Jordan (2018)

"Checks over stripes, that's what I like." Toronto-born actor-turned-rapper, Drake, is a pop superstar. Over the years, Drake has proved that he is team Nike for life. Drake has dabbled with multiple Jordan retros such as the Jordan 1, 3, 4, 6, 8, and 10. You can always count on Drake's sneaker designs to include his iconic OVO Owl. It's safe to say that you should expect more Drake and Nike/Jordan collaborations in the future.

195

5. Jay-Z x Reebok (2003)
Jay-Z x Nike (2002)
Jay-Z x Puma (2017)

"It's like I'm searching for kicks like a sneakerhead." Jay-Z, one of the greatest rappers of all time and self-made billionaire, has made some power moves in the sneaker world. In 2017, Jay-Z collab'ed with Puma on the classic Puma Clyde silhouette when his album *4:44* dropped. In 2018, Jay-Z became Creative Director of Puma Basketball. Perhaps Hova's most notable collab was when he linked up with Nike in 2002 on an exclusive Air Force 1 for his *Blueprint 2* record. This sneaker is known for the iconic Roc Nation logo placed on the side of the silhouette.

Source: Stadium Goods

Source: Stadium Goods

7. Kanye West x Louis Vuitton (2009)

These rare and iconic luxury sneaker designs are one of the main reasons Ye earned the moniker "The Louis Vuitton Don." In addition to the Don silhouette, Kanye and LV dropped two more sneakers as a part of the 2009 Kanye West x Louis Vuitton sneaker collection—the Mr. Hudson and Jasper. In total, the entire collection featured ten different colorways across the three different models.

6. Kanye West x BAPE (2007)

"So go ahead, go nuts, go apesh*t. Specially in my Pastelle, on my BAPE sh*t." Long before Kanye joined forces with adidas to launch the YEEZY brand, he collab'ed on some groundbreaking and now iconic sneakers. One of Kanye's earliest sneaker collabs was with BAPE, and featured his debut album mascot, the *College Dropout* bear, on the heel. Inspired by the colors and materials of a Louis Vuitton keepall, this sneaker is arguably one of the rarest pairs of kicks out there; if you have these grails, protect them at all costs.

Source: Stadium Goods

8. Kendrick Lamar x Nike (2018)

"Y'all don't want me to win. I'm tryna follow dreams, you want me to follow trends." Grammy award and Pulitzer Prize-winning Kendrick Lamar is one of the most prolific rappers of all time. In 2016, Kendrick collab'ed with Reebok for the CL Leather KL Kendrick Lamar, a classic Reebok silhouette. In 2017, Kendrick teamed up with Nike on another timeless model, the Nike Cortez. The word "DAMN." is plastered on the side of this sneaker to commemorate Kendrick's multi-platinum album. In 2019, Kendrick and Nike collab'ed on another model, the React 55 Kendrick Lamar. Nike and Kendrick definitely have some more heat on the way.

SNEAKER LAW

9. DJ Khaled x Air Jordan (2017)

"Another one." DJ Khaled is more than just an inspirational hip-hop hitmaker, he is a born collaborator and sneaker king. Known for flexing some of the rarest sneakers on social media, Khaled has been blowing the minds of sneakerheads with his social media sneaker closet tours for some time. Even though Khaled is not a basketball player, he has always been inspired by Michael Jordan's greatness, so it was a dream come true when Khaled got to collaborate with Jordan Brand on the Air Jordan 3 Retro DJ Khaled Grateful and Father of Asahd models. These collabs are known for including DJ Khaled's We The Best logo on the back of the sneaker.

Source: Stadium Goods

Source: Stadium Goods

11. Pharrell Williams x adidas (2016)

"Wealth is of the heart and mind, not the pocket." This is the motto of Pharrell Williams and his streetwear brand, Billionaire Boys Club. In 2016, Pharrell collab'ed with adidas on the NMD Hu, a truly innovative version of the adidas NMD. This sneaker used the traditional configuration of the NMD with a restructured lace system with large "Human Race" lettering emblazoned across the upper of both sneakers. After the success and popularity of the OG versions, a string of alternate NMD models released, each bearing a word or two about the beauty of humanity. In addition, Pharrell and adidas have collab'ed on various other styles. This long-standing collab shows no sign of slowing down.

LICENSING & COLLABORATIONS

10. Kid Cudi x Giuseppe Zanotti (2015)
Kid Cudi x adidas (2018)
Kid Cudi x A.P.C. (2019)

Source: adidas

Source: Stadium Goods

"Bury me in 501s and 10 Deep. And please keep the BAPEs on the feet. So I can watch the devil ice-grill me." Kid Cudi is one of the most influential artists of his generation. Cudi is notorious for fulfilling personal, life-long dream collaborations, not only in music, but in all forms of pop culture. It comes as no surprise that he has influenced the sneaker world as well. In 2015, Cudi and Giuseppe Zanotti, the Italian footwear and fashion designer, collaborated on a rather unique sneaker with oversized puffy leather straps. In 2019, Cudi collab'ed with the French brand, A.P.C., to release a Kid Cudi collection that included sneakers, leather jackets, t-shirts, and jeans. Prior, in 2018, adidas Originals teamed up with Cudder on his own sneaker for the Asterisk Collective Project, an adidas campaign aimed at empowering individuals through music, sports, and creativity. Shortly after, in 2019, Cudi officially signed a deal with adidas and his first signature sneaker, the adidas Originals x Kid Cudi Torsion Artillery, released in 2020. More heat is definitely in store for the Moon Man and three stripes.

12. Pusha T x adidas (2014)

"If you know you know." Pusha T is more than a rapper. The former member of the Virginia Beach duo Clipse, and G.O.O.D. Music artist has been a long-time collaborator in the fashion world, but when he signed with adidas in 2014, he broke into the sneaker collab scene in a big way. Two of his collabs include the Equipment Running Guidance King Push and adidas Ozweego Pusha T. King Push renewed his contract with adidas in 2019, and as he would say,"YUUGH!"

Source: Stadium Goods

14. Travis Scott x Nike and Air Jordan (2019)

"It's lit!" Travis Scott, the Grammy award winning hip-hop mogul, is one of the most influential artists and sneakerheads in the hip-hop game. Also known for his insane sneaker collection, Travis often rocks some of the most limited kicks in existence, which made him a prime candidate for his own sneaker collab with Nike and Jordan. Travis first collab'ed with Jordan in 2017, on the Jordan Trunner LX model, followed later by the classic Air Force 1 silhouette. Travis has also collab'ed on the Jordan Retro 1, 4, 6, and 33, as well as Air Max 270 and Nike SB. Travis is known for reconstructing classic retros that Michael Jordan introduced years ago. These collaborations will go down in history, and sneakerheads most certainly can't wait for more.

LICENSING & COLLABORATIONS

13. Rihanna x Puma (2017)

"Shine bright like a diamond." That's exactly what the nine-time Grammy award winning pop star Rihanna does. Rihanna began a lucrative partnership with Puma in 2014. Shortly thereafter, the duo dropped the Fenty Puma Creeper, a sneaker that became so popular it won Shoe of the Year by Footwear News in 2016. Since then, Rihanna and Puma have released several additional colorways of the Creeper, and other styles like the Rihanna Fenty Bow, a chic design, complete with an actual silk bow attached to the tongue of the sneaker.

Source: Stadium Goods

Source: Stadium Goods

15. Tyler the Creator x Vans (2015)
Tyler the Creator x Converse (2017)

"I'm a businessman, you ain't ever been the man." Tyler the Creator is the king of weird, celebrated for his unorthodox style when it comes to music and fashion that sits somewhere at the intersection of skate, street, and avant-garde. Tyler isn't your typical sneakerhead, and yet he is still a trendsetter in the game. In 2015, Tyler launched a collection with Vans, and then teamed up with Converse in 2017. All of Tyler's sneaker designs consist of the playful Golf Wang flower style that Tyler is famous for.

Fashion Brand Collaborations

As consumer demand evolved and sneakers became important fashion staples, sneaker producers had to make sure their kicks performed well and also looked good. Before long, prominent sneaker brands began collaborating with fashion brands that could enhance their image. These brands produced fresh takes on existing sneaker silhouettes and, in some cases, completely new and iconic designs. Here is a list of some of the most noteworthy collaborations between fashion brands and sneaker companies that have pushed the game forward and created serious heat for our feet.

LICENSING & COLLABORATIONS

1. Nike Air Max 1 Atmos Elephant
2. adidas Ultra Boost 4.0 BAPE Camo
3. adidas Chanel Human Race
4. Concepts x Nike SB Dunk Purple Lobster
5. Air Jordan 1 Dior
6. Nike SB Low Diamond Supply Co.
7. Nike Air Fear of God 1
8. Air Jordan 1 Fragment
9. Air Jordan 2 Retro Just Don
10. Nike Air Force 1 Low Kith
11. Air Jordan 1 Retro High Off-White Chicago
12. adidas Samba OG Oyster Holdings

13. Prada x adidas Superstar
14. Air Jordan 12 Retro PSNY
15. adidas Ozweego Raf Simons
16. Nike Dunk SB Low Staple NYC Pigeon
17. adidas Rick Owens Tech Runner
18. Nike LDWaffle Sacai
19. adidas Ultraboost Stella McCartney
20. Air Jordan 5 Retro Supreme
21. Air Jordan 4 UNDFTD
22. Nike Air Yeezy 2 Pure Platinum
23. adidas YEEZY Boost 750

1. Atmos x Nike (2006)

There are countless classic Air Max 1 styles, but we have to admit, the Atmos Elephant colorway is one of the best. This collaboration between the Tokyo-based brand and Nike originally released in 2006 and was retro'ed in 2017. The design consists of a black suede upper, white midsole, elephant print accents throughout the sneaker, and a teal Nike swoosh for the perfect finish.

Source: Stadium Goods

2. BAPE x adidas (2016)

BAPE and adidas have collab'ed on more sneakers than we can count; some noteworthy ones include the adidas Superstar, Campus 80s, NMD R1, and Dame 4. One of our favorites though, is the adidas Ultra Boost BAPE Camo. adidas introduced the Ultraboost model in 2015. After Kanye West was seen rocking a pair, the sneaker blew up, and everyone wanted them. The sneaker is known for its perfect blend of style and comfort. The BAPE version features their iconic camo with black and white accents. Whenever adidas and BAPE link up, you can always expect fire.

3. Chanel x adidas x Pharrell (2017)

French luxury fashion house Chanel teamed up with rap superstar Pharrell and adidas for a three-way collaboration on the adidas PW X CC HU NMD Chanel. The sneaker retailed for $1,160 and was released in extremely limited quantities at a pop-up shop in the now-closed Paris department store, Colette.

Source: Stadium Goods

Source: Stadium Goods

5. Christian Dior x Air Jordan (2020)

In 2020, French luxury fashion house Christian Dior and Jordan Brand dropped a highly coveted and ultra-luxe take on the Air Jordan 1, generating instant hype in the sneaker world. The high-top and low-top versions retailed for $2200 and $2000, respectively. A short while after their limited release and immediate sellout, they were seen reselling for over five times their retail price.

LICENSING & COLLABORATIONS

4. Concepts x Nike (2008)

Boston skateboard and sneaker shop Concepts takes their brand name seriously. Over the years, they have thought up some of the wildest sneaker collaborations and turned them into reality. Perhaps their most well-known collab was with Nike on a very New England-themed sneaker called the Lobster Dunk. In 2008, the Lobster Dunk originally released in several colorways with appropriate details such as speckled uppers, a tablecloth print lining, and lobster claw rubber bands around the toe box. Each colorway is exclusive and the resell value is extremely high.

Source: Stadium Goods

6. Diamond Supply Co. x Nike (2005)

Diamond Supply Co. is a skateboarding and clothing brand founded in 1998. In 2005, Nike SB and Diamond Supply Co. collab'ed on one of the most hyped sneakers ever, the Nike SB Tiffany Dunk. The sneaker was extremely limited, with only 4,000 pairs released to the public. The design got its inspiration from the Tiffany & Co. jewelry box. The resale value on these are off the charts, making the sneaker a grail in anyone's collection. In 2014, Diamond Supply Co. and Nike collab'ed again on a high version of the sneaker.

SNEAKER LAW

7. Fear of God x Nike (2018)

Jerry Lorenzo, founder of the luxury streetwear brand, Fear of God, is highly regarded in fashion and sneaker design. Fear of God has collaborated several times with Nike. In 2018, Nike and FoG collab'ed on a brand new silhouette, the Nike Air Fear of God 1. The sneaker has released in an assortment of colorways. It was designed to be a basketball sneaker and many pro basketball players have rocked them on the court. In addition to the Air Fear of God 1, Nike and FoG have collab'ed on other sneakers such as the Nike Air Fear of God Moccasin and Nike Air Skylon 2 Fear of God.

Source: Stadium Goods

Source: Stadium Goods

LICENSING & COLLABORATIONS

8. Fragment x Nike & Air Jordan (2014)

Fragment is a Japanese clothing brand run by designer Hiroshi Fujiwara. Fragment is a long-time collaborator with many brands, including Nike. In 2014, the two collaborated on an ultra clean black, sport-blue, and white Air Jordan 1. The sneaker, which came subtly branded with the Fragment lightning bolt logo on the heel, sold out in seconds, and is one of the most iconic Jordan 1 collabs to date. Since then, Nike and Jordan Brand has collaborated with Fragment on many other silhouettes including the Air Force 1, Air Jordan 3, and Air Cadence.

Source: Stadium Goods

9. Just Don x Air Jordan (2015)
Just Don x Converse (2018)

American streetwear designer, Don C, is well known for his Chicago based store RSVP Gallery and his Just Don sports-inspired luxury apparel and accessories brand. In addition to these lucrative ventures, Don C is a sneaker legend and has collaborated on some iconic sneakers. In 2015, Just Don and Jordan Brand collaborated on the Jordan Retro 2 in several colorways. In 2018, Just Don also collaborated with Converse on the Converse ERX 260 Just Don, which released in various colorways and versions. The same year, Don dropped a signature Jordan dubbed the Legacy 312. In 2020, Just Don collab'ed with Nike on the Nike Air Force 1 High Just Don and Nike KD 12 Don C. Just Don has proven time and time again that everything it touches is fire.

10. Kith/Ronnie Fieg x The World

KITH, the retail store and fashion brand founded by Ronnie Fieg, has collaborated with pretty much every major sneaker brand. What Ronnie has done with KITH is unbelievable, to say the least. Collaborating with the mega companies of the world like Coca-Cola, Disney, Levi's, Versace, Nike, adidas, New Balance, ASICS, Columbia, and others is what Ronnie Fieg and KITH are known for. Fulfilling lifelong dream collaborations is what separates Ronnie and Kith from most designers and fashion brands. Everything has meaning when it comes to KITH.

Source: Stadium Goods

Source: Stadium Goods

12. Oyster Holdings x adidas (2019)

"Traveling is a sport," and the adidas Samba is a classic sports silhouette that first released in 1950. Flash forward to 2019, when lifestyle brand Oyster Holdings collab'ed with adidas on the adidas Samba OG Oyster Holdings. The duo created three unique and stylish colorways, which was a refreshing take on a timeless sneaker.

LICENSING & COLLABORATIONS

Source: Stadium Goods

Source: adidas

11. Off-White x Nike & Air Jordan (2018)
Off-White x Converse (2018)

Virgil Abloh is a DJ, artist, architect, designer, and founder of the Milan-based fashion house, Off-White. One of Off-White's most notable collaborations is with Nike, a collection of co-branded sneakers called "The Ten." This collection consisted of a series of classic silhouettes that Virgil redesigned and reimagined with an Off-White spin. Every sneaker in this collection is extremely limited and most sneakerheads around the world took Ls trying to get a pair. Additional models have since been released, like the Off-White Air Jordans 4 and 5, and you can expect more fire Off-White x Nike collabs in the future.

13. Prada x adidas (2019)

Italian luxury fashion house Prada joined forces with adidas in 2019 to release the adidas Superstar Prada. The two took the classic adidas sneaker and added high quality leather and other premium materials. The sneaker released in various colorways and was sold separately with a luxurious leather bowling bag. As adidas and Prada continue their partnership, it will be interesting to see what the brands conjure up.

211

14. Public School (PSNY) x Air Jordan (2015)

Public School NY, the American fashion brand and retailer, teamed up with Jordan Brand in 2015 and dropped the Air Jordan 12 Retro PSNY. Along with the sneaker, this collaboration included a collection of PSNY branded clothes. PSNY and Jordan Brand subsequently dropped the sneaker in different colorways, and have collab'ed on other Jordan models such as the Jordan 15 and Horizon.

Souce: Stadium Goods

16. Jeff Staple x Nike (2005)

Jeff Staple, the American fashion and graphic designer, is known for designing arguably one of the most hyped sneakers of all time—the Nike SB Pigeon Dunk. The sneaker released in 2005 and goes down as one of the craziest sneaker releases ever. The lines of people trying to cop the sneaker were so insane that NYC Police came in full force to prevent riots and ensure everyone's safety. This sneaker is extremely limited, with a total of only 150 pairs produced. The Pigeon Dunk resells for around $20,000, making it one of the most expensive sneakers the resale market has ever seen.

Source: StockX

15. Raf Simons x adidas (2013)

Raf Simons is a Belgian fashion designer who started his own menswear brand in 1995. In 2020, Raf became the co-creative director of Prada. Raf and adidas collaborated on the adidas Ozweego Raf Simons in 2013, which started their partnership. This sneaker is known for its chunky lower platform sole, and there are an assortment of colorways that have been released. Raf and adidas have also collab'ed on a variety of Stan Smith silhouettes and other sneakers.

Source: Stadium Goods

17. Rick Owens x adidas (2017)

Rick Owens is a fashion designer and CEO of his eponymous luxury brand. In 2017, adidas and Rick Owens got together to create the adidas Level Runner Low Rick Owens in black and white colorways. This design is unique with a leather upper and ultra-thick midsole, which gives this sneaker a very futuristic vibe. Rick and adidas have also collab'ed on additional sneakers such as the adidas Rick Owens Tech Runner and adidas Springblade Low Rick Owens.

Source: StockX

Source: Stadium Goods

19. Stella McCartney x adidas (2005)

Stella McCartney is an English fashion designer and the daughter of former Beatles member and singer-songwriter sensation, Sir Paul McCartney. In 2001, Stella launched her own luxury fashion brand, focused on sustainable and vegan-friendly materials. In 2005, she collaborated with adidas on a sports performance collection for women that initially included vegan leather Stan Smith sneakers. Ten years later, the two brands renewed and expanded their collaboration deal through 2020, launching adidas StellaSport under McCartney's creative direction. You can find a wide array of sporty styles and colors from the Stella McCartney x adidas collab.

18. Sacai x Nike (2019)

Sacai is a Japanese fashion brand. In 2019, Nike and Sacai collaborated on a silhouette that meshed the Waffle Daybreak and LDV models. This sneaker is a wild one, featuring double everything—tongues, swooshes, shoelaces, and midsoles. The LDWaffle came in multiple colorways and marked the beginning of a series of sneaker collabs between the two brands.

Source: Stadium Goods

20. Supreme x Nike (2002)
Supreme x Air Jordan (2015)

World famous. Supreme is a skateboarding, clothing, and lifestyle brand that made its entrance in the streetwear world in the 1990s. Over the past few decades, Supreme has collaborated with some of the best brands on extremely unique products, including of course, sneakers. Supreme and Nike have collaborated many times on some of the most classic Nike models, including the Dunk Hi, Air Force 1 Mid and Low, Air Foamposite One, Air Max and even Air Jordan Retros. You can surely expect more Supreme x Nike collaborations in the future.

Source: Stadium Goods

Source: Stadium Goods

22. YEEZY x Nike (2009)

"Yeezy's all on your sofa, these the Red Octobers." Considered by some as Kanye's most rare and celebrated collaboration to date, the Air Yeezy models are grails for anyone's collection. On the Nike Air Yeezy 1 and 2, Kanye and Nike collaborated on a total of six different colorways, including the most sought after model, the Red October. However, we have seen some insane unreleased Nike Air Yeezy samples.

LICENSING & COLLABORATIONS

21. UNDFTD x Air Jordan (2005)

Undefeated, the famous sneaker store and apparel brand, has a strong resume of collaborations. UNDFTD's most highly sought-after sneaker collab is their Air Jordan Retro 4, which released in 2005. At the time, UNDFTD was the first sneaker boutique to collaborate with Jordan Brand, making the sneaker a historic release. The design features a military aesthetic, using colors like green, orange, and black. If like most of us, you wanted this sneaker, you were likely out of luck; only 72 pairs were released.

Source: Stadium Goods

Source: Stadium Goods

23. YEEZY x adidas (2015)

"YEEZY YEEZY YEEZY just jumped over Jumpman." Kanye West departed from Nike in 2013 to pursue something bigger, and he achieved that with adidas. adidas signed the YEEZY contract at a time when Kanye was roughly $50 million in debt, and just a short while later, YEEZY became a billion-dollar brand. What Kanye has done with adidas is revolutionary, and he is showing no signs of exhaustion.

Other Collaborations

We've just seen how athletes, musicians, and fashion brands have joined forces with sneaker companies to produce some amazing kicks. Occasionally, however, a collab comes along that breaks the mold and defies expectations in terms of marketing and other pop culture influence. Our journey through the best collaborations wouldn't be complete without exploring some of these clever deals. Let's take a look!

LICENSING & COLLABORATIONS

1. adidas Continental 80 Vulc Arizona Iced Tea
2. adidas Ultraboost 4.0 Game of Thrones White Walkers
3. Nike SB Dunk Low Heineken
4. adidas Jonah Hill Superstar
5. Air Jordan 4 Retro KAWS
6. K-Swiss CR-Terrati Lil Jupiterr
7. adidas Ultraboost 19 Star Wars Millennium Falcon
8. Nike Kyrie Irving 5 Spongebob
9. Nike Blazer Mid Stranger Things Hawkins High School
10. Skechers Kim K Shape-Ups (not pictured)
11. K-Swiss Gary Vee 001 (not pictured)

1. AriZona Iced Tea x adidas (2019)

AriZona Iced Tea and adidas collaborated in 2019 on the Continental 80 and Yung-1 silhouettes. The sneakers had the AriZona Iced Tea plant and logo included in its design. The collab had sneakerheads thirsty for more!

Source: Stadium Goods

Source: Stadium Goods

3. Heineken x Nike (2003)

In 2003, Nike and Dutch beer company, Heineken, collaborated on the Nike SB Dunk Low Heineken. The sneaker consists of a white-leather, green nubuck, and black suede upper, with the iconic Heineken star on the heel. The Heineken SB quickly became a classic and is a grail for many sneakerheads.

LICENSING & COLLABORATIONS

2. Game of Thrones x adidas (2019)

Fantasy novel turned HBO TV series *Game of Thrones* teamed up with adidas in 2019 to celebrate the show's final season with a series of G.O.T.-themed kicks. One of the more noteworthy designs was the White Walker adidas Ultraboost, that even sneakerheads who never watched the show could appreciate.

Source: Stadium Goods

4. Jonah Hill x adidas (2020)

Jonah Hill is an actor, director, writer, and comedian. From a young age, Jonah had a passion for pop culture, streetwear, skating, and sneakers. Fulfilling a lifelong dream, Jonah Hill signed with adidas in 2019, and in 2020, they officially released Jonah's first signature sneaker, the adidas Superstar Jonah Hill. adidas and Jonah also dropped a new version of the adidas Samba in 2020. We definitely expect more adidas x Jonah Hill collaborations will release in the future.

Source: StockX

Source: StockX

6. LilJupiterr x K-Swiss (2019)

LilJupiterr became known on social media through his Instagram mood board. Always focused on bigger things, Jupiterr linked up with K-Swiss in 2019 on two models with several colorways. Expect more to come from this trendsetter and fashion influencer.

LICENSING & COLLABORATIONS

5. KAWS x Air Jordan (2017)

Brian Donnelly, otherwise known as KAWS, is an artist and designer. Among other things, KAWS is known for replacing the eyes of iconic toy figures with "X's." In 2017, KAWS and Jordan Brand collaborated on two Air Jordan Retro 4 models in grey and black colorways. The design consists of a premium smooth suede upper and KAWS logo on the back of the sneaker, which replaced the iconic Jumpman logo.

Source: Stadium Goods

7. Star Wars x adidas (2019)

Star Wars and adidas collaborated in 2019 on a *Star Wars* Millennium Falcon themed adidas Ultraboost. This is one of many collaborations between adidas and *Star Wars*. The force is strong with this collaboration!

Source: Stadium Goods

Source: Stadium Goods

9. Stranger Things x Nike (2019)

Stranger Things, a sci-fi Netflix television series based in the 1980s, debuted in 2016, and became an instant hit. In 2019, to celebrate the release of the show's third season, *Stranger Things* collab'ed on a Nike Cortez and Nike Blazer, both prominent 1980s sneakers that remain staples to this day.

8. Spongebob x Kyrie Irving (2019)

This collaboration is a fun one. In 2019, Nike, Kyrie Irving, and *SpongeBob SquarePants* collab'ed on a version of the Nike Kyrie 5. This collab fulfilled the inner kid in Kyrie and likely hit home for many hoopers in their 20s, considering *SpongeBob* was a show that many grew up watching. Six different versions were created for each of the main characters in *SpongeBob*. Getting your hands on a pair of these could be harder than finding the Krabby Patty secret formula!

10. Kim Kardashian x Skechers (2011)

The Kim Kardashian x Sketchers collaboration in 2011 is an entertaining moment in sneaker history. Sketchers and Kim Kardashian debuted the Kim K Shape Ups during the Super Bowl in a controversial commercial. The sneaker eventually led to a lawsuit due to false advertisements about its toning and shaping abilities.

11. Gary Vee x K-Swiss (2017)

Gary Vaynerchuk is an entrepreneur, author, CEO, and motivational speaker. Known for his social media presence and entrepreneurial spirit, Gary Vee started from nothing and built a media empire. In 2017, K-Swiss and Gary Vee collab'ed on the Gary Vee 001 and 002, which was followed by additional models.

By now, you have an understanding of the critical roles that licenses and collaborations play in the creation of your favorite sneakers. A sneaker's success is also heavily dependent on how it is marketed. In our next chapter, we take a look at what marketing is and how it is used to effectively promote sneakers and sneaker products to consumers, both in traditional mediums and, most recently, in the digital world.

Marketing

"It's gotta be the shoes."

—MARS BLACKMON

Marketing is a tool brands use to strategically position their products and set them apart from their competitors. If you recall, we briefly discussed creating a marketing plan back in chapter 2, so you already know that marketing is an important consideration at the outset of your sneaker business. Marketing can also be used anytime a company wants to introduce a new product or even breathe new life into an existing one. Without marketing, so many of us would be unaware of all the new sneaker products that release on an almost-daily basis.

What makes good marketing in the sneaker world? In this chapter, you will learn about the marketing formats sneaker companies use to promote their products, from print to digital and more. But first, you must have a successful marketing strategy, which is primarily achieved through creating what is called the marketing mix.

The Four Ps of the Marketing Mix

If you think of marketing as a cake (be sure to make it a sneaker cake), the marketing mix would be the ingredients you need to create the best cake possible. The ingredients of your cake are referred to as the four Ps of marketing: product, place, price, and promotion. Now let's get baking (or cooking, for all of the sneaker cook groups out there).

Product

In any successful marketing mix, creating a product that consumers need or want is key. Since we are talking sneakers here, you should already know the product pretty well. Sneaker marketing should be based in a clear understanding of the product, why it may be desired by consumers, and what makes it different from the products competitors offer. If I am a serious runner, and I want to buy a pair of performance running sneakers, should I buy HOKA ONE ONE, Brooks, ASICS, Saucony, On, Allbirds, Under Armour, adidas, Nike, New Balance, or Mizuno? What makes the Nike Air cushioning system better than the ASICS Gel, adidas Boost, New Balance Fresh Foam, Puma LQDCELL, Saucony Grid, Converse REACT, or Reebok Hexalite? This is just a small segment of the overwhelming number of product offerings in sneakers today. If you intend to introduce a new running sneaker or midsole cushioning product, you should carefully consider how your product will be unique and attract consumers who already have a myriad of options.

Price

The second P is simply the amount of money a consumer is expected to pay for a product. For some products, price may seem trivial, but it is an essential component of the marketing mix; if a sneaker is priced too high or too low, it may not sell. In the early 1990s, it was rare for a sneaker to command a retail price over $100. Over the last three decades, as sneakers have grown immensely in popularity, product offering, and technology, so have the prices. It is now commonplace for a pair of high-performance sneakers to retail anywhere from $200 to $300 a pair, while designer kicks can run in excess of $1,000. Not everyone can afford sneakers in these price ranges; a brand could lose customers if its price is unattainable or unjustifiable. On the other hand, if a sneaker is priced too low, it may devalue the brand, which could make consumers skeptical about whether it is worthwhile or create the impression that the sneaker is poorly made. Marketing should therefore account for the consumer's appetite, the quality of the goods, and the price of comparable products.

Place or Placement

The third P determines how the product will reach consumers. Remember our discussion about distribution channels in chapter 4? Hope so! Any good marketing mix should consider the most suitable distribution channels, including where you intend to sell it, how it will get there, and how it will be positioned among the products it shares space with. For example, you can find almost all New Balance sneaker styles in New Balance's retail stores or on the New Balance website. New Balance performance sneakers are also sold at running and sports retail stores, such as Fleet Feet, Road Runner Sports, and Dick's Sporting Goods. Certain limited edition New Balance sneakers, including the Jaden Smith x New Balance Vision Racer, which dropped on July 24, 2020, make their way to exclusive sneaker boutiques such as Nice-Kicks, SNS, End, and others. New Balance must consider where it will position each product it sells and how to best target that product's consumers.

Promotion

The fourth and final P deals with how a company will communicate to its consumers. Promotions include advertisements, events, offers, activities, and other public relations. Promotion must come after all the other Ps, because you cannot promote something until you know what you are promoting (product), how you will promote it (price), and where it will be promoted (place).

In the sneaker business, how you promote your product or service may be the most significant aspect of the marketing mix. Whether it's through traditional mediums, such as print and TV, or today's internet and social media influencers, this chapter will cover all the marketing angles like elephant print on a Jordan 3.

Traditional Marketing Channels

Traditional marketing channels include print advertising as well as advertisements on TV and product placements in movies and TV shows.

Print

Extra, extra—read all about kicks! Long before sneaker blogs and Instagram feeds, sneakers were primarily marketed through print magazines, newspapers, and catalogs. Although in rapid decline since the rise of the internet, print was the earliest and most effective means of sneaker marketing.

Magazines

The most popular form of print marketing for sneakers is the magazine. One could (and still can) find sneaker ads and images in magazines of all kinds: sports magazines such as *Sports Illustrated*, *Runner's World*, *BMX*, *Slam*, or *Thrasher*; style magazines such as *GQ*, *Vogue*, *Maxim*, or *InStyle*; and even general news magazines such as *Time*, *People*, *Newsweek*, or *The New Yorker*. There are even specialty magazines such as *Sneaker Freaker*, *Sneaker Magazine*, *Sole Collector*, or *Complex*, which primarily target sneakerheads. Each of these mags now has its own online presence as well, typically in blog or vlog format (which we discuss later in this chapter).

Newspapers

Another effective but less frequently used form of print marketing tool for sneakers is the newspaper. Circulated newspapers can be traced back to as early as the fifteenth century, when Johannes Gutenberg invented the printing press. By the mid- to late twentieth century, at the same time sneakers began to grow in popularity, newspaper readership reached its peak. Sneakers were often advertised in retail circulars, which were widely distributed printed advertisements containing coupons you could cut out and redeem in store.

Mailers and Catalogs

Although used less frequently since internet and email marketing have taken over, some companies still utilize print mailers, or catalogs to market their sneaker products. For example, Eastbay, the multi-brand retailer founded in Wisconsin in 1980, has been mailing sneaker catalogs to its customers ever since. That's over forty years of sneaker sales, and still going strong!

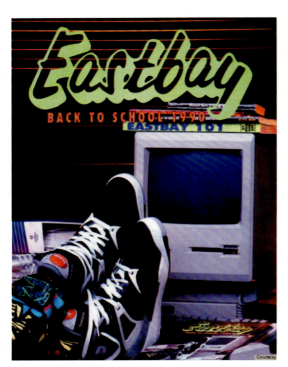

Source: Eastbay

Source: Eastbay

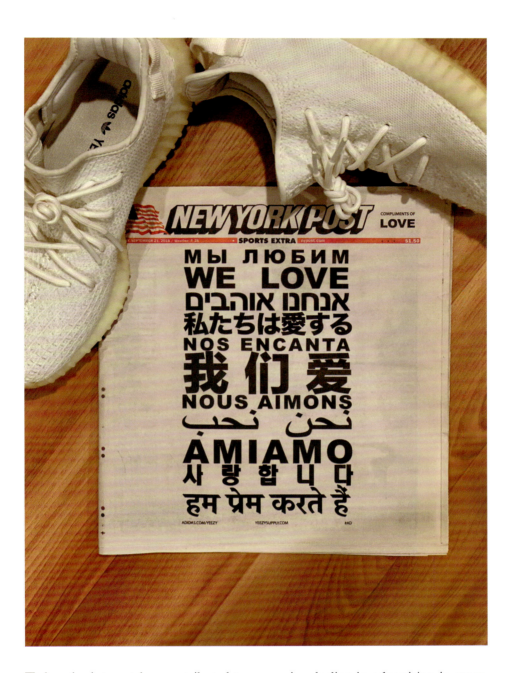

Today, the internet has contributed to a massive decline in advertising in magazines, newspapers, catalogs, and other print media. But sneaker brands still use print as an effective marketing tool. On September 21, 2018, adidas took out full-page ad spreads in ten major US newspapers to advertise the global release of the YEEZY Boost 350 V2 "Triple White." Each ad read "We Love" in various languages, including Russian, English, Hebrew, Japanese, Spanish, Chinese, French, Arabic, Italian, Korean, and Hindi.

On March 3, 2019, Skechers took out a newspaper ad in *The Oregonian* trolling Nike over a pair of sneakers that split on the recently Nike-signed basketball star Zion Williamson. Instead of Nike's famous slogan "Just Do It," the ad read "Just Blew It" and below a photo of the ripped open sneaker, a promise from the brand stating "Skechers—We won't split on you."

Billboards

Although not used as frequently as print, billboards are another effective form of sneaker marketing, typically reserved for large sneaker campaigns. Billboards are large advertisements that appear outdoors in highly visible and populated areas. Billboards are effective primarily due to the high number of people who see them and the engaging imagery and messaging they can display. Take, for example, the Nike-sponsored LeBron James "We Are All Witnesses" and "Cleveland" banners that appeared between 2005–2010 and 2014–2018, respectively. These famous billboards were featured on the side of the Sherwin-Williams building in downtown Cleveland and spanned an enormous ten stories, covering 25,000 square feet.

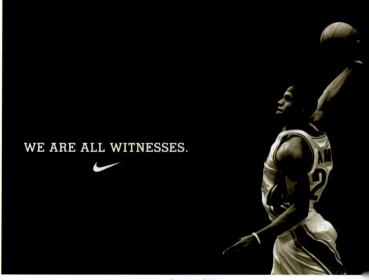

Source: Nike

Television and Film

As more people were able to have television sets in their home and could afford to go to movie theaters, marketing via TV and film grew in popularity.

Source: Nike

Commercials

The earliest television advertisement dates to 1941 and cost only $9 to air. Within just ten years, the TV ad business was booming at around $128 million in annual spend. Fast forward to 2019, and the TV ad spend reached over $70 billion. Even with the internet, TV remains a massive marketing platform, especially for sneakers.

Historically, sneaker companies have used commercials to market their products to massive audiences. Over the years, there have been some pivotal sneaker commercials. Some are unforgettable: the iconic Spike Lee and Michael Jordan spots—"Money, it's gotta be the shoes"; or when adidas superimposed boxer Laila Ali into old fight footage of her father, Muhammad Ali (the greatest of all time), so the two looked as if they were fighting each other. Classic! Whether it was Larry Bird rapping about the Converse Weapon, Charles Barkley fighting Godzilla in his Nike Air Forces, Dennis Rodman telling you to "Pump up...and air out" for the Reebok Pump, sneaker commercials have been humorous, moving, and impactful. In fact, an entire book could be written about the range and impact of sneaker commercials. We urge every reader to search online and spend some time watching sneaker commercials; it may inspire how you market your own product!

Product Placement in TV and Film

A sneaker company can always fork over cash to air a commercial, but what about the more subtle ways to market kicks on-screen? Memorable silver screen sneaker moments include Michael J. Fox auto-lacing his futuristic Air Mags in *Back to the Future Part II*, Tom Hanks unboxing a fresh pair of Cortezes in *Forrest Gump*, Michael Jordan schooling the Monstars in his Jordan 11 Concords in *Space Jam*, or Miles Morales swinging through New York in his OG Chicago Jordan 1 in *Spider Man: Into the Spider Verse*.

These are only a few of the creative ways Nike has marketed its sneakers through product placement in film. There were great product placement moments on TV as well. Who could forget all the J's worn by Will Smith in the classic '90s sitcom *The Fresh Prince of Bel-Air*? Even Jerry Seinfeld rocked everything from Huaraches, Bo Jackson Air Trainers, and Mowabb ACGs on his eponymous 1990s TV show.

Sneakers aren't just for comedies and sitcoms, and Nike isn't the only company to have benefited from on-screen placement. Bruce Lee wore Onitsuka Tiger Mexico 66s in *Game of Death*, a moment that later inspired Uma Thurman's bloody, Onitsuka-clad fight scene in Quentin Tarantino's *Kill Bill*. In chapter 1, we discussed the Reebok Alien Stomper, which appeared in the movie Alien in 1986. adidas is no stranger to movie features either. Bill Murray wore a custom pair of adi Rom's in Wes Anderson's *The Life Aquatic with Steve Zissou*, Sylvester Stallone clobbered his opponents in three-stripe boxing kicks in *Rocky*, and Run DMC dripped from head to toe in adidas in the hip-hop classic *Krush Groove*.

Today, it is hard to find a movie or TV program that is not influenced in some way by sneaker marketing. We could go on for pages atbout the sporting moments made even more iconic by the sneakers worn by triumphant athletes or the heat on the feet of musicians, comedians, and other entertainers during live concerts and other rebroadcast events. If you want to create a real story around your product, product placement is where it's at.

Digital Marketing Channels

As technology and digital media evolved, so did digital marketing to promote sneaker products. Online advertising began in 1994, when AT&T paid $30,000 for a banner ad to a website that later became *Wired* magazine. The ad campaign was a huge success. From that point on, brands realized the value of online advertising, and publishers recognized that selling ad space on their websites could be a viable revenue stream. Since then, online advertising has increased in popularity year after year, and this has been the case for the sneaker industry as well. In 2019, Nike's total advertising and promotional spend was a whopping $3.75 billion, and its annual spend has been steadily increasing since 2000; a sizable portion of its budget is utilized for the digital space.

On the flip side, sneaker publishers and media companies derive significant income from selling digital ad space. For example, Complex, a publisher, media company, and video network that creates a wealth of sneaker-related content, sells advertising on its digitally owned and operated properties, and this makes the company a substantial amount of money each year.

The options for online advertising have expanded over time. We will explain all of these in this section. Make sure your pop-ups are enabled!

Online Marketing

Digital Advertising

The OG form of digital marketing is advertising through websites viewed on a desktop or laptop computer. Brands typically buy advertising space on publishers' digital properties to promote their products or services. If they are represented by digital agencies, the agency buys digital advertising on their behalf. As time has passed, digital advertising has expanded from desktop computers to mobile phones, tablets, and apps.

Understanding the many types of digital advertising can be complicated, and the options can be quite technical, so we have done our best to list each while providing practical examples for clarity.

01 Display ads are presented in image or video form. An ad can technically be considered a display ad as long as users can see it online. Example: a video ad by Li-Ning promoting a new Way of Wade sneaker featured on *Sole Collector*'s website.

02 Banner ads are generally images embedded on websites. These often feature text to entice the user to click on the ad. The ads come in many different sizes and can appear on any part of the website. Example: an ad by Stadium Goods featuring three new sneaker releases with the text, "Purchase the most recent drops at Stadium Goods now," in the shape of a vertical rectangle on the side of Highsnobiety's website.

03 Pop-up ads are a form almost everyone knows. As annoying as they can be, they are also effective. As the name suggests, these ads pop up on a user's screen when visiting a website. Example: a Sneaker Con ad that pops up when a user visits Hypebeast's mobile website.

04 Native advertising is advertising that matches the look and feel of the website, app, or platform on which it appears. With this type of advertising, it is often hard to tell that the ad is actually an ad because it feels like part of the content. Example: an ad by Golden Goose for a new Super-Star sneaker that appears on a Facebook user's news feed right under a friend's post.

05 Sponsored content a form of native advertising, is sponsored and paid for by a brand and is usually featured on a publisher's website in the form of an article or video. Sponsored content can also appear on social media, as banner and display ads, and in other forms of digital content. Example: an article that Yeezy Mafia pays *Sneaker News* to post on its website.

06 Search advertising also referred to as paid search advertising, is advertising that appears in search engine results. When a user searches for something on Google, Yahoo!, Bing, and other search engines, an ad appears in the search results. Example: an ad for the new adidas x Kid Cudi sneaker collab appearing in search results after a user Googles "Cudi."

07 Email advertising involves a brand sending promotional emails and newsletters to its consumers. Email advertising can also take the form of ads that appear in email newsletters from brands. Example: an ad for Complex's *"Sneaker Shopping"* show (s/o to Joe La Puma!) appearing in an email newsletter that Foot Locker sends its customers.

08 Social media advertising is done through platforms that include Facebook, Instagram, Twitter, Snapchat, TikTok, LinkedIn, YouTube, Pinterest, and others. These ads are tailored to the specifications of the applicable platform. All of the social media platforms offer distinct services where you can purchase and launch ads. For example, Instagram has Instagram Business services, where users can create stories, videos, photos, carousels, and collections, explore ads, and buy these ads through the ads manager within the app, or through Instagram partners that can help with the ad creation and delivery process. Many sneaker companies engage in social media advertising due to its ability to connect directly with users; nowadays, almost everyone uses social media, so this gives sneaker companies an opportunity to promote their products and services in an effective and engaging way. Example: the sneaker store Concepts creating a Facebook ad campaign through the ads manager tool, serving video ads promoting its online store to sneakerheads' news feeds. We will cover more about social media marketing in the sneaker industry later in this chapter.

Data and Targeting

None of the types of digital advertising we've just described are effective unless the ads reach the right consumers, in our case, sneakerheads. An essential way of doing this is through targeting. This is the process of serving ads based on data related to users' demographics, interests, traits, online behavioral history, and certain tendencies, preferences, and purchase behaviors. Retargeting focuses on users who already visited a website or app. Have you ever browsed the web for a pair of sneakers and noticed a flurry of sneaker ads follow? Well, you have retargeting to blame for that!

Targeting only works if you have good data. Data is generally collected on websites, apps, devices, social media channels, and other digital properties that users visit and can be captured through the following:

01 Pixels are pieces of code that are placed on websites that collect information about users who visit. This helps companies capture data used with retargeting, analytics, building custom audiences, personalized user experiences, conversions, and more.

02 Tags are also placed on websites and often control data that is passed to a pixel. Tags can be set to look for certain sets of information and can help with tracking, reporting, analytics, conversions, optimization, and more.

03 Cookies are files that are located and saved on web browsers, and store data and information related to the user's online behavior.

04 IP addresses are unique addresses used to identify a specific computer, computer network, or mobile device that browses the internet and, as a result, can be extremely useful for targeting.

05 Mobile advertising IDs are IDs that are assigned to mobile devices, used to serve relevant advertising.

Other Digital Advertising Technologies

There are many players in the digital advertising space. As a sneaker company looking to advertise, it is important to know your options. You'll find various software as a service (SaaS) companies out there that specialize in technologies related to digital advertising. These companies assist with more effective advertising. Programmatic advertising is another digital advertising medium. It enables companies to purchase ads automatically from a wide array of publishers rather than directly and individually from publishers. This process is done in real time and occurs through demand-side platforms (DSPs), which allow companies/advertisers to buy ads automatically, and supply-side platforms (SSPs), which allow a publisher to sell ad space on its digital properties. Generally, sitting in the middle of programmatic advertising are ad exchanges, which help DSPs transact with SSPs. With all of these digital advertising technologies, data is essential to effective advertising.

Benefits of Digital Advertising

Effective digital advertising can benefit sneaker companies in several ways. First, it creates brand awareness. When digital advertising is effective and data is used successfully, the ad reaches consumers who are interested in the products or services that the ad promotes. When this happens, the impressions, or the number of times the ad is displayed on someone's screen or device, can be abundant and lead to brand awareness. For example, if a new sneaker brand runs an effective digital ad campaign for one month and the campaign garners 400,000 impressions, chances are that more people will know about the brand.

Second, digital advertising can help with sales. If a digital advertising campaign is effective, relevant consumers are targeted. There is a good chance that individuals who are interested in the company's products or services will see the ad and click on it. When users click on the ad, it can lead to potential sales, also known as conversions. For example, say Balenciaga spent $200,000 on digital advertising related to new iterations of its Triple S and Track sneakers. Balenciaga, of course, will want to see a good conversion rate, meaning that a good number of consumers who actually saw the ad purchased the sneakers. The conversion rate is calculated by taking the number of conversions and dividing by total ads during the same period. If you ran 10,000 ads over a three-month period and got 2,000 conversions, your conversion rate would be 20 percent.

Third, digital advertising is measurable. The insights and analytics that typically accompany digital advertising campaigns give companies the ability to measure the success of the campaigns and overall behaviors of consumers. This allows companies to see what is and isn't working. For sneaker companies, this can be hugely beneficial because they can learn relevant information about consumers and formulate business plans accordingly.

Source: Worapol Kengkittipat / Shutterstock.com

Privacy Concerns

Data collection and usage for digital advertising is highly regulated. There are various international, federal, and state laws and regulations as well as self-regulatory organizations that set forth requirements and restrictions when it comes to digital advertising and data collection and usage. For example, internationally, there is the EU General Data Protection Regulation (GDPR); in California, the California Consumer Privacy Act (CCPA); at the federal level, the Federal Trade Commission (FTC) and Federal Communications Commission (FCC); and there are also self-regulatory organizations such as the Network Advertising Initiative (NAI), Interactive Advertising Bureau (IAB), and Digital Advertising Alliance (DAA).

One could probably write a separate book on data protection; just make sure your company is aware of these laws, regulations, rules, and guidelines to ensure compliance with all parties involved.

Mobile Apps

Another form of digital marketing is through mobile apps. Nowadays, almost every sneaker company has a mobile app that accompanies its products or services. By using apps, sneaker companies can sell their products or services, share news, post content, offer rewards programs, and provide other features. Many of the types of digital advertising previously described can occur on mobile apps as well. Popular sneaker apps include the Nike SNKRS app, adidas and Confirmed apps, J23, KicksOnFire, apps for Finish Line, Champs, Eastbay, Footaction, and Foot Locker, and the Kith app.

Social Media

The internet has been bringing small groups of people together since the earliest iterations of chat rooms like IRC (Internet Relay Chat) and messenger apps like AIM (AOL Instant Messenger). Back then, if you wanted to hop online and talk to someone about sneakers, there were very limited options, and until the early 2000s, social media was relatively unknown. In fact, before social media became the behemoth and household necessity that it is today with platforms such as Facebook, Twitter, and Instagram, there were only online forums or discussion boards where you could post and reply to other users' messages. One of the first forums for sneakers was NikeTalk. Not affiliated with Nike, NikeTalk has been around since 1999, where sneaker discussions, collecting, and questions could be exchanged and answered among the earliest sneakerheads. For those of us who were in the game back then, NikeTalk was the OG sneaker social media platform.

The NikeTalk forums still exist today, but as we will see in the sections to follow, the sneaker community has drastically evolved through social media. It is estimated that 3.1 billion people worldwide are on social media every single day. That's just under half the world's population! When you think about those staggering numbers, it is no wonder why social media has evolved so quickly and become such an important part of our global society. Social media is no longer just about connecting and finding old friends, sharing pictures, music, or building a small, dedicated following. With social media, businesses can market and amplify their brand message across the globe with unlimited potential. As you will soon find out, this is undoubtedly true for the sneaker world.

In this section, we take a look at social media and what it has done for the world of sneaker marketing today. We examine each of the primary social media platforms in turn, explaining how they can be used to market sneaker products and services. We also will provide some concrete examples of the ways in which sneaker brands have used these platforms to drive demand, sales, and general exposure. Since we covered social media advertising in the digital advertising section, we will not cover it here. However, as mentioned, we want to stress the importance of advertising on social media; all players in the sneaker industry can greatly benefit from it and help increase revenues. So without further ado (we know that you are anticipating this like a SNKRS drop), let's get into it, and of course, make sure you smash that like button and give us a follow back (our Instagram account is @snkrlaw)!

Instagram

#sneakerhead #igsneakercommunity #kicksoftheday #wdywt #kickstagram. It goes down in the DM (and on Instagram overall when it comes to sneakers)! Instagram is a go-to platform for sneaker companies, designers, and others in the sneaker industry to market their products and services. Almost all players in the sneaker industry have an Instagram profile consisting of posts, highlights, reels, and stories, all of which feature photos or videos. Other Instagram users can interact by liking, commenting, and direct messaging the user who posted the content. Through Instagram, you can build a strong profile that showcases whatever sneaker products or services you wish to market, which can lead to large numbers of followers and sales.

To build a strong profile on Instagram, you need to create engaging content. With all of Instagram's posting options, there is a large opportunity to be creative and engage current and potential followers. When marketing sneakers on Instagram, the majority of brands feature the sneakers through creative graphics, images, and video clips. Influencers (which we will discuss in detail later in this chapter), athletes, and celebrities are frequently shown rocking sneakers and promoting the brand. In 2018, for its #YEEZYSEASON6 campaign, which included the YEEZY 500 sneaker, YEEZY created a paparazzi-inspired Instagram campaign where various models, celebrities, and influencers posing as Kim Kardashian West were all decked out in the same YEEZY gear and YEEZY 500s. The IG campaign was an instant hit and sneakerheads and non-sneakerheads alike took notice. When YEEZY and adidas dropped the YEEZY 500s, in classic YEEZY fashion, they instantly sold out.

For others in the sneaker industry, outside of brands, it is also important to create engaging content. For example, Yeezy Mafia, an exclusive news source for everything YEEZY related, often creates engaging videos every time they leak a new YEEZY model. This has worked for them; they have almost 3 million followers and are successful in their preorder services and merchandise sales.

To have a strong Instagram page, you need a substantial number of followers. Engaging content can certainly lead to more followers, but to gain a strong following, you have to do much more. You can jointly market, or collaborate, with other sneaker companies and people in the sneaker industry. By collab'ing, each party can get exposure to the other party's followers. Collabs can involve influencers, celebrities, athletes, and other prominent figures, actual sneaker collabs, and collabs involving contests, sweepstakes, and promotions. Studying insights and analytics related to posts and interactions can also increase your followers by helping you focus on what works.

YEEZY MAFIA

Source: Yeezy Mafia

Selling on Instagram

Instagram is more than just a place to post sneaker-related content; it has become a massive market for selling sneakers and sneaker-related products and services. With the right content and messaging on IG alone, your sneaker business can truly blow up from sales.

So how do you sell products or services on Instagram? Unlike other social media sites, such as Facebook, you cannot embed links on IG photo posts. This can make it a bit tricky to sell on IG, but there are ways. You can add captions to your photo and instruct your followers to click the link in your bio, sending them to your main shoppable website where they can make the purchase. Instagram allows only one clickable link on your entire account, so you have to be careful about keeping the link simple and broad enough to access all your products. However, using third-party companies such as Later, you can create mobile-optimized Linkin.bio landing pages that actually look like your IG feed, and each post can be a separate link taking you to any web page of your choosing.

Another way to sell products is through shoppable posts. These posts have embedded tags that allow users who click on them to be redirected to a product page where they can purchase. Your account will need to be set up as a business account and then approved by Instagram to be eligible to feature your sneaker products or services in posts.

Over time, IG has evolved from one photo feed per user to a multifaceted platform with variety of posting options, including the main IG feed, stories, which last for only twenty-four hours unless highlighted, and their latest addition, reels, meant to directly compete with rival TikTok. Selling products and services on IG has never been easier, and truly IG-savvy sneaker businesses can generate massive sales with the right content, engagement, and marketing strategy.

Facebook

Facebook is the most-used social media platform in the world and it kick-started the game of social media and digital marketing that we all know and love today. Facebook is a popular digital medium for sneaker companies to engage with fans and keep them updated on news and releases. Facebook owns Instagram; because of this, the platforms share similar functionalities. As with Instagram, Facebook users can post photos, videos, and stories to their feeds. However, Facebook is bigger and more robust. As of the second quarter of 2020, Facebook boasted over 2.7 billion monthly active users and, as of the writing of this book, has a market capitalization of over $700 billion.

Facebook has an array of features that Instagram does not offer. On Facebook, you can post GIFs, statuses without any images or videos, and also include clickable links in any post. Customers can leave reviews on business profiles, and businesses can also use a chatbot, which is an automated messaging software that responds to and messages users who contact them. Facebook also has groups, which we will discuss in the next section. Since Facebook is the owner of Instagram, sneaker companies can run ads that are placed on both Facebook and Instagram, making it a multiplatform powerhouse.

Facebook has a lot to offer and can be extremely valuable. For example, And1 Basketball (yes, we're bringing it way back to the mixtape days!) has a Facebook page with over 1 million followers. And1 posts engaging videos and images and sells its sneakers and other products on its page. The brand also has a chatbot that automatically responds to messages and assists with purchases.

Facebook Groups

In addition to being a great platform to promote your sneaker brand or business, Facebook is home to over 10 million groups, or user communities. There are groups for everything from learning Spanish to securing leftover tickets to your favorite music festival. Sneakerheads are no different.

Before we dive into the depths of sneaker groups on Facebook, there are a few things you should know. First, not every group is public. Many of the best sneaker communities are set up as closed groups managed by an administrator/moderator (or several) who decide who can and cannot join. Once you're allowed into a group, you must follow its rules, or you could get kicked/banned. The Facebook group Yeezy Talk Worldwide has over 200,000 members, with strict guidelines about posting things related to only Kanye West and YEEZY. You want to talk about Drake and OvO? Find another group!

In addition, most groups have requirements about what you can post. For example, personal brand promotional posts usually need prior approval from the admin, and you definitely cannot post any fake kicks or you will be booted. (Pun intended.) With that being said, the right approach in the right group can have a profound effect on your brand's marketing and exposure, so find your community today and start marketing yourself through Facebook Groups.

Twitter

Twitter is another major social media platform that is a lot more basic in terms of design and functionality than Instagram and Facebook but just as effective in terms of reach. Users send out tweets, which is what posts on Twitter are called, and they appear on the timelines of users who follow the account that posted the tweet. Tweets can also appear on the timelines of people who don't follow that account if a user they follow retweets it. Tweets can also be liked, and users can send direct messages to each other. Tweets are limited to 280 characters, so users are forced to tweet short messages or split longer messages across multiple tweets. Tweets can contain images, videos, GIFs, and links. For the sneaker industry, Twitter is used to share news and to market and sell products and services. Twitter can also be used for customers and sneaker brands to interact with each other through tweets and retweets.

Twitter is a viable means of selling sneakers. When a new sneaker drops, brands and retailers often tweet links to the product. In fact, Twitter has acted as an exclusive platform for purchasing certain sneakers. For example, in 2012, Nike implemented the Twitter Link Only strategy, where consumers could purchase limited and exclusive sneakers only through a Twitter link. For the most part, after Nike posted a link, the releases would sell out in seconds, and hundreds of thousands of users would view the tweet and click the link. This was great marketing for Nike. Not only were they able to sell sneakers, but they were also able to gain followers on Twitter and increase engagement through the platform. Although Nike no longer uses the Twitter Link Only method, the authors of this book still have mobile notifications enabled for Nike tweets just to make sure we don't miss out on any drops. That's a testament to Nike's brilliant marketing.

Twitter can also act as a community forum for sneakerheads. Because of Twitter, sneakerheads across the world can tweet at each other and talk about sneaker news, upcoming releases, reselling, and more. The community vibe of Twitter can bode well for sneaker companies and others in the sneaker industry because of the hype and dialogue that take place on the platform. However, the Twitter sneaker community is not always so nice; people have no problem roasting a brand and handing out Ls if they aren't feeling a certain sneaker. So tread (or tweet) lightly!

Snapchat

Snapchat allows users to exchange pictures and videos (called snaps) that are meant to disappear after they are watched. What started in 2011 as a person-to-person private photo exchange app has evolved into something much bigger. It is reported that over 3 billion snaps are sent and posted on the platform every day, which is why it is an effective digital sneaker marketing platform.

There are several ways to use Snapchat. Like other social media platforms, you can build a following by creating engaging content and interacting with other Snapchatters. This is primarily done by taking photo or video snaps, either by using the built-in camera or importing from your phone's camera roll. You can add filters, graphics, text, and other add-ons to dress up your snaps. Snapchat was the first to launch a stories feature, where you can publish a collection of snaps.

The app's premise may seem childish when you first fool around with it, but major sneaker companies and others in the sneaker industry are utilizing Snapchat in a very serious way. About 75 percent of Snapchat users are under age thirty-four, and the primary consumers of sneakers are millennials and Gen Z. This makes the app a perfect medium for reaching the target sneaker audience. To have a comprehensive social media presence, you can use Snapchat to repost your main (multiplatform) social content and then supplement that with exclusive, Snapchat-only material. Creating engaging content on Snapchat will make your business memorable, which may translate into sales when a consumer comes across your product elsewhere and it comes time to check out.

For example, Snapchat can be a great way to give fans a temporary behind-the-scenes look at your business, how your products are made, and who is involved. Celebs and other influencers do this best, so take notes from them: in 2018, DJ Khaled gave Snapchatters an exclusive look at his Air Jordan collaboration, including a look inside his Nike business meetings and the whole product creation from start to finish. Khaled, no stranger to Snapchat (or social media in general), has been known to grace fans with exclusive snaps, and unless they tune in right away, the info disappears. It's a brilliant way to keep customers engaged and glued to their phones. Some of the earliest YEEZY sneaker designs were "leaked" on Snapchat by Kim Kardashian West, where she racked up over 40 million views before they disappeared, only to reappear and immediately sell out online.

Snapchat is not just for celebs and influencers. Companies are finding serious value in the social platform. In June 2020, Snapchat and Gucci teamed up to launch a shoppable augmented reality (AR) tool. Using a custom filter, consumers in select countries were able to hold their phone cameras over their feet and virtually try on Gucci sneakers; if you liked the look, you could purchase directly through the Snapchat app. adidas ran a similar Snap AR campaign in December 2018 with its Ultraboost 19 running sneakers. The next time you think Snapchat is only good for filter that put freckles, glitter, or dog ears on your face, think again.

Reddit

Reddit, the self-proclaimed "front page of the internet," is one of the most popular websites. Unless you are familiar with how it works, Reddit can be quite confusing. Essentially, it is a massive collection of forum topics, where people can share news, content, and comment on other people's posts about anything they like (or don't like). These forum topics, called subreddits, are open to subscribers, much like Facebook Groups or other social media communities. Unlike other social sites, however, Reddit is neither flashy nor eye-catching.

Reddit's primary purpose is to spread news and discussions in a no-frills bulletin-board style, allowing readers the ability to promote or "upvote" a user post if they believe more people should see it, or "downvote" if they think it was a waste of time. The more upvotes your post receives, the more karma you earn. Karma is displayed on your profile; users with good karma scores are thought of as effective Reddit contributors.

Reddit was founded in 2005. As of 2008, there were nearly 10,000 subreddits; by 2020, that number skyrocketed to 1.2 million. The same year, it was estimated that there were more than 190 million posts across all subreddits, and over 40 million searches were conducted on the site per day, ranking its user engagement higher than other social media behemoths such as Instagram, Twitter, or LinkedIn. With those numbers, it is easy to see why Reddit is not just a good information source but a strong marketing tool as well.

There is a massive subculture for sneakers on Reddit. Popular sneaker subreddits, such as r/sneakers, with over 1.5 million subscribers, have substantial reach. How can you engage with and attract this audience to your sneaker business? Marketing on Reddit is not as easy or user-friendly as on some social sites. The best way is to start posting and engaging, hopefully building karma while you go. Unlike other social media sites, Reddit doesn't care how many friends or followers you have; as long as your posts are enjoyable and engaging, you will get upvoted. On the other hand, should you post something readers find to be inauthentic, they will be sure to let you know, so consider your posts wisely.

If you have a sneaker product or service you want to promote, the best thing to do is find a great story to build around it and share it with the right sneaker community. If your post catches fire, Reddit might promote it to its front page, which could increase its exposure exponentially. Post the right content and be on your way to unlocking one of the largest subsections of social media and engaging with a vast community of potential sneaker customers.

LinkedIn

LinkedIn refers to itself as the largest professional network on the internet. In chapter 3, we discussed the importance of networking and how, in 2016, LinkedIn helped bring the authors of this book together to start the Sneaker Law conversation. Without LinkedIn, there would be no *Sneaker Law* today! LinkedIn can also be used as a viable marketing platform for sneaker products and services.

Aside from purchasing targeted ads (as we discussed previously), LinkedIn users can use the social feed as an organic way to find customers, grow email lists, and post quality content about sneaker products and services. Like Facebook and Reddit, there are LinkedIn Groups, divided into companies, organizations, and other communities of interest. Joining and participating in these group discussions with a clever bend toward your business can be a useful marketing strategy.

As with Reddit, blatant self-promotion or hard-sell advertising within LinkedIn posts is generally frowned upon, since LinkedIn is a networking site above all else. With the right story and timing, however, your business and personal brand could find engagement on the site. If your post gains momentum, LinkedIn will promote and increase its chances of going viral. Also, if your business has employees, create a company page where your employees can connect and highlight their skills and experience to the general public. Business exposure on every level!

TikTok

Launched in 2017, TikTok is relatively new. Users upload videos with music clips, sounds, or effects playing in the background. TikTok videos can be up to fifteen seconds long, and users can like, share, and comment on the videos. Also, users can follow different accounts. TikTok has recently become a phenomenon. In 2019, it was downloaded 738 million times. Sneaker brands, others in the sneaker industry, and sneakerheads alike use TikTok to market their products and services in an engaging and fun way. For example, Nike posted a TikTok of the Greek Freak, Giannis Antetokounmpo, dancing and dunking on a kids basketball hoop while rocking his Nike Zoom Freak 2 signature sneaker. The post got over 200,000 likes and was a fun and effective way for Nike to market its sneakers.

MARKETING

Blogs, Vlogs, Podcasts, & Other Content Conglomerates

Blogs

Blogs, short for weblogs, are essentially online journals, diaries, or informational websites with a consistent theme. To bloggers and their readers, however, they are much more. Blogging began in the late '90s and really picked up steam in the early 2000s. People with different interests began blogging about any and every little thing. It was not long before sneakers became a heavily blogged-about topic. Over time, many popular sneaker blogs have evolved into multiplatform marketing machines.

Sole Collector, for example, was founded in Portland, Oregon in 2003 and began as a print magazine. The company would later reach a larger audience with its blog, which quickly became a primary source of sneaker news. The platform now reports on everything sneaker related: trends, niche cultures, and sneaker designs. It even has its own app, and was purchased by Complex in 2010.

Another major sneaker blog is *Sneaker News*. Blogging about kicks since 2006, it has become the go-to source for all official news about release dates, previews of upcoming kicks, and more. Through its website and other social media channels, Sneaker News claims a reach of over 20 million consumers per month. But *KicksOnFire* claims it is actually the most-read sneaker blog in the world. The *KicksOnFire* publishing platform has 1.3 million Facebook fans and 920,600 Twitter followers in addition to its heavily trafficked blog.

Today, there are literally thousands of other blogs of all formats that cover sneakers. Some are written by the average sneakerhead with a handful of loyal followers, others by a team of marketing professionals at massive sneaker brands like Nike or publishers like Complex with global reach in the millions. For those looking to get the word out about a specific product or service, creating a sneaker blog or approaching an existing, well-known sneaker blog to post on your behalf can be a great organic way to market.

Vlogs

Vlogs are the video counterpart (and at times supplement) to blogs. The definition of a vlogger is somewhat loose, as it can be anyone with a social media account who posts short videos that tell a consistent story. Although you can certainly vlog on many social media platforms, the most prominent by far is YouTube. Searching on YouTube can bring up sneaker vlogs of all kinds. Jacques Slade, Mr. Foamer Simpson, Tony Mui, Harrison Nevel, Brad Hall, and Roszko specialize in sneaker unboxing and product reviews. Other vlogs like *Complex* take you sneaker shopping, where you can live vicariously through the grail purchases of other notable sneakerheads, athletes, and celebrities. Wary sneaker buyers can count on vloggers like Yeezy Busta, Scoop208, and RealorFakeOfficial to teach them how to spot the differences between authentic and counterfeit kicks, while those looking to beat the bots on release day (see chapter 9 for more on reselling and bots) can watch live cop vlogs from Botter Boy Nova, ayobooka, and NoKapCole. Finally, there are those that just flex harder than all the others, like the Perfect Pair, the Mayor, Mark Bostic, and the Chicks with Kicks; their personal collections rival some of the top reselling stores in the world and are often filmed and vlogged about by others. If you have a sneaker product or service you're looking to market, find a niche and create your own dope vlog or contact the vloggers we just mentioned.

Podcasts

Unlike a blog or vlog, which are visual mediums, a podcast is an audio transmission and the online equivalent of a radio show. But podcasts can offer much more than a typical radio show; they can cover any topic, be any length, and have any format. As of mid-2020, there were over 1 million podcasts with over 30 million episodes. Statistics show that over 55 percent of Americans have listened to a podcast; 37 percent of Americans listen to podcasts on a monthly basis. There are a handful of great sneaker podcasts focusing on a variety of sneaker-related topics, usually with regular and engaging guests and content. Marketing on existing podcasts or creating your own can be a powerful way to reach a captive audience in a creative way.

Source: Roszko

Content Conglomerates

Some of today's largest sneaker content producers began as print magazines or small blogs and have grown so popular that they became their own publishing conglomerates. Hypebeast, for example, was created by Kevin Ma in 2005 as a blog to cover the sneaker industry. Today, it is known as the go-to source for men's contemporary fashion and streetwear and has more than 8 million visitors per month. Recognized by *Fast Company* as one of the most innovative companies, Hypebeast also has a creative services division, online marketplace, annual sales of $96 million, and over 300 employees. Highsnobiety is another blog-turned-content publisher known for its sneaker coverage. Billed as a daily news website covering streetwear, sneakers, cars, lifestyle, and the arts, Highsnobiety started in 2005 and has expanded massively with the help of its own branded content and e-commerce platform.

Finally, there is Complex Media, which started as a bimonthly magazine founded by streetwear designer Marc Ecko; today, it is a jointly owned subsidiary of media mammoths Verizon and Hearst with annual revenue in excess of $200 million, its own video broadcasting platform with several video series, podcasts, and even a yearly streetwear culture and content convention called ComplexCon, where exhibitors can purchase booths and promote their goods in front of hypebeasts from all over.

Much more could be said about these marketing giants, but the main takeaway is that at some point, they all started with one magazine article, blog post, or video. For those looking to market, consider how each of these bloggers, vloggers, and publishing conglomerates started out just creating content and grew to be authorities in the sneaker game. So what are you waiting for? Start creating some dope sneaker content and get it out there. If we can do it, so can you!

Sneaker Conventions

Sneaker conventions are another relatively new way for players in the sneaker industry to market their products and services. These are large events where sneakerheads can buy, sell, and trade sneakers from brands, resellers, and others. Typically, there are booths that people buy to showcase the sneakers they have for sale. Additionally, companies offering other products or services may have booths. (In fact, we hope to have a *Sneaker Law* booth at future sneaker conventions.) By way of example, Crep Protect, a company that offers sneaker cleaning and protection products, had a booth at the 2019 Sneaker Con in London. Sneaker Con is the OG. The first Sneaker Con took place in 2009 in New York City. Since then, Sneaker Con has had over 1 million people attend its many conventions in more than forty cities around the world. In addition to physical events, Sneaker Con also has an online marketplace where people can buy, sell, and trade sneakers. Other famous sneaker conventions include ComplexCon, Sole Exchange, and Dunkxchange. If you see us at the next sneaker convention you attend, say what up!

Source: Eudaimonic Traveler / Shutterstock.com

Influencers & Sponsored Posts

Influencers are popular figures tied to particular industries. These individuals have a level of social influence in that industry and can sway a consumer to purchase a product or service solely due to their endorsement. In addition to celebrities, athletes, and other prominent figures, influencers are used frequently by sneaker brands and other sneaker companies to promote their products and services. This is referred to as influencer marketing.

The Growth and Economics of Influencer Marketing

With the prominence of social media, influencer marketing has exploded in recent years, particularly in the sneaker industry. Many major sneaker brands and companies now have huge budgets dedicated to influencer marketing because of the positive results it yields. Getting the right influencer with the right following can change the trajectory of a company overnight. According to a 2019 report, Kylie Jenner earns around $1.2 million for a single post on Instagram. With over 191 million followers, Kylie is an extreme example, but influencer marketing can be pricey even at lower levels. Micro-influencers are experts in particular industries, typically with followers in the 1,000 to 100,000 range. Although they have far fewer followers than mega-celebrities like Kylie, brands are turning to micro-influencers because their followers are comprised of a more focused market.

There is no uniform metric for determining how much an influencer can charge. Although many digital marketers suggest that one cent per follower is the golden rule, it really depends on the situation. You may find that an influencer who really digs your sneaker product or service is more willing to cut you a deal than if you asked them to sponsor your flat tummy tea or high-powered massage gun. Welcome to the bizarre world of influencers.

Who Are Influencers in the Sneaker Business?

When it comes to influencers, who has the most clout? Athletes and celebrities typically come to mind. In the world of social media, there is, at times, a blurred line separating athletes, celebrities, and influencers. athletes and celebrities are certainly influencers in their own right, but today, we are seeing an increase in influencers who become celebrities. When we refer to influencers in the sneaker business for the purposes of this section, we mean someone who might appeal to sneakerheads or anyone else interested in purchasing products and services related to sneakers.

Use of Influencers to Endorse Sneakers

Influencers are used for campaigns that run on many of the major social media platforms, including Instagram, Facebook, Snapchat, Twitter, YouTube, and TikTok. Sneaker companies generally use Instagram the most for influencer marketing. Say, for example, that we wanted to engage with an influencer to create an Instagram campaign to promote *Sneaker Law*. We decide to ask DJ Clark Kent, the world-famous sneakerhead and DJ (who also co-hosted the Complex show *Quickstrike* with Russ Bengston). As a part of the deal, we ask Clark to create engaging content that features him holding and talking about the book. The content will be posted on Clark's Instagram as a post and story. Clark has a huge following on Instagram, and many of his followers are sneakerheads, so we think that the campaign would be a good investment. Hopefully, Clark won't charge us too much!

Disclosures & FTC Requirements

One last thing you should know about influencer marketing on social media is that it is now regulated by the Federal Trade Commission (FTC). Each sponsored post must meet certain government-mandated requirements to avoid fines and penalties. Why? Well, years ago, as social media and influencer marketing began to take off, it became almost impossible to tell whether an influencer was promoting a product because they really liked it or were just paid to do so. And what about the loads of products that companies send to influencers for free in hopes that they might wear or post about them?

As you can imagine, it can be quite deceiving if someone with serious influence posts a photo wearing a pair of kicks, raves about how comfortable they are, and never discloses the fact that they were paid to wear the product and comment on how great it is. What if your favorite rapper posts a picture of himself in the studio wearing a pair of sneakers, never writes anything about the sneaker, but gets paid $500,000 for the sneaker to be in the shot? Don't you think you deserve to know that? The FTC does.

The FTC's primary purpose is to protect consumers by stopping unfair, deceptive, or fraudulent practices in the marketplace. The FTC, which already had rules regulating the use of product endorsements and testimonials,[1] realized that it needed to address how those rules should apply to influencer marketing. Accordingly, they put together a document called "Disclosures 101 for Social Media Influencers."[2] This brief guide outlines the requirements for sponsored posts and highlights the rules for distinguishing between an effective and ineffective disclosure.

In brief, the disclosures apply whenever there is a financial, employment, personal, or family relationship with a brand. In those instances, product endorsements or sponsored posts should be clearly communicated to the viewer; the disclosure should be easy to see and hard to miss. The disclosure should be communicated in simple and clear language—for example, using words like *advertisement*, *ad*, or *sponsored*. It is also acceptable for the influencer to write "Brand Ambassador" or "Brand Partner" where "Brand" is the brand name being promoted.

These guidelines apply no matter the social media platform. The same thing goes for Snapchat as for Twitter. Companies that do not comply with the guidelines could receive warning letters and if not heeded, face penalties. For example, in 2016, the FTC cracked down on department store Lord & Taylor for having a group of fifty influencers promote photos of themselves wearing the same paisley dress. After the dress sold out, it became apparent to the FTC that Lord & Taylor made no requirement that their influencers disclose the fact that they were given the dress for free and were paid thousands of dollars to wear it on the same day. Lord & Taylor settled the case but can no longer misrepresent its paid ads and must have its influencers disclose when they are paid for their product endorsements.

---

[1] 16 CFR Part 255, "Guides Concerning the Use of Endorsements and Testimonials in Advertising."

[2] Federal Trade Commission, https://www.ftc.gov/system/files/documents/plain-language/1001a-influencer-guide-508_1.pdf (last visited Sept. 1, 2020).

We all agree that sneakers are popular, but we now know that marketing plays a huge role in a sneaker's success. Whether for a print ad, digital campaign, or celebrity influencer, sneaker companies will spend millions of dollars to ensure their products are seen and heard. In our next chapter, we turn to another behind-the-scenes component of what makes the sneaker business so successful—law. Without the law and lawyers, none of the business would exist, or if it did, it would be a complete mess. If you ever wanted to know what a sneaker lawyer does and the many aspects of sneakers that are impacted by the law, keep reading!

45

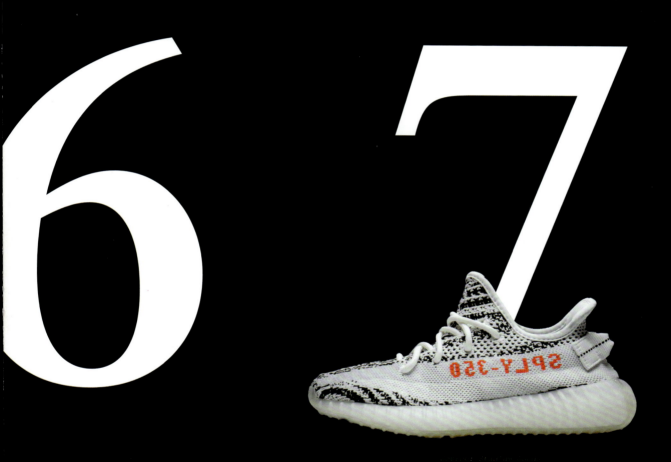

6 7

The Law of Sneakers
Part 1: The Law & Litigation

"In addition to excellence and courage, I encourage you to practice diplomacy as you practice the law. Cultivate your own style of disagreeing without being disagreeable. And, what's perhaps hardest of all, at least for me, is to learn to lose gracefully. (Well, everywhere but in court. There, zealous advocacy will require you to leave it all on the field.)"

—*HILARY KRANE*

And now a word from the authors.

What's going on? How's everyone feeling out there? We hope you're enjoying this book so far. Here's a little sidebar…Before we became lawyers, we were sneakerheads, and when we attended law school, we were among the few students who rocked sneakers and streetwear to class. At times, we felt out of place and struggled to connect with outdated and dense classwork that did not appeal to our interests. Over the years, however, we learned through our experience and knowledge of sneakers that law doesn't have to be boring. Through the next two chapters, we hope to reach people who were, like us, looking for a more engaging way to learn about law. The material that follows is essential legal knowledge for many industries, but by using sneakers as the foundation, you will see that law can, in fact, be pretty cool!

We now return to our regularly
scheduled *Sneaker Law* programming.

Most sneaker companies, whether big or small, have lawyers who oversee many of their essential legal tasks. Their work can make or break a project. When your favorite athlete or celebrity gets a lucrative sneaker deal, lawyers on both sides will draft and negotiate lengthy legal documents that consider every possible aspect and outcome to protect their clients before the parties ultimately sign off. Brands looking for every edge in the lucrative and competitive world of kicks can find themselves in court, calling foul on a competitor or defending their latest edgy move, with lawyers on the front lines and millions of dollars at stake. Sure, sneakers would not look as cool without the designers or generate long lines on release day without all the businesspeople whose job it is to market and generate revenue, but without lawyers, the sneaker business would be lost.

To illustrate just how important law is to the sneaker business, we've devoted the next two chapters to many of the issues these sneaker lawyers encounter, in and out of the courtroom. We added real-world examples to illustrate complex legal principles, because as we said, law doesn't have to be boring. Whether you are a seasoned lawyer, law student, or someone with no legal experience at all, in the following two chapters, we will teach you all you need to know about the Law of Sneakers.

Chapters 7 and 8 break the Law of Sneakers into two parts: (1) The Law and Litigation and (2) The Art of the Sneaker Deal. In chapter 7, or part 1, we provide an explanation of intellectual property law in the United States, as well as other areas of the law relevant to the sneaker industry. We also explore areas of sneaker law that have been the subject of public dispute, either in the courtroom or at an administrative level. For us, nothing is more exciting than two sneaker companies going at it, in and out of the courtroom!

In chapter 8, or part 2, we offer a look at what we call The Art of the Sneaker Deal, a comprehensive yet practical overview of sneaker transactions and their critical components. This includes licenses, endorsements, collaborations, and other related deals. Once you make it through this section, you will be well on your way to understanding how lawyers craft a complicated sneaker deal, and you'll be able to identify key issues that arise in negotiations.

Intellectual Property

Let's start our chapter on The Law and Litigation with an overview of intellectual property law in the United States, which we believe is the most critical component of the law of sneakers. What is intellectual property? According to the World Intellectual Property Organization (WIPO), intellectual property refers to creations of the mind, such as inventions, literary and artistic works, designs, and symbols, names, and images used in commerce. There are many types of intellectual property, and the protections countries provide to the owners of these works vary. These laws are designed to encourage innovation and grant certain protections, usually for a limited time, to people and entities that create such works.

Intellectual property in the United States can be divided into four main categories: (1) trademarks and trade dress, (2) copyrights, (3) patents, and (4) trade secrets. Each of these is important to the sneaker business and we will examine them in turn. Here are some examples of what we're talking about:

01 Trademark: the brand name Li-Ning

02 Trade dress: the visual appearance of the adidas Superstar

03 Copyright: the striped pattern on the YEEZY Boost 350

04 Patent: Nike's Flyknit technology

05 Trade secrets: proprietary, confidential brand secrets and methods used in the creation of New Balance sneakers

Some countries and regions, such as the European Union, have other types of protection that are not covered in this book.

Trademarks

A trademark or service mark is any word, name, symbol, or device used to identify and distinguish one manufacturer's goods or services from another's and to indicate their source. A "trademark" applies to goods, and a "service mark" applies to services, but the laws and concepts are essentially the same. Trademarks can be names (such as Nike and Reebok), slogans (Just Do It), and even logos (the adidas three stripes, Nike swoosh, and the Puma cat logo).

In this section, we will explore where trademarks originate, types of trademarks, how to obtain a trademark, and how they are enforced and disputed in the marketplace.

The History of Trademarks

Trademarks originated in the Middle Ages when craftsmen placed signatures, or "marks," on their artistic works or functional products. These craftsmen often worked for trade guilds, and their marks were a guarantee of the guild's craftsmanship and reputation. In those days, there was severe punishment for copying another guild's mark—off with their head!

The importance of trademarks grew rapidly during the Industrial Revolution, as inventions spurred technological progress. Inventors and the companies that employed them often turned to trademarks as a way to distinguish their brand and goods from the competition. As you can imagine, brands with a superior reputation and quality were favored, and these brands were often copied by aggressive competitors trying to gain market share.

The widespread and unauthorized copying of companies' trademarks became a real problem, and as a result, during the nineteenth century, many countries began developing laws governing the registration and protection of trademarks. In 1881, the United States Congress passed the first trademark act, which was later revised in 1905. In 1946, the US Trademark Act received a major overhaul and was renamed the Lanham Act, after Congressman Frederick Garland "Fritz" Lanham, the lead sponsor.

The Lanham Act provides a federal system for registering and protecting trademarks. That system is designed to help consumers identify and purchase a product or service based on whether its characteristics and quality—as indicated by its unique trademark—meet their needs.

In addition to federal law, many states recognize common law trademark rights, a form of protection for marks that are used in a certain state but not federally registered. Some states also have statutory trademark laws, which are laws passed by state legislatures designed to afford additional protection. However, the majority of trademark cases are brought under the federal Lanham Act. The state and common law rights are secondary in such actions since their requirements and findings typically mirror the requirements under federal law.

What Does the Lanham Act Do?

We know the Lanham Act is a law designed to protect trademarks in the United States, but what does it actually do? The act governs trademarks, service marks, and unfair competition. It sets forth, among other things, (i) what a trademark is, (ii) what kinds of acts constitute trademark infringement (simply put, an unauthorized use of the mark or a mark that is confusingly similar),[3] (iii) how one can demonstrate their trademark was infringed upon, (iv) what arguments a defendant might have to offer against a claim of trademark infringement, and (v) what damages are available to someone who can prove their trademark has been infringed. Thus, when one sneaker brand rips off the design of another, the lawsuit will be brought under the Lanham Act, and these factors will be considered to determine whether a claim for trademark infringement is established. In this section, we will explain each of these elements and then take a look at some notable sneaker trademark cases to illustrate how the Lanham Act is used to interpret and resolve trademark disputes.

---

[3] The Lanham Act is also used for trademark dilution and false advertising claims, but we are not covering those claims in this chapter.

What Is a Trademark?

The Lanham Act defines a trademark as "any word, name, symbol, or device, or any combination thereof" that a person or business either actually uses in commerce to distinguish their product or service from others or "has a bona fide intention to use in commerce" when they apply for registration. The distinction of "actual use" versus "a bona fide intention to use" simply means whether you can demonstrate that goods or services bearing a trademark or service mark are being sold in interstate commerce at the time you apply for a trademark, or whether you plan to use the mark on goods or services in the near future.

There are four categories of trademarks, ordered from weakest to strongest: (1) generic, (2) descriptive, (3) suggestive, and (4) arbitrary or fanciful.

A generic term is the common name for the goods or services and can never function as a trademark (e.g., SNEAKERS for sneakers, HIGH HEELS for footwear).

A descriptive trademark is one that describes an ingredient, quality, characteristic, function, feature, purpose, or use of the goods or services and cannot be protected without a showing of "secondary meaning" (e.g., AMERICAN APPAREL for apparel).

A suggestive trademark is one that when applied to the goods or services requires imagination, thought, or perception to reach a conclusion as to the nature of those goods or services (e.g., DRI-FIT for Nike's technology that keeps clothing dry, THE NORTH FACE for apparel).

An arbitrary trademark is a word that is in common use, but when used to identify particular goods or services, the mark does not suggest or describe them (e.g., NIKE and CONVERSE for sneakers and apparel). A fanciful trademark is a term that has been invented for the sole purpose of functioning as a trademark (e.g., adidas and YEEZY for sneakers and KID CUDI for music and entertainment).

What Constitutes Trademark Infringement?

Under Section 1114(1)(a) of the Lanham Act, infringement of a registered trademark involves the use, in commerce, of any reproduction, counterfeit, copy, or imitation used to sell, offer for sale, distribute, or advertise goods and services that are likely to cause confusion, mistake, or to deceive the consumer. Trademark counterfeiting is a subset of trademark infringement for which a registered trademark is necessary and which allows for additional damages.

A trademark registration is not necessary to enforce your rights under the Lanham Act, but it makes things easier. Under Section 1125(a)(1) of the Lanham Act, even if you do not have a registered trademark, you can still bring a claim against someone who uses an unregistered trademark that is likely to cause confusion or deceive a buyer by suggesting a connection with you or your trademark. Without a registration, however, you must be able to prove that the trademark is yours, valid, and protectable.

Thus, if you started your own sneaker brand named Yahm, for the purposes of this example, and another brand began creating sneakers under the same name, you could initiate an action against the other brand for trademark infringement even if you never registered the trademark for Yahm. However, it is advisable to register all trademarks associated with your sneaker brand because, as we will discuss, it strengthens your ability to enforce your rights.

How Does One Demonstrate Trademark Infringement?

To demonstrate trademark infringement, the holder needs to show two things: (1) they must prove that they own a valid and protectable mark and (2) they must also demonstrate a "likelihood of confusion," that a consumer will likely be confused about the nature or origin of the product or service. There are various factors used to determine whether or not a likelihood of confusion exists, and these depend on the state in which the case is brought. In New York, for example, the factors are referred to as the "*Polaroid factors*," after a case the Polaroid camera company brought against another company called Polarad.[4] Likely to confuse, no?

---

[4] Polaroid Corp. v. Polarad Elect. Corp., 287 F.2d 492 (2d Cir. 1961).

The *Polaroid* factors below are intended as a guide, and not all may be helpful in any given case. Courts will balance the factors to determine whether or not there is a likelihood of confusion, and no one factor is determinative on its own.

Strength of the senior user's mark. The stronger or more distinctive the senior user's mark, the more likely the confusion.

Similarity between the marks. The more similarity between the two marks, the more likely the confusion.

Similarity of the goods or services. The more that the senior and junior user's goods or services are related, the more likely the confusion.

Likelihood that the senior user will expand into the junior user's product area or bridge the gap. If it is probable that the senior user will do so, the more likely there will be confusion.

The junior user's intent in adopting the mark. If the junior user adopted the mark in bad faith, confusion is more likely.

Evidence of actual confusion. Proof of consumer confusion is not required, but when the trademark owner can show that the average reasonably prudent consumer is confused, it is powerful evidence of infringement.

Sophistication of the buyers. The less sophisticated the purchaser, the more likely the confusion.

Quality of the junior user's products or services. In some cases, the lesser the quality of the junior user's goods, the more harm is likely from consumer confusion.

Proximity of the goods in the marketplace. Are the goods sold in the same stores, and are they sold near each other in those stores?

Is a Trademark Registration Necessary?

In the United States, a trademark owner acquires trademark rights at the time they start using the trademark in US commerce. The Lanham Act defines "commerce" as "all commerce which may lawfully be regulated by Congress." That most commonly means interstate commerce: commercial transactions that cross state boundaries or involve more than one state.

A trademark registration is not necessary for protection in the United States, but you'll find that most sneaker lawyers highly recommend it. That's because registration (1) gives the mark a presumption of validity, (2) puts others on notice of your rights, (3) is beneficial in preventing counterfeiting, (4) allows you to record your trademark with US Customs, and (5) allows you to obtain assistance from law enforcement to stop counterfeit goods.

Foreign considerations are also important for sneaker companies. Companies should consider whether they will be selling or manufacturing outside of the United States. Trademarks are typically filed on a country-by-country basis; however, in some instances, one trademark registration can cover multiple countries (e.g., one can get an EU trademark registration to cover all of the countries in the European Union). Unlike in the United States, in many countries trademark rights are acquired by the first entity to file a trademark application. This leads to issues with trademark squatters, who will file a trademark application in a foreign country before a brand does, hold the trademark hostage, and demand large sums from the legitimate brand owner. In some cases, these trademark squatters even open stores using the trademark to capitalize on the goodwill of the legitimate owner. For example, Supreme has been in a trademark battle with a company called Supreme Italia, which filed trademarks in countries outside the United States and has even gone so far as to open knockoff stores. If a shopper did not know about the knockoff Supreme, they likely would not have realized that the store was not affiliated with the real brand. Supreme has had some recent successes in court, but it has been a long and expensive process.

Jordan Brand, YEEZY, and New Balance have all had similar problems in China. In fact, China is the source of many of these trademark squatters. Thus, when coming up with a new brand name, companies should not only file for their trademark in the United States but immediately file in China as well. Spending more money on trademark filings up front can save significant sums in litigation down the line, especially if your brand has plans to expand internationally.

Source: Hu Siyuan / Shutterstock.com

Registration and Protection of a Trademark in the United States

Applying for a trademark does not guarantee that it will be approved. Applications submitted to the US Patent and Trade Office (USPTO) are assigned an application serial number and reviewed by an examining attorney, who checks to see if the proper fees were paid and whether the mark complies with all rules and requirements for trademark protection in the United States. Typically, it takes the USPTO four to six months to review an application. If there are any technical or substantive deficiencies in your application, the examining attorney will send you a letter, referred to as an office action, refusing the application. The reasons for an office action may be technical, such as rewording the description of goods or services, or more complex, such as the mark is likely to be confused with another mark. You must respond to the office action within six months of the date the office action is issued or your application will go abandoned.

Provided that your office action response is submitted on time and addresses any deficiencies raised by the examining attorney, the USPTO will initiate the next step, which is to publish the mark for opposition. Once a mark is published, third parties have thirty days to challenge the registration of the mark. If no challenges are filed, the mark will be registered in the case of a use-based application or a Notice of Allowance issued in the case of an intent-to-use application. (We covered the different types of trademark applications in chapter 2.)

For an intent-to-use application, you have six months after the Notice of Allowance is issued to use the mark in commerce and file an Amendment to Allege Use. You can extend that deadline for up to three years in total if you file for extensions every six months along the way. If you do not file an Amendment to Allege Use in time, your application will be abandoned. If you submit a timely Amendment to Allege Use, it will be reviewed by the examining attorney, and if acceptable, the application will proceed to registration. Once approved, the USPTO will issue your trademark registration (usually within two months).

You now have a registered trademark—congratulations! However, there are a number of things you must do to keep the registration active, or "live," so make sure you read and comply with all subsequent correspondence from the USPTO about your mark. If you have an attorney file your trademark application, the attorney will receive all legitimate correspondence from the trademark office. Be careful, because a lot of scammers send fake correspondence to trademark owners to try to swindle them.

Int. Cl.: 25

Prior U.S. Cls.: 22 and 39

United States Patent and Trademark Office　Reg. No. 1,370,283
　　　　　　　　　　　　　　　　　　　　　　　　　Registered Nov. 12, 1985

TRADEMARK
PRINCIPAL REGISTER

AIR JORDAN

NIKE, INC. (OREGON CORPORATION)
3900 S. W. MURRAY BOULEVARD
BEAVERTON, OR 97005

FOR: FOOTWEAR AND ATHLETIC CLOTHING, NAMELY, SHIRTS, PANTS, SHORTS, AND WRIST BANDS, IN CLASS 25 (U.S. CLS. 22 AND 39).

FIRST USE 11-28-1984; IN COMMERCE 11-28-1984.

SER. NO. 536,336, FILED 5-7-1985.

TERESA M. RUPP, EXAMINING ATTORNEY

Protecting Your Trademark

Merely owning a trademark is not enough. It is also your responsibility to police the mark in the marketplace. This means that it is on you to stop others from using your mark if you are aware of it. It is also in your best interest to protect your brand!

Often, the first step to stopping someone who is using your trademark or one that is confusingly similar is to send them a letter demanding that they stop. This is called a cease and desist (C&D) letter. If you are not able to work matters out on your own or through your lawyer, then you may need to sue.

In cases of counterfeiting, which we will cover in chapter 9, you may decide that sending a C&D letter is not the most effective option and instead resort immediately to litigation to get the counterfeit products out of the marketplace.

You can also send a C&D letter if someone files a trademark application for a mark that you believe is too similar to yours, or if someone has a trademark registration for a trademark that you have prior rights to (even if you don't have a federal registration). If the parties are not able to resolve the matter, the party who believes they are being harmed can file a proceeding before the Trademark Trial and Appeals Board (TTAB). This is not a court filing but instead an administrative proceeding handled by a division of the USPTO. The TTAB can only determine whether a trademark can be registered, not whether the trademark can be used in the marketplace.

Trade Dress

Another form of intellectual property protection related to trademarks is trade dress. Trade dress is the form or manner of display in which a product or service is offered to the market. Trade dress includes the product's total image and overall appearance, as well as the elements that make it up. This includes the size, shape, color, color combinations, texture, graphics, configuration, decor, or architecture of the product. It can include the packaging or, in some cases, even the product design itself. It can also include the decor of a restaurant or retail establishment. Sneaker designers and companies seeking trade dress protection should consider which elements of the design, either alone or combined, make the design unique compared to other products or services.

What are some examples of trade dress? The shape of the Coca-Cola bottle, Tiffany & Co.'s blue box, the McDonald's Golden Arches, the overall design of a Ferrari, the red tab on Levi's jeans, the White Castle restaurant's castle design, and the clean white appearance of Apple's stores and packaging. As we will discuss later in this chapter, Christian Louboutin successfully used trade dress law to protect his red-soled shoes. Other examples include Burberry's plaid and Vans's black-and-white checkerboard pattern. Converse has registered the trade dress of its hi- and low-top Chuck Taylor sneakers with the USPTO, and K-Swiss, ASICS, Fila, Camper, Off-White, and Superga have all registered the trade dress for their sneakers with the patent office, too.

How to Protect Trade Dress

If a product or service's trade dress is not registered with the USPTO, it can still be protected under federal and state unfair competition laws, although it can be difficult to enforce. How, then, does trade dress qualify for protection?

Trade dress must be (1) distinctive and (2) nonfunctional.

Trade dress can either be inherently distinctive or acquire secondary meaning.

Trade dress is inherently distinctive if the total impression it gives the consumer almost automatically identifies it as coming from a specific origin or source, whether or not that source is known to the consumer. Inherently distinctive trade dress helps consumers identify the product or service, distinguishing it from those produced by others. When determining whether something is inherently distinctive, the total visual impression of the trade dress should be considered, and not each element in isolation; it is the combination of elements and the total impression that determines if the trade dress is distinctive.

If a trade dress is not inherently distinctive, it can still acquire distinctiveness through "secondary meaning." This means that in the consumer's mind, the trade dress clearly identifies a single source of the product or service, regardless of whether consumers know who or what that source is. When determining whether trade dress has acquired a secondary meaning, courts will consider various factors depending on the jurisdiction, including (1) direct consumer testimony, (2) consumer surveys, (3) exclusivity, length, and manner of use, (4) amount and manner of advertising, (5) amount of sales and number of customers, (6) established place in the market, and (7) proof of intentional copying. No single factor is determinative, but some jurisdictions consider proof of intentional copying to be particularly significant.

A trade dress is nonfunctional if, taken as a whole, the collection of trade dress elements is not essential to the product or service's use or purpose or does not affect its cost or quality, even though elements of the trade dress may be functional. If something is functional, it does not qualify for trade dress protection.

Trade dress can be difficult to establish and enforce; however, it can be a powerful tool in a brand's intellectual property portfolio.

By way of example, let's examine Off-White's iconic red zip tie. Anyone who knows Off-White knows about the red zip tie—it accompanies its clothing, accessories, and sneakers. Given its importance to the brand, Off-White's lawyers applied to obtain a trademark for it. But the USPTO denied the trademark application through an office action on the grounds that the red zip tie is not distinctive, it is functional, and that there was a likelihood of confusion between the red zip tie and two other registered marks.

Off-White's lawyers took issue with the USPTO's reasoning. First, with respect to functionality, Off-White's lawyers argued that the red zip tie is used purely as an indicator of the source of the trademark and that it has no functional purpose. Second, in terms of distinctiveness, they asserted that the red zip tie was distinctive by providing evidence of its use as a source indicator in advertising, promotional, and explanatory literature along with other information. Last, for the likelihood of confusion, Off-White's lawyers claimed that the red zip tie differed in appearance from the other registered marks and that the other marks were used on different goods than Off-White's.

TSDR	ASSIGN Status	TTAB Status	*(Use the "Back" button of the Internet Browser to return to TESS)*

Goods and Services IC 018. US 001 002 003 022 041. G & S: Handbags; wallets; backpacks. FIRST USE: 20160615. FIRST USE IN COMMERCE: 20160615

IC 025. US 022 039. G & S: Tops; bottoms; headwear; footwear. FIRST USE: 20160515. FIRST USE IN COMMERCE: 20160515

Mark Drawing Code (2) DESIGN ONLY

Design Search Code 14.11.09 - Ball and Chain (restraints) ; Handcuffs ; Leg irons ; Manacles ; Restraints (ball and chain, handcuffs, leg irons, manacles)
29.02.01 - Red or pink (single color used for the entire goods/services)
29.03.01 - Red or pink (single color used on a portion of the goods)
29.04.01 - Red or pink (single color used on packaging, labels or signs)

The USPTO conceded on the consumer confusion issue but rejected the functionality and distinctiveness arguments. Off-White's lawyers sent a second office action response. In terms of functionality, the attorneys stressed that the red zip tie has zero performance value and is a status symbol, which serves the purpose of identifying Off-White as the source of the goods. In regard to distinctiveness, they stated that the red zip tie is akin to product packaging and, again, is a powerful source indicator. Once again, the USPTO stood by its functionality and nondistinctiveness refusals. We will have to wait to see how Off-White's attorneys respond next.

Notable Trademark and Trade Dress Cases

Now that you know the basics of trademark and trade dress law, let's look at some real-world examples of how these laws are used to protect and enforce sneaker brands and their iconic products.

adidas v. Payless

What is more classic than the adidas three stripes? When people around the world see three stripes on a sneaker, they instantly connect it with adidas. But what about two stripes or maybe four? When the discount retailer Payless introduced sneakers with just those patterns, adidas sued its competitor in Oregon federal court.[5]

Claiming trademark and trade dress infringement, as well as trademark dilution, adidas fought to protect its famous three stripes, which have been displayed on its sneakers and clothing since 1952. adidas alleged that Payless had planted its stripes on sneakers that bore a striking resemblance to a series of signature adidas silhouettes, including the adidas Superstar, Country Ripple, Tuscany, adi Racer, Pranja, Copa Mundial, Campus, Samoa, Stan Smith Millennium, and Mei.

Payless clapped back, arguing that there was no likelihood of confusion between adidas's three-stripe trademark and its use of two and four stripes on footwear. Under the Lanham Act, the question before the judge and jury was whether "a reasonably prudent consumer" (one who uses good judgment or common sense in purchasing goods) was likely to be confused because of the similarities.

The Ninth Circuit, where adidas filed its lawsuit, determines a likelihood of confusion by evaluating the *Sleekcraft* factors. These are similar to the Polaroid factors, but are named after a Ninth Circuit trademark infringement case that involved two competing companies that sold recreational boats. The *Sleekcraft* factors are (1) the similarity of the marks, (2) the relatedness of the parties' goods, (3) the similarity of trade or marketing channels, (4) the strength of the plaintiff's marks, (5) defendant's intent, (6) evidence of actual confusion, (7) the degree of care exercised by the average purchaser, and (8) the likelihood of expansion into other markets.[6] Applying the *Sleekcraft* factors, the court found substantial evidence that a likelihood of consumer confusion existed between the adidas three-stripe trademark and Payless's use of two and four stripes on its sneakers. The court also posited that the similarities in the stripes were unmistakable and that the design as a whole was too similar. Following a three-week jury trial, the jury found in favor of adidas and held that "Payless acted willfully and maliciously, or in wanton and reckless disregard of adidas's trademark and trade dress rights."

The jury awarded adidas a staggering $304.6 million, encompassing $30.6 million in actual damages, $137 million in Payless's profits, and $137 million in punitive damages. The judge eventually reduced the accounting of Payless's profits to $19.7 million, because the jury had not factored in all the company's expenses, while also lowering the jury's punitive damages award to $15 million.

---

[5] adidas-America, Inc. v. Payless Shoesource, Inc., 546 F. Supp. 2d 1029 (D. Or. 2008).

[6] AMF Inc. v. Sleekcraft Boats, 599 F.2d 341, 348-49 (9th Cir. 1979).

adidas Superstar

Payless Imitation

adidas Tuscany/adi Racer

Payless Imitation

adidas Country Ripple

Payless Imitation

This case is important because it demonstrates that sneaker brands should be entitled to trademark protection for their iconic marks and that other companies generally cannot take a brand's trademark, slightly alter it, and use it on sneakers of their own. When this happens, courts will use the *Polaroid* or *Sleekcraft* factors to determine whether a likelihood of confusion exists.

Christian Louboutin v. Yves Saint Laurent

As Cardi B said, "these expensive, these is red bottoms…these is bloody shoes." If you know shoes, you know that red-bottomed heels and sneakers are associated with the designer Christian Louboutin. That is essentially what his company's lawyers argued when they sued designer brand Yves Saint Laurent (YSL) for using the lacquered red-sole high heel on its own design.[7] Louboutin brought its case in the US District Court for the Southern District of New York, where it argued that YSL's line of monochrome-style shoes infringed its Red Sole trademark, covering the red lacquered outsole of a woman's high-fashion shoe. Louboutin also sought a preliminary injunction to prevent YSL from marketing any shoes with red outsoles identical to the Red Sole trademark while the lawsuit was pending. YSL counterclaimed, seeking cancellation of Louboutin's Red Sole trademark and damages for tortious interference with business relations and unfair competition. The district court denied Louboutin's request for a preliminary injunction and held that "a single color can never serve as a trademark in the fashion industry."

Louboutin appealed the decision, and the US Court of Appeals for the Second Circuit reversed, holding that a single color may, in fact, serve as a legally protected trademark in the fashion industry. After considering Louboutin's evidence, the second circuit found that its Red Sole trademark "ha[d] acquired limited secondary meaning as a distinctive symbol that identifies the Louboutin brand." This was a huge win for Louboutin and its red bottoms, but it did not apply to all bloody shoes. The court limited Louboutin's Red Sole trademark to "uses in which the red outsole contrasts with the remainder of the shoe." Thus, competitors like YSL could continue to market shoes with red outsoles, such as their monochromatic line of shoes, as long as the shoes' red outsole did not contrast with the remainder of the shoe. All-red everything!

---

[7] Christian Louboutin S.A. v. Yves Saint Laurent Am. Holding, Inc., 696 F.3d 206 (2d Cir. 2012).

adidas v. Skechers

The adidas Stan Smith sneaker has been known as a classic silhouette since 1970. It has transcended generations, becoming a fashion staple and one of adidas's best-selling sneakers of all time. So it should come as no surprise that over the years, some companies have made attempts to produce their own versions. In 2015, Skechers gave it a try, releasing a freakishly similar sneaker to the Stan Smith called the Onix. adidas simply was not having it.

According to a company-issued statement, adidas sued Skechers "to protect its valuable intellectual property and to put an end to a long-term pattern of unlawful conduct by Skechers to sell two sneaker styles that infringe adidas's rights."[8] The thirty-five-page complaint, including 318 pages of exhibits, alleged that the Skechers Onix sneaker infringed upon its unregistered Stan Smith trade dress and that the Cross Court sneaker infringed upon adidas's three-stripe trademark.

adidas successfully obtained a preliminary injunction prohibiting Skechers from selling the sneakers, and Skechers immediately appealed. On appeal, the US Court of Appeals for the Ninth Circuit affirmed the lower court's decision to the extent that it prevented the sale of the Onix, finding that the Stan Smith sneaker had acquired secondary meaning and that there was a substantial likelihood of confusion between the two.

In support of its decision, the court of appeals held it was likely that the public would reasonably think that the two sneakers came from the same source, that Skechers intended to confuse consumers, and was blatant in its conduct. For example, Skechers used metatags on its website so that anyone searching for Stan Smith on the internet would be directed to the Skechers website; the court said doing this was like posting a sign with another company's trademark in your storefront window. The court also found stark similarities between the two sneakers, including the same white leather upper, raised green heel path, angled stripes with perforations, identical stitching, and flat white rubber outsole.

Given the evidence, the ninth circuit held that the lower court had not erred in finding that adidas was likely to succeed on its trade dress claim and would suffer irreparable harm if Skechers continued to sell its Onix sneakers.

On the other hand, the appeals court found with regard to the Cross Court sneaker claims based on the adidas three-stripe trademark, a preliminary injunction was not justified. The court found that there was no evidence that Skechers harmed adidas's ability to control its brand image.

Interestingly, Skechers continues to sell the Onix sneaker to this day, although we note that the silhouette has been fairly modified from its original "Stan Smith-like" design.

---

[8] adidas America, Inc. v. Skechers USA, Inc., 890 F.3d 747 (9th Cir. 2018).

Skechers Onix	adidas Stan Smith

Converse v. ITC

The Converse Chuck Taylor All Star has been an iconic sneaker since it was created for basketball players in 1917. Sneakerheads and novices alike rock the Chuck Taylor all around the world. It is not surprising that a myriad of other brands have attempted to replicate it. After watching this happen for years, Converse finally got fed up and, in 2014, filed a massive trademark infringement complaint with the US International Trade Commission (ITC) that targeted thirty-one companies (referred to as the "Respondents") and one hundred infringing sneakers.[9] Among other claims, the ITC complaint alleged trademark infringement and requested that the ITC order the companies to cease the production and importation of further infringing products into the United States. The Respondents included companies such as Wal-Mart Stores, Inc., Skechers U.S.A., Inc., and New Balance Athletic Shoe, Inc. Converse also brought additional trademark infringement actions in federal court.

Converse's ITC infringement complaint was based on three of its federally registered trademarks: (1) Registration No. 4398753, referred to as the '753 Midsole Trademark ("the design of the two stripes on the midsole of the sneaker, the design of the toe cap, the design of the multi-layered toe bumper featuring diamonds and line patterns, and the relative position of these elements to each other"); (2) Registration No. 3258103, referred to as the '103 Outsole Trademark (the three-dimensional tread design located on the outsole of the sneaker); and (3) Registration No. 1588960, referred to as the '960 Sole Trademark (the three-dimensional sole design of the sneaker, including the lining and stippling elements of the sole design).

In 2015, an Administrative Law Judge (ALJ) of the ITC held that the allegedly infringing products violated Section 337 of the Tariff Act and recommended a general exclusion order, preventing infringing products from entering the country. But on review, the ITC reversed the ALJ's finding on the validity of Converse's '753 Midsole Trademark and held the trademark was "invalid based on lack of secondary meaning." Accordingly, the ITC held there was no violation of Section 337 of the Tariff Act and reversed the exclusion order. Nonetheless, in a partial victory for Converse, the ITC upheld the validity of the '103 Outsole Trademark and '960 Sole Trademark, and the general exclusion order for goods infringing those two marks.

Converse appealed the ITC's holding, and numerous parties filed amici curiae briefs (legal documents filed by nonlitigants that have a vested interest in the issues at hand) to the ITC on its behalf, including eleven law professors and the Fashion Law Institute. On October 30, 2018, Federal Circuit Judge Timothy B. Dyk vacated the ITC's ruling that Converse lacked a valid trademark, holding that the ITC applied the incorrect standard. But he also noted that even if Converse's trademark is valid, Converse would not be entitled to a presumption of secondary meaning since Converse had not federally registered its trademark until 2013, and competitors, such as some of the Respondents, have been selling sneakers for the past eighty years. The case was remanded back to the ITC, where Chief ALJ Charles E. Bullock found that with respect to Skechers, Converse's '753 Midsole Trademark was not infringed because there was no likelihood of consumer confusion. Additionally, Judge Bullock found that Converse's trademark had not yet acquired secondary meaning in 2001, when Skechers started using the designs in question. The decision applied to only Skechers; we presume the other Respondents all settled or were dismissed from the action.

---

[9] Converse, Inc. v. ITC, 909 F.3d 1110 (Fed. Cir. 2018).

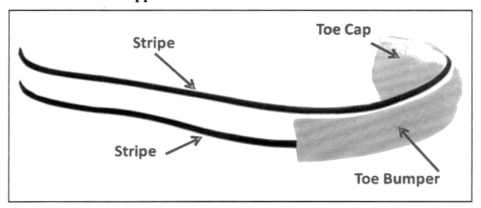

FIGURE 1: Appearance of the Converse Midsole Trademark

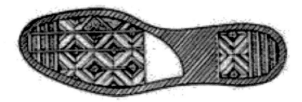

FIGURE 11: Design Depicted in the '960 Registration

FIGURE 14: Representative Images of Respondents' Accused Products

Other Trademark Cases

2007: ASICS v. Skechers[10]

ASICS claimed that Skechers, Brown Shoe Company, and Brown Group Retail were selling multiple sneakers that infringed on its incontestable stripe design trademark and trade dress. ASICS's motion for a preliminary injunction was denied because it failed to demonstrate that the marks were confusingly similar. The court considered the total components of the sneakers and concluded that the Skechers designs, which featured a single stripe on a portion of the side of the sneakers, were different from ASICS's designs, which featured two curved stripes displayed on the entire side of the sneaker.

2009: New Balance v. LVMH Moet Hennessy[11]

New Balance brought a lawsuit against LVMH Moet Hennessy, alleging that Louis Vuitton's "Minstrel" sneaker infringed upon the NB 574's trade dress, specifically its shape and color. The parties ultimately reached a private, out-of-court settlement and LVMH agreed to pull the sneaker from stores permanently.

2013: Already v. Nike[12]

In this case, the topic of sneakers made it all the way to the US Supreme Court (pretty cool, we think), which was asked to resolve a dispute between Nike, Inc. and Already, LLC d/b/a Yums. Nike sued Yums for selling two sneaker styles that allegedly infringed upon Nike's classic Air Force 1 (AF1) sneaker, which has sold millions of pairs since it debuted in 1982. Nike alleged that it had a registration protecting the stitching design, exterior panels, and their relative positioning on the AF1. Yums counter-sued, seeking to invalidate Nike's trademark, claiming that it should never have obtained a registration and the AF1 design should therefore be placed in the public domain. Perhaps recognizing this potential threat to its AF1 mark and design protection, Nike moved to dismiss its own lawsuit, agreeing to no longer sue Yums on any of its existing sneaker designs. But Yums did not let up, arguing that Nike's covenant not to sue should not preclude Yums's counterclaim against Nike, because Nike's registration could still cause injury to Yums in the future. The Supreme Court ultimately sided with Nike, stating that Nike's voluntary agreement to no longer sue Yums made the counterclaims against Nike moot. One of the takeaways from this case is that trademark holders should be careful about who they sue in infringement actions, as the alleged infringer could fight and file counterclaims to invalidate the plaintiff's trademark.

---

[10] Asics Corp. v Skechers U.S.A., CV 07-0103 (C.D. Cal. 2007).

[11] New Balance Athletic Shoe, Inc. v. LVMH Moet Hennessy, Louis Vuitton SA et al., CV 09-11497 (D. Mass. 2009).

[12] Nike, Inc. v. Already, LLC, 663 F.3d 89 (2d Cir. 2011).

Source: Mia2you / Shutterstock.com

2017: MCH Swiss Exhibition Basel v. adidas[13]

The contemporary art fair organizer MCH Swiss Exhibition Ltd. sued adidas for selling at least 1,000 pairs of adidas EQT Support ADV sneakers bearing the name Art Basel on the tongue. MCH alleged that Art Basel was its registered trademark and that adidas did not obtain consent to use its mark on the EQT sneaker. The parties settled out of court, and adidas released a statement conceding that it "did not obtain a license to use the Art Basel mark," "regrets these actions and is pleased that the lawsuit filed by Art Basel has been settled amicably."

---

[13] MCH Swiss Exhibition (Basel) Ltd. v. adidas America, Inc. and adidas AG, CV 17-22002 (S.D. Fla. 2017).

Copyrights

Copyright law is another type of intellectual property that is increasing in importance to the sneaker world. In this section, we will explain what a copyright is, the history of copyrights, and how copyrights apply to sneakers.

What Is a Copyright?

Trademarks, as we just learned, help protect commercial words, names, slogans, and logos. A copyright, on the other hand, helps protect creative or intellectual works. A copyright exists at the time of creation and protects against the unauthorized copying or exploitation of someone's work.

Copyright protection applies to original works that are fixed in a tangible form. Examples of copyrightable things include literary works, songs, movies, or computer software. The holder of a copyright has the right to reproduce the work, create derivative works (which are new but modified versions of the original), distribute copies of the work, and to perform and display the work publicly.

A work must meet three basic requirements to be protected by copyright. It must be:

01 Original
the work must be independently created, and not a copy of something else

02 Creative
the work must demonstrate some (usually very small) amount of creativity

03 Fixed
the work must be fixed in a tangible medium of expression. In other words, it must be in a format that can be seen directly or with the help of some device. For example, a literary work is usually fixed on paper or stored in an electronic file available on a computer. A song's copyright is fixed in a record, CD, MP3, or some other electronically playable file. If you have an idea for a movie script or song in your head but haven't written it down, it's not fixed under the law. Ideas and concepts are not protectable under copyright law; only the expressions of ideas and concepts are.

History of Copyright

The history of copyright law dates to 1710, when British Parliament enacted the Statute of Anne.[14] Named after Queen Anne of Great Britain, the Statute of Anne afforded authors of new books sole publication rights for fourteen years (or twenty-one years if the book was already in print). This was the first copyright statute in the world.

In the United States, copyright law began in 1787 with the drafting of the US Constitution and was based on Britain's Statute of Anne. Article I, Section 8 of the Constitution specifies the necessary and proper powers of Congress:

"Congress shall have the power...To promote the progress of science and useful arts, by securing for limited times to authors and inventors the exclusive right to their respective writings and discoveries."

Using the Constitution as a framework, Congress passed the first Copyright Act in 1790. This act established the principle that an author of a work may reap the fruits of his or her intellectual property for a limited time. The original copyright law was very limited and provided protection for books, maps, and charts for fourteen years, with another fourteen-year renewal period thereafter.

In the years that followed, Congress would amend the Copyright Act many times, expanding authors' rights to include other types of works.

The Copyright Act received its most recent overhaul by Congress in 1976. Signed into law by President Ford, the Copyright Act of 1976 extended protection to all works, as long as they are fixed in a tangible form. It also extended the copyright term of protection to last for the entire life of the author plus fifty years thereafter. Since the enactment of the Copyright Act of 1976, it has been amended several times to include provisions for new technologies and longer terms for protection, but otherwise remains intact.

Generally, the current term of protection in the United States for works created after January 1, 1978, is the life of the author plus seventy years—or for an anonymous work, a pseudonymous work, or a work made for hire, the copyright term is ninety-five years from publication or one hundred and twenty years after creation, whichever expires first.

What Do Copyrights Protect, and How Do They Apply to Sneakers?

Copyright typically protects works of authorship, such as books, songs, movies, and other similar creations. Fabric patterns, certain jewelry designs, computer software, and architectural designs are also copyrightable.

But what about sneakers? Under US copyright law, useful articles, which are works that have a utilitarian function, such as clothing or footwear, are generally not copyrightable. Historically, sneaker designs have been considered useful articles and, as a result, ineligible for copyright protection.

However, many sneaker companies these days are applying for copyright registrations to protect their most coveted silhouettes. How? And why? As we will soon discuss, adidas filed and successfully obtained a copyright registration for the YEEZY 350 Boost. But what does this copyright protect, and how did adidas manage to obtain a registration? Keep reading and we'll find out!

Additionally, copyrights are important in the sneaker business in other ways. Copyright protection typically exists in sneaker company's logos, websites, promotional materials, and photos. It is also important to ensure that your designs don't infringe on other companies' copyrights when running your sneaker business.

---

[14] The full title of the Statute of Anne was, *An Act for the Encouragement of Learning, by Vesting the Copies of Printed Books in the Authors or Purchasers of Such Copies, during the Times therein Mentioned.*

Notable Copyright Cases

Star Athletica v. Varsity Brands

To understand how copyright protection can be applied to sneakers, we begin with the *Star Athletica* U.S. Supreme Court case.[15] By way of background, Varsity Brands, Inc. ("Varsity") designs and manufactures clothing and accessories for athletic activities, including cheerleading. Design concepts for the clothing at issue incorporated elements such as colors, shapes, lines, and other features and did not consider the functionality of the final clothing. Varsity received copyright registrations for various two-dimensional designs, five of which were very similar to designs that Star Athletica, LLC ("Star") later offered for sale. Varsity sued Star Athletica and alleged that Star infringed upon Varsity's copyrights, among other claims. Star asserted counterclaims, including one that alleged Varsity made fraudulent representations to the copyright office when it knew that the designs at issue were not copyrightable.

After a drawn-out battle in the lower courts, the case was decided by the US Supreme Court. The Supreme Court held that federal copyright protection extends to the "arrangements of lines, chevrons, and colorful shapes" ("Designs") appearing on Varsity's cheerleader uniforms. In doing so, the Supreme Court articulated a new test for determining whether elements of useful articles, such as clothing, are eligible for copyright protection: "a feature incorporated into the design of a useful article is eligible for copyright protection only if the feature (1) can be perceived as a two- or three-dimensional work of art separate from the useful article and (2) would qualify as a protectable pictorial, graphic, or sculptural work—either on its own or fixed in some other tangible medium of expression—if it were imagined separately from the useful article into which it is incorporated."

By this standard, the court concluded that Varsity's Designs were protected by federal copyright law. If imagined separate from the uniform, the court held, the Designs would qualify as two-dimensional works of art under Section 101 of the US Copyright Act because they have pictorial, graphic, or sculptural qualities when separated from the uniform and applied in another medium—"for example, on a painter's canvas." The court noted, "the only feature of the cheerleading uniform eligible for a copyright in this case is the two-dimensional work of art fixed in the tangible medium of the uniform fabric." Thus, even though Varsity has a valid copyright in the Designs of the cheerleader uniforms, Varsity does not have the "right to prohibit any person from manufacturing a cheerleading uniform of identical shape, cut, and dimensions." Varsity may only prohibit "the reproduction of the surface designs in any tangible medium of expression—a uniform or otherwise."

---

[15] Star Athletica, L.L.C. v. Varsity Brands, Inc., 137 S. Ct. 1002 (2017).

Design 0815
Registration No. VA 1-675-905

Design 078
Registration No. VA 1-417-427

Design 299B
Registration No. VA 1-319-226

Design 299A
Registration No. VA 1-319-228

This case is important because prior to the Supreme Court ruling, fashion designs generally were not considered copyrightable. Now fashion designers are able to apply for copyright protection in the designs if they meet the Star Athletica standard. For the sneaker industry, brands can now potentially obtain copyright protection in their designs. An example of this is the adidas YEEZY 350 Boost, V1

Puma v. Forever 21

In April 2017, Puma sued Forever 21, Inc. in the Central District of California, alleging that Forever 21 infringed on its intellectual property rights in the Creeper Sneaker, Bow Slide, and Fur Slide, known collectively as the "Fenty" sneakers.[16] One of Puma's claims was for copyright infringement because Puma had obtained copyright registrations for the three styles. Forever 21 argued that the Fenty sneakers were not eligible for copyright protection. In support of its copyright claims, Puma cited the then-recent *Star Athletica* Supreme Court decision and argued that the designs of the Fenty sneakers were eligible for copyright protection because they can be perceived as two- or three-dimensional works of art separate from the sneakers and would qualify as protectable pictorial, graphic, or sculptural works—either on their own or fixed in some other tangible medium of expression. The court declined to consider whether the designs of the Fenty sneakers were eligible for copyright protection, and the parties ultimately settled the lawsuit.

This case is important because it was one of the first cases to cite the Supreme Court's decision in *Star Athletica* in connection with its copyright infringement claims.

---

[16] Puma SE v. Forever 21, Inc., CV 17-02523 (C.D. Cal. 2017).

Source: Puma

The adidas YEEZY 350 Boost Copyright Registration

Capitalizing on the *Star Athletica* case, the folks over at adidas were able to score a huge win in pursuit of the copyright registration for their iconic design of the adidas YEEZY 350 Boost V1 and V2.

In 2017, adidas applied for a copyright registration for the design and was initially denied protection by the copyright office, which held that copyright protects only creative, separable elements of useful articles, not the articles as a whole. The company requested reconsideration, and the application was rejected again. This time, the copyright office said that although the sneakers did contain separable designs, those designs did not meet the originality requirement.

Unsatisfied, adidas appealed to the Copyright Review Board and, citing *Star Athletica*, managed to convince the board to grant its copyright applications. The board held that the design elements can be perceived as two- or three-dimensional works of art separate from the useful article, meaning that the sneaker design can be considered separate from the article.

`The Star Athletica holding, initially considered a huge win for the apparel world, is already having an immense impact on the sneaker world. There is no question that we will see more designers and sneaker companies turn to copyright for design protections moving forward.`

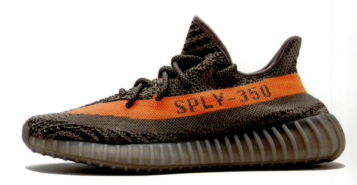

Source: Stadium Goods

Source: Stadium Goods

Stewart v. adidas

What happens when someone obtains a copyright for a drawing or graphic and another company uses the copyrighted work on a sneaker without permission? In *Stewart v. adidas*, this was the issue at hand.[17] In 1995, Scott Stewart, a designer, sued adidas America Inc., Kinney Shoe Corp., and The Athlete's Foot Stores, Inc. (collectively, the "Defendants") alleging copyright infringement of his "Jack Stickman" stick-figure basketball graphic design. In 1991, adidas met with Stewart, and both parties agreed that Stewart would design graphics for the company, and they would be used only on adidas T-shirts. Shortly after, Stewart created the Jack Stickman design and adidas accepted it. The proposed agreement called for Stewart to assign his rights to the copyright of the design, but adidas never sent him a copy.

Years later, adidas sold an array of sneakers and apparel featuring Stewart's design—but the agreement was limited to T-shirts. In 1994, adidas, unable to find Stewart's signed assignment agreement, asked him to sign a new one. Stewart refused, objecting to the use of his designs on products other than T-shirts and submitted an application to the US Copyright Office to register the Jack Stickman design. In 1995, Stewart's counsel sent adidas a letter about the dispute, and quickly after receiving the letter, adidas stopped the production, marketing, distribution, importation, and sale of all products featuring the disputed copyrighted design. Stewart subsequently filed a lawsuit against the Defendants, and the Defendants responded by filing a motion for summary judgment arguing that the claims were barred because Stewart failed to bring the complaint in a timely manner. The motion was denied because there were material issues of fact in connection with the alleged infringements of the copyright. Thereafter, Stewart and adidas ended up settling the case.

[17] Stewart v Adidas A.G., 95 CIV. 4824 (S.D.N.Y. 1997).

Although this case settled, it is a great example of how copyrighted works can be featured on sneaker designs, provided the sneaker company has lawfully obtained the rights from the copyright holder. If adidas had obtained a license or assignment of the copyright to use on sneakers, which the company thought it had, the dispute would have never happened. However, since adidas did not have the rights to use the copyright on its sneakers, litigation ensued.

Patents

A patent is a grant of property right to an inventor issued by the USPTO in the United States. Patents are governed by Title 35 of the United States Code and protect inventions such as machines, devices, methods, processes, and pharmaceuticals. Generally, the term of a new utility or plant patent is twenty years from the filing date, and the term of a design patent is generally fourteen or fifteen years depending on when the application was filed (fourteen years from the date of grant for design patent applications filed before May 13, 2015, and fifteen years from the date of grant for design patent applications filed on or after that date). A patent gives the owner an absolute monopoly on the protected property for the life of the patent.

There are three types of patents:

01 A **utility patent** covers any new and useful process, machine, article of manufacture, or composition of matter.

02 A **design patent** covers any new, original, and ornamental design for an article.

03 A **plant patent** covers any distinct and new variety of plant.

How Are Patents Used in Sneakers?

Design patents can be used to protect sneaker designs in some instances, such as their ornamental and aesthetic features. Novelty and nonobviousness are essential when seeking a design patent. This means the sneaker must be unique and display a considerable amount of ingenuity. Design patent protection can be afforded to a certain portion of a sneaker and to a sneaker as a whole. For example, adidas has a design patent for the entire design of the YEEZY Boost 350.

Nike had a design patent for its air bubble feature (officially called an adjustable viscoelastic unit in the patent application), which is a gas-inflated insert that is contained within shock-absorbing material in the sole. The air bubble design patent has since expired.

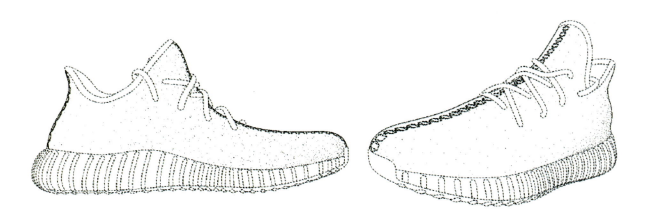

There is a problem with design patents: the application process is lengthy and costly. Since it can take up to two years to obtain a design patent for a sneaker, other companies may copy that particular sneaker style while the patent is pending. Thus, applying for a design patent can be a fruitless endeavor. Additionally, courts are reluctant to enforce the validity of design patents in the area of fashion, finding infringement in only about half the cases. Despite this, there are still a wealth of design patents that exist for sneakers, especially ones that have proven their commercial success.

Utility patents, which cover functional aspects, can be used to protect new, useful, and innovative technologies in a sneaker. Compared to design patents, which provide fifteen years of protection from the date of grant, utility patents afford twenty years of protection from the date the application is filed. But securing a utility patent can take even longer than that of a design patent—in some cases up to five years!

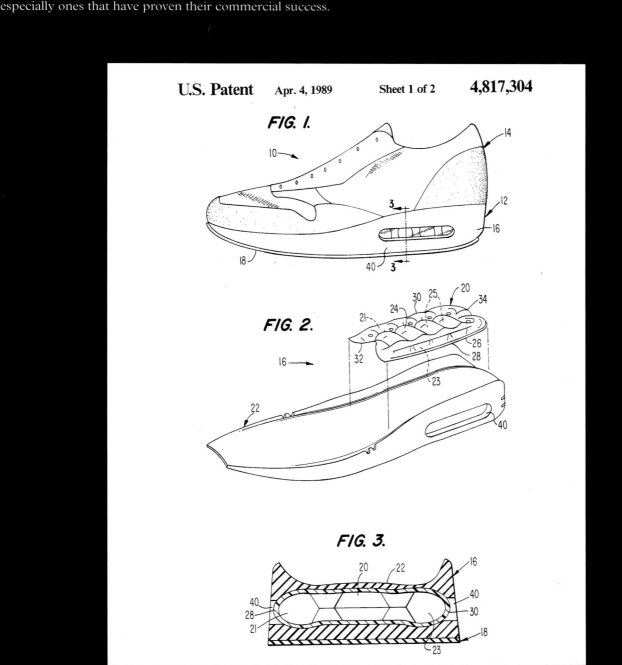

Auto-lacing

An example of a utility patent is Nike's automatic lacing system. First seen on the feet of Marty McFly (played by Michael J. Fox) in the 1989 film *Back to the Future Part II*, auto laces accompanied the silhouette of the Nike Mag. Auto laces are a self-lacing system that enables sneakers to tighten automatically with no human assistance. Originally only a movie prop, the Nike Mag was an instant grail for sneakerheads globally. In 2011, Nike shocked the world and released the Mag in extremely limited quantities but without the auto-lacing system. On October 21, 2015, the actual fictional date that Marty McFly traveled to the future in the movie, Nike shocked the world again by re-releasing the Mag, this time equipped with light-up midsoles and, yes, Nike's fully functional, utility patented automatic lacing system! Great marketing, right? Shortly thereafter, Nike raffled off eighty-nine pairs of the sneaker with the automatic lacing technology, and all proceeds went to the Michael J. Fox Foundation to support research toward finding a cure for Parkinson's disease, from which the actor suffered. Today, the extremely rare 2016 auto-lace sneaker resells anywhere from $25,000 to $50,000.

Source: Dylan Ratner

Nike continues to employ the automatic-lacing system utility patent in some of its sneakers, including the Nike HyperAdapt and Adapt BB. The technology is definitely the future (pun intended)!

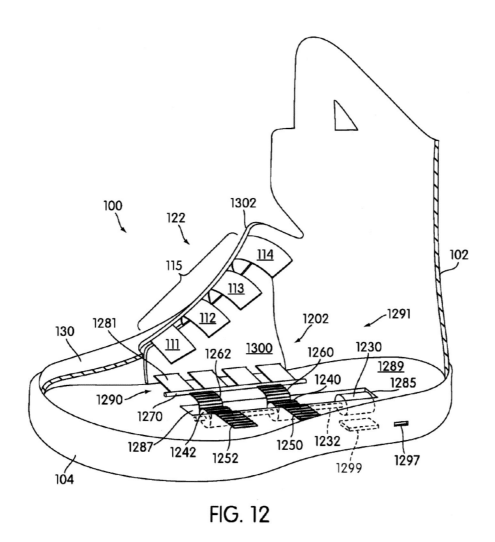

FIG. 12

Plant Patents

Because plant patents are typically utilized for distinctive and new varieties of plants, this type of patent is not yet applicable to sneakers. However, maybe Cactus Plant Flea Market has something up its sleeves. You never know!

How to Apply for a Patent in the United States

Like trademarks, patent applications are filed online with the US Patent and Trademark Office. The USPTO has many resources on its website to help guide you through the filing process, but patent applications can be extremely technical and must meet very specific requirements. If you are serious about your invention, we highly recommend using an attorney skilled in patent law. Many applicants have wasted time and money only to find their application was rejected and, as a result, lost the opportunity to protect a potentially valuable invention. With that being said, let's go over the basics of patent filings.

Before applying for a patent, you must determine whether you will need a design patent (e.g., the Air Max bubble) or a utility patent (e.g., Nike Mag auto-lace technology). We've already covered the difference between the two, so you should be able to figure out which one is right for your invention. Next, perform a search to ensure that no similar application or registration exists. This can be tricky, as there are countless patents in the USPTO database, so make sure your search is thorough and encompasses any possible keywords or descriptions. By doing this, you decrease the chances of overlooking anything that is relevant. You can also hire third-party search companies to perform a comprehensive search for you.

If you believe your patent is new and no similar patents are pending or registered, you should next decide whether to file a provisional or formal application. A provisional patent application (PPA) is a temporary application that can be filed immediately and at a lower cost with fewer formalities. This may be useful if you want to get immediate protection for your invention and may not have had the time to perfect it and secure investors, licensees, and others. The PPA is temporary, and you have twelve months from the date of its filing to file a nonprovisional (or formal) patent application. Unlike intent-to-use trademark applications, however, the PPA is nonextendible, so either you file the formal application within a year or you lose the benefit of the PPA filing date. A PPA requires a cover page (form SB/16), written description, any necessary drawings, and a fee submitted within the prescribed time limit. The written description should provide enough detail to allow someone with ordinary skill in the same technology to make and use the invention.

If you filed the PPA, you will need to submit your nonprovisional application within one year. The nonprovisional application must contain a specification, which includes an abstract, background, summary, detailed description, and a conclusion. All of these documents should be highly detailed and well worded, so again, unless you know what you are doing, we stress the importance of having an attorney assist with the application and filing.

The review process can take up to three years (almost as long as we've been waiting on new YEEZY 750 colorways!), so be prepared to wait. A patent examiner may correspond with you or your lawyer about questions or issues with the application. You or your counsel must respond promptly. If you fail to respond to the examiner in the specified timeframe, your application will be deemed abandoned.

If your application is rejected twice, you can appeal to the Patent Trial Review Board. If it is not rejected, congratulations (you did not play yourself), and you will receive a Notice of Allowance indicating that your patent has passed to registration. You will have to pay a fee for issuance and publication of the patent. (Yay, more fees!) These fees are due three months from the date of the Notice of Allowance. When the issue fee is paid and all other requirements have been met, the application will be forwarded to the printer for final issue preparation. The application is then assigned a patent number and you will be informed of the patent number and issue date. Finally (at last!), a bond paper copy of the patent grant will be ribboned, sealed, and mailed to you by the Office of Patent Publication.

Notable Patent Cases

Reebok v. J. Baker

Reebok International Ltd. ("Reebok") brought a patent infringement action against J. Baker, Inc. ("Baker"), claiming Baker's Olympian sneaker infringed upon Reebok's design patent for the ornamental design of Reebok's SHAQ I, the signature sneaker of NBA superstar Shaquille O'Neal.[18] By the time Reebok filed its complaint, Baker's Olympian sneaker had been discontinued, but approximately 33,000 pairs remained in inventory. Reebok sought to enjoin Baker from selling the remaining sneakers. Reebok argued that the sale would result in the public mistaking the Olympian sneaker, a product of inferior quality, for a Reebok product. The US District Court for the District of Massachusetts denied Reebok's motion for a preliminary injunction, holding that Reebok failed to establish that Baker's sale of the remaining Olympian sneakers would cause irreparable harm to Reebok's reputation.

On Reebok's appeal, the US Court of Appeals for the Federal Circuit affirmed the district court's ruling and held that although the district court erred by placing the burden of establishing irreparable harm on Reebok without first determining Reebok's likelihood of success, the error was harmless. Baker successfully rebutted the presumption of irreparable harm to Reebok's reputation by proving that Reebok no longer advertised or sold the SHAQ I beyond a *de minimis* extent, so purchasers of Baker's Olympian sneaker would not likely mistake it with Reebok's SHAQ I.

This case highlights how irreparable harm to reputation is difficult to prove, especially in situations where the patent owner is no longer advertising and selling the product embodying the patent.

Nike v. Wal-Mart

Nike Inc. ("Nike") brought a patent infringement action against Wal-Mart Stores, Inc. ("Wal-Mart") for alleged infringement of Nike's well-known "Shox" midsole, which are columns in the heel of a sneaker that incorporate shock absorption and additional cushioning.[19] The United States District Court for the Eastern District of Virginia held that Wal-Mart infringed Nike's "Air Mada Mid" sneaker design patent and awarded Nike Wal-Mart's profits under 35 U.S.C. Section 289. Wal-Mart appealed to the United States Court of Appeals for the Federal Circuit and argued that Nike was precluded from recovering its profits because the Air Mada Mid was not sufficiently marked with a patent number, and thus, Nike failed to comply with the patent marking requirement. Nike responded to this technicality, stating that the patent marking requirement does not apply to the recovery of the infringer's profits under 35 U.S.C. Section 289, the remedy that Nike sought and was awarded. Nike also argued that even if the marking requirement was necessary, 96.6 percent of all of its unmarked Air Mada Mid sneakers had been replaced with marked ones by the time of the infringement and thus Nike complied with the patent marking requirement.

The court of appeals reversed the district court's ruling and held that the marking requirement applies to design patents regardless of whether the recovery is for damages under 35 U.S.C. Section 284 or for profits under 35 U.S.C. Section 289. The appellate court held that for Nike to satisfy the constructive notice provision of the marking statute, Nike must have shown that substantially all of its Air Mada Mid sneakers were marked and that the marking was substantially consistent and continuous. The appellate court remanded the case to determine whether Nike complied with the patent marking requirement. There is no further history available, so it is likely the parties settled the case outside of court.

---

[18] Reebok Int'l Ltd. v. J. Baker, Inc., 32 F.3d 1552, 1556 (Fed. Cir. 1994).

[19] Nike Inc. v. Wal-Mart Stores Inc., 138 F.3d 1437, 1441 (Fed. Cir. 1998).

THE LAW OF SNEAKERS PART 1: THE LAW AND LITIGATION

Chart 1: Images Depicting Infringement of NIKE Design Patent D498,914 by the Wal-Mart Shoe	
D498,914	Wal-Mart Shoe

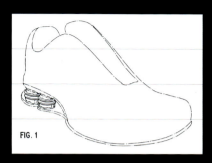

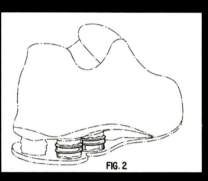

Regardless of whether Wal-Mart acted innocently and did not know whether Nike had a patent for the Air Mada Mid, this case shows the importance of marking a patented article with its patent number. Doing so will provide the public with constructive notice that an article is patented and helps avoid a potentially innocent infringement.

Crocs v. ITC

Crocs, Inc. ("Crocs") almost lost its patent after filing a complaint with the US International Trade Commission ("ITC") alleging unfair competition pursuant to 19 U.S.C. Section 1337.[20] Crocs argued that numerous companies were importing foam footwear infringing upon its '858 utility patent of breathable footwear pieces and its '789 design patent of the ornamental elements of Crocs footwear. The alleged copycat sneakers were sold at large stores such as Wal-Mart and K-Mart. Crocs named twelve Respondents in the ITC investigation; however, after settlements and determinations of noninfringement, five Respondents remained in the case: Collective, Double Diamond, Effervescent, Gen-X, and Holey Soles (collectively, "Respondents"). Crocs filed a motion for summary determination on infringement of its '789 patent, and the Respondents answered with motions for summary determination of noninfringement. An Administrative Law Judge ("ALJ") of the ITC found in favor of the Respondents, granting its motions for summary determination of noninfringement of Crocs's '789 patent and invalidating Crocs's '858 patent on the basis of obviousness, stating the '858 patent was simply a combination of elements found in prior art. On remand, the ALJ again found in favor of the Respondents, holding the imported foam footwear did not infringe Crocs's '789 patent and upheld the invalidation of Crocs's '858 patent. Crocs filed a petition for review, and on final determination, the ITC affirmed the ALJ's findings.

Crocs appealed the ITC's final determination with the United States Court of Appeals for the Federal Circuit. There, the court reversed the ITC's findings and held the accused product infringed Crocs's '789 patent because an ordinary observer would believe the accused product was the same as the patented design. The court held that the ALJ and ITC relied on the written description of the patented design too much, instead of focusing on the design illustration, which caused them to place too much emphasis on minor differences between the infringing product and Crocs footwear. The court concluded that illustrations depict the design better than any written description, and the proper infringement analysis is to compare the infringing product with the patent illustration to see whether an ordinary observer would be confused. The court also reversed the ITC's invalidation of Crocs's '858 patent, holding the '858 patent is not simply a combination of elements found in the prior art, but that Crocs's use of a foam strap riveted to a foam base with direct contact was an inventive combination and, as a result, not obvious.

---

[20] Crocs, Inc. v. International Trade Com'n, 598 F. 3D 1294 (Fed. Cir. 2010).

(12) United States Design Patent
Seamans

(10) Patent No.: **US D517,789 S**
(45) Date of Patent: ** **Mar. 28, 2006**

(54) FOOTWEAR

(75) Inventor: Scott Seamans, Boulder, CO (US)

(73) Assignee: Crocs, Inc., Niwot, CO (US)

(**) Term: 14 Years

(21) Appl. No.: 29/206,427

(22) Filed: May 28, 2004

Related U.S. Application Data

(63) Continuation-in-part of application No. 10/803,569, filed on Mar. 17, 2004, which is a continuation-in-part of application No. 10/602,416, filed on Jun. 23, 2003, and a continuation-in-part of application No. 10/603,126, filed on Jun. 23, 2003.

(51) LOC (8) Cl. 02-99
(52) U.S. Cl. D2/969
(58) Field of Classification Search D2/903, D2/916–918, 919, 969, 926, 932; 36/4, 8.1, 36/10, 11.5

See application file for complete search history.

(56) References Cited

U.S. PATENT DOCUMENTS

1,392,350 A	10/1921	O'Brien	
2,180,924 A	11/1939	Dunbar	
2,470,089 A	5/1949	Booth	
3,407,517 A *	10/1968	Gessner	36/11.5
3,698,107 A	10/1972	Fukuoka	
4,032,611 A	6/1977	Fukuoka	
4,100,685 A	7/1978	Dassler	
4,408,401 A	10/1983	Seidel et al.	
4,476,600 A	10/1984	Seidel et al.	
4,888,887 A	12/1989	Solow	
4,967,750 A	11/1990	Cherniak	
D350,021 S *	8/1994	Stein	D2/969
5,369,895 A	12/1994	Hammerschmidt	
5,438,767 A	8/1995	Stein	
5,528,841 A	6/1996	Pozzobon	
5,561,919 A	10/1996	Gill	
D381,794 S	8/1997	Gelli	

(Continued)

FOREIGN PATENT DOCUMENTS

CA	2375957	9/2002
EP	0 802 039 A2	10/1997
EP	0 802 040 A2	10/1997
EP	0 802 041 A2	10/1997
EP	0 884 005 A1	12/1998
GB	2322286	8/1998

OTHER PUBLICATIONS

http://web.archive.org/web/19980420230857/www.birkenstock.com/featprof.htm (3 pages).
Birkenstock®, Spring & Summer 2003 Catalog, Birkenstock Orthopudie GMbh, Germany (82 pages).
Cindy MacDonald, *The Entrepreneurs: they're bilingual, multicultural and talented. Distance and language present no barriers to Quebec plastics processors and mold makers as the province's plastics industry continues to increase its level of exports and welcome new companies*, Canadian Plastics, O'99, v. 57(10), pp. 35–50 (9 pages).
Comfortable Walking, Italian Technology, Oct. 1999, n. 3, p. 168 (abstract, 1 page).

(Continued)

Primary Examiner—Dominic Simone
(74) *Attorney, Agent, or Firm*—Faegre & Benson, LLP

(57) CLAIM

The ornamental design for footwear, as shown and described.

DESCRIPTION

FIG. 1 is a front perspective view.
FIG. 2 is a right side view.
FIG. 3 is a left side view.
FIG. 4 is a front view.
FIG. 5 is a rear view.
FIG. 6 is a top view; and,
FIG. 7 is a bottom view.
The broken line showing of the sole and surface treatment of the upper is for illustrative purpose only and forms no part of the claim design.

1 Claim, 4 Drawing Sheets

(12) United States Patent
Seamans

(10) Patent No.: **US 6,993,858 B2**
(45) Date of Patent: **Feb. 7, 2006**

(54) BREATHABLE FOOTWEAR PIECES

(75) Inventor: Scott Seamans, Longmont, CO (US)

(73) Assignee: Crocs, Inc., Niwot, CO (US)

(*) Notice: Subject to any disclaimer, the term of this patent is extended or adjusted under 35 U.S.C. 154(b) by 133 days.

(21) Appl. No.: **10/603,126**

(22) Filed: **Jun. 23, 2003**

(65) **Prior Publication Data**

US 2004/0231189 A1   Nov. 25, 2004

Related U.S. Application Data

(60) Provisional application No. 60/473,360, filed on May 23, 2003, provisional application No. 60/473,371, filed on May 23, 2003.

(51) Int. Cl.
A43B 7/06 (2006.01)
A43B 3/12 (2006.01)
(52) U.S. Cl. .... 36/3 A; 36/11.5; 36/50.1
(58) Field of Classification Search .... 36/3 R, 36/3 A, 3 B, 7.5, 11.5, 98, 29

See application file for complete search history.

(56) **References Cited**

U.S. PATENT DOCUMENTS

2,180,924 A	*	11/1939	Dunbar	36/3 B
4,476,600 A	*	10/1984	Seidel et al.	12/142 V
4,888,887 A	*	12/1989	Solow	36/3 R
4,967,750 A	*	11/1990	Cherniak	36/140
5,369,895 A	*	12/1994	Hammerschmidt	36/3 A
D381,794 S	*	8/1997	Gelli	D2/916
5,814,254 A		9/1998	Bisconti	
D416,667 S	*	11/1999	Lamstein	D2/916
D431,346 S	*	10/2000	Birkenstock	D2/916
6,237,249 B1	*	5/2001	Aguerre	36/11.5
6,256,906 B1	*	7/2001	Matis et al.	36/11.5
6,640,464 B2	*	11/2003	Hsin et al.	36/11.5

FOREIGN PATENT DOCUMENTS

EP	0802039 A2	10/1997
EP	0802040 A2	10/1997
EP	0802041 A2	10/1997
EP	0884005 A1	12/1998

OTHER PUBLICATIONS

Rhoda Miel, *Snowshoe walks away with best design*, Plastics News, Apr. 22, 2002, v14, n8, p4 (2 pages).
Luisa Zargani, *One Fine Year; Anton Magnani's Quirky Dry-Shod Designs Have Gained the Italian Designer Respect, Recognition and a Deal With Comme Des Garcons*, Footwear News, Aug. 2, 1999, p. 102 (2 pages).
Finproject Brews an Extralight (Evasol Plastics and Finproject signed a joint venture agreement to introduce a range of new block and net-fit soles for shoes), FN World, Aug. 4, 1997, v. 53, n.31, p. 8 (1 page).

(Continued)

Primary Examiner—Jila M. Mohandesi
(74) *Attorney, Agent, or Firm*—Townsend and Townsend and Crew LLP

(57) ABSTRACT

Among other things, the present invention provides various footwear pieces, and methods for manufacturing such pieces. In various cases, the footwear pieces are molded from a lofting material. Further, in various cases, the footwear pieces include one or more ventilators formed in the footwear piece that are surrounded by liquid conductors capable of channeling liquid spilled on the surface of the footwear pieces away from a foot within the footwear pieces.

2 Claims, 12 Drawing Sheets

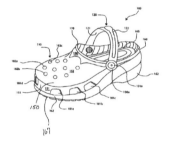

This case shows the inconsistencies between the courts and the ITC on patent issues, and it is remembered for the concept that, when evaluating design patent infringement claims, it is best to base the analysis on a visual comparison between the design patent and the infringing product rather than verbal descriptions of the design patent, which can easily lead to confusion, erroneous application of law, and

L.A. Gear v. Thom McAn

As we have discussed, design patents are not often used in the sneaker industry because of the high cost, slow registration period, and difficulty in obtaining protection. However, this is an example of a case showing the value of a design patent—here, the design patent was defended, held valid, and allowed for a basis for recovery in favor of the sneaker company L.A. Gear, Inc.

In the lawsuit, L.A. Gear argued that Thom McAn Shoe Company, the Melville Corporation, and Pagoda Trading Company, Inc. (collectively "Defendants") copied and sold a line of athletic sneakers similar to L.A. Gear's "Hot Shots" sneakers, for which L.A. Gear held United States Design Patent No. 299081 (the "'081 Patent").[21] Since Pagoda had ceased importing the allegedly infringing sneakers before L.A. Gear was issued its '081 patent, L.A. Gear charged Melville Corporation and its division Thom McAn Shoe Company (together "Melville") with only patent infringement.

The US Court of Appeals for the Federal Circuit affirmed the US District Court for the Southern District of New York's ruling, holding Melville liable for infringing L.A. Gear's '081 Patent with respect to four styles of sneakers. On appeal, the court rejected Melville's defenses of patent invalidity and noninfringement. Instead, the court held that L.A. Gear's design patent was valid and met all the criteria—the patent-protected designs were primarily ornamental and thus not functional, and the '081 Patent was not obvious because the design elements had not previously been combined into a single sneaker design.

Further, the federal circuit held that the infringement was willful, reversing the district court's holding.

---

[21] L.A. Gear, Inc. v. Thom McAn Shoe Co., 988 F.2d 1117 (Fed. Cir. 1993).

This case is important because even though individual elements of a patented sneaker design may not be novel, the combination of elements can still be considered novel for purposes of design patents.

adidas v. Skechers

adidas America, Inc., et al. ("adidas") filed a patent infringement action against Skechers USA, Inc. ("Skechers") in the US District Court of Oregon in July 2016.[22] adidas argued that Skechers copied and sold a line of sneakers similar to adidas's Springblade design, for which adidas held two patents. adidas claimed that Skechers blatantly copied the Springblade technology in developing its Mega Flex sneakers (bearing the "Mega Blade" design) without bearing the cost of developing the technology and that Skechers harmed adidas's reputation and market share by cutting into the Springblade's pricing power, "coolness," and "cachet." adidas sought an injunction against any infringements and damages.

US District Judge Michael Simon held that Skechers did not willfully infringe the two adidas patents by selling its less expensive Mega Flex sneakers. He also denied adidas's request for a preliminary injunction to block Skechers from selling its Mega Flex sneakers because adidas did not prove that it faced irreparable harm without a preliminary injunction or that it was likely to win the case. Judge Simon found there was no willful infringement because, although adidas launched the Springblade in 2013, Skechers began selling its "Mega Blade" design one year before the adidas patent registrations were issued in May 2016.

---

[22] adidas Am., Inc. v. Skechers USA, Inc., 16-cv-1400 (D. Or., 2017).

This case illustrates how pending patent filings
can be susceptible to duplication.

Nike Flyknit v. adidas Primeknit

Nike has several utility patents for its Flyknit technology, which is a knitted and elastic material that flows throughout the exterior of sneakers. Within five months of Nike debuting its Flyknit technology, adidas introduced a similar technology called Primeknit, which also featured woven materials and an overall appearance that was similar to Flyknit.

As a result, Nike filed a patent infringement lawsuit in Germany seeking to stop the production of the Primeknit.[23]

Although Nike initially got a temporary injunction, in the litigation, adidas argued that the knitted construction technique of the Flyknit upper has been used since the 1940s and, therefore, was obvious and not proprietary to Nike. The court agreed and invalidated Nike's European patent.

Fresh off its win in the European Union, adidas brought its Primeknit fight stateside and filed a petition to invalidate Nike's Flyknit patents with the US Patent Trial and Appeal Board (PTAB). Nike sensed they were in trouble and tried to amend their patent applications to show why their Flyknit techniques were novel and patentable, but the PTAB did not agree and invalidated the patents because they employed obvious and well-known stitching techniques.

Nike appealed the PTAB decision to the Court of Appeals for the Federal Circuit. On April 9, 2020, the court ruled that the PTAB did not give Nike proper notice or opportunity to respond to adidas's challenges and has now sent the case back to the PTAB for additional consideration.

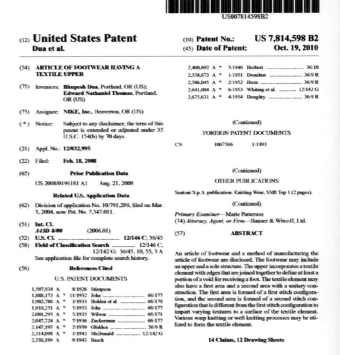

---

[23] Nike, Inc. v. adidas AG, 19-1262 (Fed. Cir. 2019), appeal from the United States Patent and Trademark Office, Patent Trial and Appeal Board in No. IPR2013-00067.

THE LAW OF SNEAKERS PART 1: THE LAW AND LITIGATION

The ongoing fight has been long and expensive for the parties but is both a fly and prime example of the patent infringement wars that occur in the sneaker industry. Disputes such as these can be commonplace when a company has a patent pending for a successful sneaker design.

Trade Secrets

Trade secrets protect business methods, customer lists, patterns, ideas, formulas, and other information that is not publicly known. To be a trade secret, the information must be used in business and create an opportunity to obtain an economic advantage over competitors who do not know or use it. A famous example of a trade secret is the formula for Coca-Cola.

Nike v. Dekovic et al.

Sneaker companies often go through great lengths to protect trade secrets. In December 2014, trade secrets were a topic of the highest level in the sneaker business when Nike sued three of its former employees, Dennis Dekovic, Marc Dolce, and Mark Miner, who quit to join adidas.[34] Under normal circumstances, a move from one company to a competitor might be harmless. In this case, however, Nike alleged the three former employees, all designers, conspired to compete against Nike, misappropriated Nike's trade secrets, and breached enforceable provisions of their employment agreements.

In its complaint, which sought over $10 million in damages, Nike alleged that the designers stole the following items, many of which it deemed to be valuable and highly guarded trade secrets: "extremely confidential and commercially sensitive strategic business plans that reflect Nike's global football business strategies for the next three-to-four years," including ways to compete directly with adidas; unreleased drawings, sketches and designs for Nike football footwear and apparel; proprietary and confidential innovations in athletic apparel and footwear technology; financial information reflecting product performance and marketing campaign materials; confidential and proprietary virtual footwear product design plans and testing methods; and blueprints for conducting successful product launches.

Nike detailed in its complaint just how much money it invests and the great lengths it goes through to protect its trade secrets. Nike maintained that it has spent more than $1.5 million, plus executive time and attention, in developing a security initiative called Keep It Tight (KIT), which provides training and education to Nike employees on how to keep a lid on company trade secrets. Every Nike executive was also required to sign a noncompete agreement, which explicitly required that they not disclose Nike's sensitive, confidential, proprietary, and trade secret information.

In a statement released by their lawyer, defendants Dekovic, Dolce, and Miner all denied the allegations, proclaiming that they "have a tremendous amount of respect for our colleagues at Nike and would never do anything to harm them. We find Nike's allegations hurtful because they are either false or are misleading half-truths. We did not take trade secrets or intellectual property when we departed Nike in September."

---

[34] Nike Inc. v. Dekovic et al., 14-cv-18876 (D. Or. 2014).

The parties agreed to drop the matter in June 2015 after they reached a private and confidential settlement. The takeaway from this case, however, is that sneaker companies can go to great lengths to protect their confidential and proprietary information. If you are a departing employee, be sure you don't violate any restrictive covenants you may have signed when you joined.

Source: Nike

Other Trade Secret Cases

At the end of 2015, Nike filed suit against another former designer, Matthew Millward, alleging he breached his contract with Nike and stole certain protected trade secrets when he left Nike to join Club Monaco, a fashion company owned by Polo Ralph Lauren.[25]

Also in 2015, Puma was hit with a $57 million trade secret lawsuit by Parigi, a New York-based company that had a license to utilize Puma's trademarks in connection with the manufacture and distribution of childrenswear.[26] Parigi alleged Puma systematically misappropriated Parigi's trade secret and proprietary business information, including financial and customer information. These trade secrets, Parigi claimed, were stolen to further Puma's own business interests and form a secret joint venture with another manufacturer and distributor.

We cannot be sure how much money changed hands in the resolution of these trade secret actions, but the takeaway is that trade secrets are expensive to protect, must be closely safeguarded, and may require swift legal action to prevent theft, perhaps by even your most trusted colleagues.

---

[25] Nike, Inc. v. Millward et al., 15-cv-02282 (D. Or. 2015).
[26] Parigi Group, Ltd. v. Puma North America, Inc. et al., 15-cv-00272 (S.D.N.Y. 2015).

Employment Law

Now that you have a full overview of intellectual property law, the next critical area of law related to sneakers involves employment. Generally speaking, employment law governs the employee-employer relationship. This body of law consists of thousands of federal and state statutes, administrative regulations, and judicial decisions, and we cannot fully cover them in this book. But having a decent practical knowledge of certain employment laws is critical when it comes to the sneaker business (and all businesses).

First, as we discussed in chapter 2, if you plan to start your own sneaker business, you should understand what laws may be implicated as your business hires talent and grows. On the other hand, if you are (or plan to be) a sneaker designer, lawyer, creator, accountant, or have some other relevant business role at a sneaker company, you will want to be hired and so you need to know your rights as a worker. For these reasons, we will focus on six areas of employment law that are most relevant to the sneaker biz: (1) wage and hour laws, (2) discrimination, (3) employees and independent contractors, (4) employment contracts and their general provisions, (5) work-for-hire agreements, and (6) confidentiality and nondisclosure agreements. As in the previous section, we will focus on US employment laws, specifically with respect to their impact on and implications in the sneaker industry, providing real-world examples where applicable. But first, let's look at the genesis of some of the more prominent US employment laws.

History of US Employment Law

The history of employment law in the United States dates to the early settling of the country and is expansive. You may be pleasantly surprised to learn that the very first American labor union was formed by a group of shoemakers. Does this mean everything can be traced back to kicks? Maybe not, but in 1794, on the brink of the Industrial Revolution, the Federal Society of Journeymen Cordwainers (shoemakers), the first trade union in America, was organized primarily to protect worker interests and advocate for better working conditions. Fresh pairs for everyone, but not at the expense of the workers!

In 1908, a law was enacted that, for the first time, protected workers who were injured on the job. At the time, railroads were a thriving mode of transportation across America, and the danger associated with railroad work was extreme. Accordingly, President Benjamin Harrison laid the groundwork for what would become today's workers' compensation law by signing the Federal Employers Liability Act (FELA, not to be confused with the sneaker brand FILA). If an injured worker was able to prove that the railroad was at least partially negligent in causing the injury, under the FELA, that worker would be entitled to compensation.

Textile mills became an integral component of the Industrial Revolution following the invention and patenting of the cotton gin by Eli Whitney in 1793. As a result of this invention, factories began sprouting all over, and people looking for jobs found long hours and steady work within them. Those in impoverished communities found that it was more beneficial to put children to work instead of sending them to school. Children could be paid less, work long hours, and complete tasks that were more challenging for less nimble adults.

During the early 1900s, child labor reform groups organized to call for regulations and were met with much resistance. Not until the Great Depression, when more adult Americans were out of work than ever, did US lawmakers realize that pulling jobs away from children was an economic interest, not just a social one. Sweeping reform under President Franklin Delano Roosevelt's New Deal brought widespread limitations to the use of child labor.

EMPLOYEE RIGHTS
UNDER THE FAIR LABOR STANDARDS ACT

FEDERAL MINIMUM WAGE
$7.25 PER HOUR
BEGINNING JULY 24, 2009

The law requires employers to display this poster where employees can readily see it.

OVERTIME PAY — At least 1½ times the regular rate of pay for all hours worked over 40 in a workweek.

CHILD LABOR — An employee must be at least 16 years old to work in most non-farm jobs and at least 18 to work in non-farm jobs declared hazardous by the Secretary of Labor. Youths 14 and 15 years old may work outside school hours in various non-manufacturing, non-mining, non-hazardous jobs with certain work hours restrictions. Different rules apply in agricultural employment.

TIP CREDIT — Employers of "tipped employees" who meet certain conditions may claim a partial wage credit based on tips received by their employees. Employers must pay tipped employees a cash wage of at least $2.13 per hour if they claim a tip credit against their minimum wage obligation. If an employee's tips combined with the employer's cash wage of at least $2.13 per hour do not equal the minimum hourly wage, the employer must make up the difference.

NURSING MOTHERS — The FLSA requires employers to provide reasonable break time for a nursing mother employee who is subject to the FLSA's overtime requirements in order for the employee to express breast milk for her nursing child for one year after the child's birth each time such employee has a need to express breast milk. Employers are also required to provide a place, other than a bathroom, that is shielded from view and free from intrusion from coworkers and the public, which may be used by the employee to express breast milk.

ENFORCEMENT — The Department has authority to recover back wages and an equal amount in liquidated damages in instances of minimum wage, overtime, and other violations. The Department may litigate and/or recommend criminal prosecution. Employers may be assessed civil money penalties for each willful or repeated violation of the minimum wage or overtime pay provisions of the law. Civil money penalties may also be assessed for violations of the FLSA's child labor provisions. Heightened civil money penalties may be assessed for each child labor violation that results in the death or serious injury of any minor employee, and such assessments may be doubled when the violations are determined to be willful or repeated. The law also prohibits retaliating against or discharging workers who file a complaint or participate in any proceeding under the FLSA.

ADDITIONAL INFORMATION
- Certain occupations and establishments are exempt from the minimum wage, and/or overtime pay provisions.
- Special provisions apply to workers in American Samoa, the Commonwealth of the Northern Mariana Islands, and the Commonwealth of Puerto Rico.
- Some state laws provide greater employee protections; employers must comply with both.
- Some employers incorrectly classify workers as "independent contractors" when they are actually employees under the FLSA. It is important to know the difference between the two because employees (unless exempt) are entitled to the FLSA's minimum wage and overtime pay protections and correctly classified independent contractors are not.
- Certain full-time students, student learners, apprentices, and workers with disabilities may be paid less than the minimum wage under special certificates issued by the Department of Labor.

WHD — WAGE AND HOUR DIVISION, UNITED STATES DEPARTMENT OF LABOR
1-866-487-9243
TTY: 1-877-889-5627
www.dol.gov/whd

In 1938, Congress passed the Fair Labor Standards Act (FLSA), which made it unlawful for manufacturers and miners in America to employ anyone under the age of sixteen. It also set the first-ever federal minimum hourly wage, a meager $0.25 per hour, and placed restrictions on the number of consecutive hours an employee could be on the job. With the act, the Wage and Hour Division of the Department of Labor was created, and to this day, it continues to enforce the act's mandates. Although the United States now has almost a century of wage and labor reforms in place, almost all sneaker production has moved overseas to areas where these labor laws were, until recent times, a novel concept. As consumers put pressure on sneaker manufacturers to be more socially responsible, a lot is being done to improve overseas factory conditions.

To this day, however, in certain countries, many impoverished workers, primarily women, are being exploited and work long hours for low wages in substandard work conditions.

Inequality in pay and opportunity for women has long been an issue in the United States workplace as well. In 1963, the Equal Pay Act was passed into law, prohibiting sex-based wage discrimination between men and women in the same establishment who perform jobs that require substantially equal skill, effort, and responsibility under similar working conditions. Although this law was a step in the right direction, to this day women are still marginalized in many male-dominated industries, including sneakers. We dive deeper into this in our section on discrimination.

Source: Abbie Rowe. White House Photographs. John F. Kennedy Presidential Library and Museum, Boston.

On July 2, 1965, the Equal Employment Opportunity Commission (EEOC) was established to enforce the laws set forth in the Equal Pay Act of 1963 and another newly passed law, Title VII of the Civil Rights Act of 1964 (Title VII). Title VII was enacted to ensure equal opportunity in the workplace, particularly on the basis of one's "race, creed, color, religion, sex or national origin." The EEOC's reach was expanded later to cover the Age Discrimination in Employment Act of 1967, which increased the scope of Title VII by prohibiting discrimination against anyone over the age of forty.

In 1990, the Americans with Disabilities Act (ADA) was passed, which prohibits discrimination on the basis of a person's disability. The ADA also requires employers to provide reasonable accommodations to employees with disabilities. In 2011 and 2012, the EEOC expanded the definition of sex discrimination to include individuals who are lesbian, gay, bisexual, transgender, or may have different gender identities.

THE LAW OF SNEAKERS PART 1: THE LAW AND LITIGATION

Source: mark reinstein / Shutterstock.com

Massachusetts passed the nation's first safety and health legislation in 1877, requiring the guarding of belts, shafts, and gears, protection on elevators, and adequate fire exits in factories. It was not until a century later, however, that the first national law was passed to enforce safety in the workplace. In 1971, President Richard Nixon signed into law the Occupational Health and Safety Act.

The act sets out to ensure safe and healthful working conditions for working men and women. It is enforced by the Occupational Health and Safety Administration (OSHA), which sets standards and provides training, outreach, education, and assistance. Over the past four decades, OSHA has helped to save many thousands of lives and reduce occupational injury and illness rates by more than half.

Source: mark reinstein / Shutterstock.com

In 1993, President Bill Clinton signed the Family Medical Leave Act (FMLA) into law. The FMLA was designed to help employees balance their work and family responsibilities by allowing them to take reasonable unpaid leave for certain family and medical reasons. Employers that meet certain criteria must grant eligible employees up to twelve weeks of unpaid leave each year for (1) the birth and care of a newborn child, (2) placement with the employee of a child for adoption or foster care (3) care for an immediate family member, and/or (4) to take medical leave when the employee is unable to work because of a serious health condition.

Now that you know a little bit about the history of employment law, we will look at present-day laws and their impact on employees in the sneaker business. A clear understanding of these laws will help business owners know how to pay and treat employees in a lawful and ethical manner, as well as help workers understand their rights.

Wage and Hour Laws

Over the years since its passing in 1938, the Fair Labor Standards Act (FLSA) has undergone a number of changes. The minimum wage is periodically updated to fall in line with the basic standard of living. States and cities are free to set their own minimum wages should they deem the cost of living higher than what the federal rate provides. For example, as of the writing of this book, the minimum wage is $15 an hour in New York City, because the cost of living is so much higher there, whereas it is $11.80 in the remainder of the state; the federal minimum wage is only $7.25 per hour. This means that if you are an employer in New York State but not New York City, you must pay the minimum wage of $11.80 per hour.[27]

The FLSA also governs overtime laws. Like minimum wage, each state may have its own nuances with respect to overtime, but federal law generally requires employers to pay an overtime rate of one and a half times the regular rate to hourly workers putting in more than forty hours per workweek.

Employers should always check with their state's labor department to ensure they are following the correct wage and hour laws and not violating the FLSA. Violations of the FLSA could be extremely costly, depending on the number of employees and the duration of the violations. For example, in 2007, a class action (a lawsuit designed to provide legal relief to large numbers of individuals who believe they were wronged in a common way) was brought against Foot Locker under the FLSA. The workers, sales associates, stock persons, and cashiers, alleged that they were not properly paid for time spent doing maintenance work and opening and closing the store. Foot Locker managed to settle the case out of court but had to pay $7.1 million to the aggrieved workers.

In 2014, Skechers settled a class action of approximately 4,800 workers who alleged that they should have been paid for missed meal and rest breaks, overtime, and earned wages.[28] The total settlement cost Skechers somewhere between $357,000 and $714,000 and was not the first time Skechers faced wage and hour troubles. In 2004, the company settled three lawsuits, paying around $1.8 million to former and current store managers, assistant store managers, and employees of the company's retail stores who accused the company of violating California's wage and hour laws.

In another sneaker employment dispute, in 2017, Nike was successful in defending a wage and hour case brought by a class of retail workers who claimed that they were not compensated for the time spent undergoing bag searches as they exited stores.[29] The California District Court held that since the average inspection time took no more than 18.5 seconds per employee bag, the time was *de minimis*, or not significant enough to be compensable under FLSA wage and hour laws.

---

[27] These rates often change annually and are set to change on December 21, 2020. Some areas in New York, such as Long Island and Westchester, have a slightly higher minimum wage than the general state minimum wage.

[28] Roneshia Sayles v. Skechers U.S.A., Inc., No. BC473067 (Ca. Sup. Ct., 2012).

[29] Rodriguez v. Nike Retail Services, Inc., 2017 U.S. Dist. LEXIS 147762 (N.D. Cal. 2017).

Discrimination

As previously discussed, Title VII was enacted in 1964 to prevent workplace discrimination, and the EEOC was later created to enforce it. Title VII and the EEOC's reach has been expanded gradually since 1965. Title VII now extends protection to applicants, employees, and former employees who are discriminated based on their race, color, religion, sex, national origin, age (forty or older), disability, and genetic information (including family medical history). Most recently, on June 15, 2020, the US Supreme Court ruled that the definition of sex under Title VII extends similar protection to gay, lesbian, and transgender workers.

The sneaker industry is no stranger to discrimination, particularly when it comes to race and sex. Although the industry is often acknowledged for its promotion of people of color and women in advertisements and endorsements, sneaker corporations have been criticized for lack of diversity and historically disparate treatment of minorities. In 2019, adidas came under fire when a *New York Times* article highlighted the lack of diversity and discriminatory workplace culture at adidas's North American headquarters in Portland, Oregon. The newspaper interviewed more than twenty current and former adidas employees, finding that they believed a pattern of discrimination and lack of promotion negatively impacts Black employees, who make up only 4.6 percent, or fewer than 75 of the 1,700 workers at adidas HQ.

adidas is not the only company to be criticized for a lack of diversity. As of 2018, it was reported that only 23 percent of Nike's American retail employees were Black; 29 percent of its vice presidents were women and 16 percent people of color. Nike's own HR chief has publicly acknowledged that the company was failing in terms of promoting and hiring a diverse workforce.

In 2018, the sneaker giant was sued by two former female employees, Kelly Cahill and Sara Johnston, who claimed that Nike's discriminatory policies and practices, including equal pay, promotion, and harassment, had created a sexually hostile and discriminatory work environment. Specifically, the two alleged that Nike "intentionally and willfully" discriminated against women with regard to pay and promotions and that its majority-male executives fostered a hostile work environment at its Oregon headquarters. Nike moved to dismiss these claims on various grounds but was denied, and other women have since come forward to join the lawsuit. On the heels of this suit, Nike announced that it would commit to new diversity initiatives and acknowledged that minorities were significantly underrepresented in leadership roles and, additionally, that women were not on equal footing with men.

In 2019, Under Armour had to beef up its diversity and inclusion policies after news broke that certain executives were fostering a toxic "boys' club" workplace culture, where strip club tabs were expensed and female employees were excluded and not allowed to advance like their male counterparts. In 2018, *Footwear News* listed its top forty under forty influential people in the footwear industry, and although a handful were female, not one was Black. Puma, on the other hand, received high marks for diversity and inclusion in a company ranking report issued by *The Financial Times*. Out of 700 progressively diverse European companies across all industries, Puma scored eighty-fourth on the list.

Systemic racism and corporate discrimination were at the forefront of the news after George Floyd, a Black man from Minneapolis, Minnesota, was brutally killed by a group of police officers on May 25, 2020. Floyd's murder, just one of countless incidents involving police brutality, sparked immediate outrage; protests in support of the Black Lives Matter movement ignited, first across the United States and then, in support, across the world. As a result, many corporations started to look at their company policies and unequal treatment of Black people in the workplace. Some companies that have historically profited from the Black community looked to find ways to speak out and make an impact on racial equality for society as a whole.

On May 29, 2020, Nike launched a "For Once, Don't Do It" campaign, urging its community and supporters to not turn their back on racism and to be part of the change in preventing racial injustice. The advertisement was so powerful that even a long-standing competitor, adidas, reposted it on its own social channels.

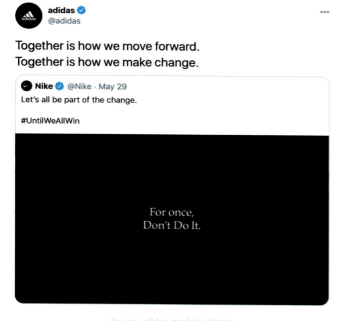

Source: adidas and Nike Twitter

On May 30, New Balance spoke up against the perpetual injustice faced daily by communities of color and asked its social media followers to support the Justice for George Floyd petition. (New Balance had previously donated 10,000 pairs of sneakers to Black community-based programs in the Atlanta area.) The same day, Puma urged its social media followers to support the Minnesota Freedom Fund, and Reebok acknowledged on social media that neither its brand nor America would exist without the Black community. On May 31, Fila announced it would make a $100,000 donation to Black Lives Matter. On June 3, Brooks committed to donating $100,000 to the Equal Justice Initiative to help with racial justice, criminal justice reform, and public education. On June 4, HOKA ONE ONE contributed $500,000 to the NAACP, the NAACP Legal Defense and Educational Fund, the ACLU Foundation, the Center for Constitutional Rights, Black Lives Matter, and the Antiracist Research and Policy Center at American University. The same day, Vans announced it would donate $100,000 to the NAACP, $50,000 to Color of Change, and $50,000 to the GSA Network.

On June 5, Nike, Converse, and the Jordan Brand committed $40 million over the next four years to Black communities and organizations that ensure racial equality, social justice, and greater access to education. The Jordan Brand separately committed an additional $100 million over the next ten years. On June 7, Reebok ended its partnership with CrossFit after its CEO, Greg Glassman, made an insensitive comment about George Floyd on Twitter. On June 8, Under Armour CEO Patrik Frisk announced to employees that the company would implement several new policies in the workplace designed to bring about more diversity and inclusion. On June 9, after four days of protests from Black workers at adidas, the company announced that it would invest $20 million in Black communities and give fifty scholarships over the next five years to Black employees.

A day later, after criticism from employees and others that the amount was insufficient, adidas pledged an additional $100 million to invest in Black communities, committed to filling at least 30 percent of all open positions with Black and Latinx candidates, and 50 percent of all new positions with diverse talent across gender, sexual orientation, disability, and veteran status. On June 12, Reebok, which is owned by adidas, made a similar 30 percent/50 percent commitment to hiring, funding Black student scholarships, and investing $15 million over the next five years to Black communities and organizations focused on ending racial injustice. On June 24, sneaker retailer Foot Locker committed to support the Black community by donating $200 million over the next five years toward educational initiatives and economic development.

Whether all this social and workplace change was entirely voluntary or due to pressure from outspoken and oppressed workers is not always clear. However, recent diversity and inclusion initiatives instituted by sneaker companies seem to show that things are starting to head in the right direction. Clearly, much work has to be done before the industry is a truly inclusive place.

On a positive note, here is one discrimination case that sneakerheads will be pleased to learn about. In 2014, firefighter Keith Daniel injured his ankle while performing on-the-job rescue duties. After the injury, his doctor gave him a prescription for "tennis shoes with arch support + high rescue boot high ankle" to help ease his pain, and provide better ankle support and comfort. Daniel wore the sneakers for six to eight weeks before the department's deputy chief told him he could no longer wear them because they did not comply with the department's dress code of wearing station shoes, or plain black leather boots. Daniel sued the city in 2015 for failing to accommodate his disability and reasonable request to wear sneakers on the job.[30] In January 2020, after a long legal battle and a favorable decision from the Minnesota Supreme Court, the city settled with Daniel for $785,000. When asked by the Minnesota Star Tribune to give his thoughts on the case's outcome, Daniel said, "For me, it was hard to believe that we went all through this for a pair of…tennis shoes." As sneakerheads know, a pair of kicks is always worth the trouble, and if it were us, we would be copping some serious grails with that settlement money!

---

[30] Daniel v. City of Minneapolis, 27-cv-16-700 (Minn. Ct. App. 2015).

Source: Zac Hancock / Shutterstock.com

Classification: Employees versus Independent Contractors

Whether you plan to hire workers or be one, understanding the distinction between an employee and independent contractor is crucial. Under the FLSA, an employee is one who, as a matter of economic reality, follows the usual path of an employee and is dependent on the business that he or she serves. An independent contractor, on the other hand, is someone who is engaged in, and dependent on, a business of his or her own. However, there is a bit more to the distinction.

One important difference between the two types of working relationships is how the individual is paid and the resulting tax implications. In an employer-employee relationship, the company will pay the employee a salary or an hourly wage (preferably a legal one, at or above the minimum federal and state requirement) from which taxes are withheld by the employer. These taxes include federal and state withholdings and other miscellaneous deductions, such as unemployment and Social Security. In an independent contractor relationship, the contractor or consultant is typically paid a fee, but taxes are not withheld by the company and are the consultant's responsibility to report and pay to the federal and state government.

If tax treatment were the only distinguishing factor between independent contractors and employees, every business owner would think, "Hmm, why don't I just hire all consultants and save a bunch of money on paying taxes?" Sadly, many do and have faced significant fines and back-tax penalties for this type of unlawful misclassification. So how can employers be sure to properly classify their workforce to reduce their legal exposure? This is a complex issue and has gone all the way to the US Supreme Court.[31] In order to have a true independent contractor relationship, the following factors must be considered:

01 The extent to which the services rendered are an integral part of the company's business (is the work similar to that which the company already performs?)

02 The permanency of the relationship (is this a short- or long-term position?)

03 The amount of the alleged contractor's investment in facilities and equipment (does the contractor invest in and provide his or her own equipment for performing the job?)

04 The nature and degree of control by the company (does the company have any say in how the contractor performs the work?)

05 The alleged contractor's opportunities for profit and loss (who bears the burden if the job takes longer and/or costs more than anticipated?)

06 The amount of initiativae, judgment, or foresight in open market competition with others required for the success of the claimed independent contractor (does the worker perform routine tasks or does the job require special skills and/or training?)

07 The degree of independent business organization and operation (does the worker have his or her own business, business cards, website, etc.?)

There is no single rule. The total activity or situation should be reviewed on a case-by-case basis. This is definitely something to keep in mind the next time you plan to hire someone to work at your sneaker company, or if you want to work for one yourself.

---

[31] United States v. Silk, 331 U.S. 704 (1947).

Employment Contracts & Offer Letters

When an employer wants to hire an individual, an employment contract must be executed. Employment contracts detail the employer and employee's relationship, responsibilities, rights, obligations, compensation, and any other employment-related details. Thus, regardless of the situation, whether a sneaker company, designer, store owner, store or company employee, reseller, distributor, or manufacturer, knowing the ins and outs of employment contracts are essential. Terms in employment contracts generally include the following:

Job Duties, Term, and Termination (start date, at-will or guaranteed term of employment)

Job Duties, Term, and Termination (start date, at-will or guaranteed term of employment): The job title will typically dictate what duties are expected from the employee and the obligations that the employer will be responsible for. But for some jobs, it may be useful to set out specific roles and responsibilities so there is no ambiguity. The "term" is the duration of an agreement, which includes the employee's start date and the agreement effective date, and how long the agreement will be in place for, which can be a guaranteed period or at-will, which means that the employment can be terminated at any time by the employer or employee (we will discuss this in more detail later).

Compensation (wages, hours, salary, commission, bonus, etc.)

The employee's compensation must be detailed in the employment contract. Will the employee be paid a salary or hourly? Will there be overtime pay? An important distinction to make is whether the employee is exempt or nonexempt, which are specifications under the FLSA. Nonexempt employees are entitled to overtime pay, while exempt employees are not. Additionally, some states have their own wage and hourly rate laws by which the employer must always abide. Other considerations, if applicable, include whether the employee will be entitled to any bonus and/or commission. If so, the structure and terms for those payments should be in writing. It is also possible to have a separate governing document or plan to cover bonuses and commissions. If any of these documents are in place, the employment contract should still mention the commission and/or bonus payments and specify that all terms governing those payments will be set forth in the respective separate document(s).

Vacation and Paid Time Off

The company's policies regarding vacation and paid time off (PTO) should be delineated in the employment contract. How many PTO days is the employee entitled to? How many days off do employees get for holidays? What happens if an employee exceeds the allotted PTO days?

Benefits & Health Insurance

Any benefits and health insurance that an employee is eligible for can be included in the employment contract. However, it is not necessary to go into detail about benefits and health insurance. These can be outlined in separate plan documents.

Confidentiality

Confidentiality is a standard term that is included in the majority of contracts regardless of what the agreement entails. With respect to employment contracts, the confidentiality provision should prohibit the employee from sharing any of the company's confidential information with individuals outside of the organization, except with permission from the company.

Restrictive Covenants (noncompetition, nonsolicitation)

Oftentimes, employment contracts contain restrictive covenants such as noncompetition (noncompete) and nonsolicitation (nonsolicit) clauses. Noncompetes typically prevent the employee from working for competitors and other companies in the same industry for a set time after the employment ends with the company. Nonsolicits generally prohibit an employee from trying to take business or employees away from the company once the employment terminates.

Intellectual Property

Although intellectual property created by the employee in the furtherance of their duties generally belongs to the company, it is advisable to explicitly state this in the employment agreement.

State Laws

As mentioned in connection with compensation, there are many state-specific laws that govern the employment relationship. These laws can impact areas other than just compensation, such as PTO, mandatory breaks, restrictive covenants, and more. Thus, it is important to consult with a local lawyer to ensure that the employment agreement is compliant with all applicable state laws.

At-Will Employment

When an employment is at-will, it means that the employer or employee can terminate the employment at any time and for any reason (or no reason). For the employer, unless the reason for termination is in violation of a federal or state law (e.g., one protecting against discrimination or retaliation), the employer incurs no legal liability for the termination. Additionally, if the employee decides that he or she wants to quit (terminate the employment), as long as the employee did not do anything illegal, there is no liability for the employee either.

In addition to being able to terminate the employee at any time, with at-will employment, employers can also change the terms of the employment contract at any time. Thus, for example, an employer can change an employee's compensation without any liability so long as no laws are violated by the employer. For the most part, employment relationships are at-will. In fact, in all US states, except for Montana, at-will employment is presumed for employment relationships. On the other hand, high-level employees and executives are generally able to negotiate terms in employment contracts that guarantee a certain level of compensation, specify that the employee can only be terminated for cause, and ensure that if the employee is terminated for another reason, they are entitled to additional compensation, such as severance. In some respects, these types of employment contracts divert from the standard terms that are included in at-will relationships.

Offer Letter versus Employment Contract

Offer letters are sometimes confused with employment agreements. Generally, when an employer makes an employment offer, the company will send an offer letter. The offer letter sets out all of the proposed terms of the employment, including the job title, compensation, exempt versus nonexempt status, PTO, benefits, and other terms. The offer letter is not an employment contract. The employee must first accept the offer and thereafter, if applicable, execute an employment agreement. In the at-will employment context, an offer letter can take the place of an employment agreement so long as it specifies all the other important and lawfully required terms we just covered.

Work-for-Hire Agreement and Clauses

When it comes to design and other roles in the sneaker industry with the potential to create valuable intellectual property, it is critical to know what work-for-hire agreements and clauses entail. The last thing you want is to create a sneaker design that blows up, only to have no ownership rights over the design once the sneakers are created.

When hiring independent designers, specialists, consultants, or other nonemployees, sneaker companies should classify the worker as an independent contractor and have them sign a work-for-hire (WFH) agreement. Under the Copyright Act (15 U.S.C. Section 101), a work made for hire is defined as "a work specially ordered or commissioned for use...if the parties expressly agree in a written instrument signed by them that the work shall be considered a work made for hire." Thus, it is always important that any WFH agreement include language that states whether ownership of the works will be assigned to the company or retained by the independent contractor if the works are not deemed made for hire.

Nondisclosure Agreements and Confidentiality

Nondisclosure agreements (NDAs), also referred to as confidentiality agreements, protect a party's confidential information from being disclosed to others. NDAs can be unilateral, meaning that the agreement protects only one party's confidential information, or mutual, meaning that the agreement protects both parties' confidential information. Within the NDA, what constitutes confidential information should be specifically defined. That said, confidential information usually includes proprietary information, trade secrets, and any information that is not known to the general public. When applied to sneakers, confidential information can include designs, strategy, release dates, financial information, unreleased sneakers, samples, manufacturing information, quantity of pairs in a release, and more.

Sneaker companies take confidential information seriously and, as a result, have NDAs executed by anyone who will receive confidential information. In addition to stand-alone NDAs, many agreements, whether they concern sneakers or not, include confidentiality provisions. These clauses have the same purpose as NDAs.

Now that we have addressed some of the major areas of sneaker law and their accompanying disputes, let's take a look at the Art of the Sneaker Deal, a practical overview of how sneaker contracts are constructed to achieve the best result for each side of the negotiation table.

The Law of Sneakers Part 2:
The Art of the Sneaker Deal

"In my adidas contract, I definitely should be able to wear Jordans."

—*KANYE WEST*

In the previous chapter, we covered some serious content involving areas of law and related disputes that have impacted the sneaker industry in a major way. Props for getting through it all, but we're just warming up (like PJ Tucker in some grails). We must move on to the practical side of *Sneaker Law*. We call this the Art of the Sneaker Deal, and it is indeed an art.

When your favorite celebrity or athlete gets his or her own signature pair of kicks, you can be sure that weeks, if not months, of negotiations will precede the release. From Serena Williams to Steph Curry, Kanye West to Stella McCartney, Beyoncé to Rihanna, every athlete endorsement, designer deal, or creative collaboration will have a contract associated with it. Lawyers on both sides will go back and forth on the details of provisions within the contract that affect the way each sneaker deal is crafted. In this section, we cover the range of typical sneaker deals and how their provisions are negotiated to advance the interests of the parties.

Types of Deals

Sneaker deals often take one of the following forms:

01 Endorsement

One or more individuals are paid to promote a sneaker or sneaker line

02 License

One or more individuals lend their name, likeness, brand, or intellectual property in connection with a sneaker or sneaker line

03 Collaboration

Two or more individuals or entities working together on a sneaker or sneaker line

04 Commissioned Work for Hire

Someone is paid to create a sneaker or sneaker line, or one is created under an employer-employee relationship (in-house designer)

No one type of deal is perfect for every scenario; the structures and nuances depend on the parties and the circumstances. For example, an athlete or celebrity could be a party to an endorsement deal, license deal, or a collaboration deal. The same is true for a designer. No matter the type of deal or the parties involved, however, certain provisions are almost always found in these contracts. We will examine each below.

Standard Clauses

No one type of deal is perfect for every scenario; the structures and nuances depend on the parties and the circumstances. For example, an athlete or celebrity could be a party to an endorsement deal, license deal, or a collaboration deal. The same is true for a designer. No matter the type of deal or the parties involved, however, certain provisions are almost always found in these contracts. We will examine each in this chapter.

Intellectual Property Ownership

The ownership of the intellectual property (IP) in any sneaker deal is of utmost importance. When considering IP ownership, a number of questions come into play, and their answers vary based on the specific circumstances of the deal. Who is creating the designs? Who will own the design and final sneaker that is created? Who will own the rights to the name associated with the deal? What trademarks and/or copyrights will be used on the sneakers, and who will own such trademarks and/or copyrights? Will any patents be involved, and if so, who will own them?

You can obtain rights to use IP in three ways. The first is by creating it; obviously, if you created the IP, you should be free to use the property as you wish unless you have given your rights away. The second way is to have the rights assigned to you, and the third is to obtain a license. Let's take a look at these last two methods.

Assignment

IP rights can be assigned, or transferred from one party, called the assignor, to another, the assignee. If a sneaker company wants to permanently own the rights to IP created by a designer or another entity, it could enter into a deal to purchase the rights. In this case, the rights would be assigned by the designer/assignor to the buyer/assignee. In a license agreement, typically, the licensor retains all IP in the work, and the licensee is granted a temporary right to exploit that work, so there is no assignment. In an endorsement deal, the sneaker company might be similarly granted a limited right to use the name, likeness, or trademark of the person endorsing the sneaker. Work-for-hire agreements typically require an independent contractor to immediately assign all work created under that agreement in exchange for a fee paid. Under the Copyright Act, works created by employees within the scope of their employment are considered works for hire, but as we discussed in the "Employment Law" section in chapter 7, it is always recommended to add assignment language into any employment agreement just to be safe. As a designer, you should always be aware of whether you are retaining ownership in the IP you create, or whether you have assigned those rights to another party, such as an investor, employer, or some other party from whom you might be receiving compensation.

License

As mentioned, a license is a deal where one party, the licensor, lends their IP to another, the licensee, for a certain period. A license is a type of stand-alone agreement, but larger agreements can also contain licensing clauses. Typically, in exchange for the use of IP, a licensee will pay the licensor what is called a royalty, or a percentage of sales. A license provision should specify the term (how long the licensee can use the IP), the territory (where the licensee can use the IP), and assignment rights (whether the licensee can transfer or sublicense its IP rights to someone else).

License agreements can be exclusive, meaning that the grant of IP rights is reserved solely for one party, or nonexclusive, meaning that the licensor is free to grant similar rights to other parties at the same time. A licensee in a sneaker deal might want to have an exclusive license, but in today's world of rapid collaborations, a nonexclusive license, or a license for a brief time, would provide more freedom for the licensor to take on other projects.

The license provision can also be exclusive in product scope, limiting it, say, to one type of product, such as sneakers. In November 2019, Under Armour obtained a license for the trademark of the famous candy brand Sour Patch Kids. Under Armour likely negotiated with Sour Patch Kids' parent company, Mondelēz International, for a limited period of exclusivity on its surprisingly sour drop of colorful, candy-coated Steph Curry 7s. By doing this, Sour Patch Kids would be free to license its mark on other types of products (such as toys or pillows), and Under Armour has assurance that, during the term of the license, the only pairs of Sour Patch Kids sneakers will be the ones released by Under Armour. Remember, if you own a brand, you want to make sure the licensee will strengthen and add value to your brand. You do not want the licensee to create a product that might damage the reputation or goodwill that the brand has built. So pick your licensee wisely, get a good royalty rate, and make sure the kicks are always fire.

Source: Under Armour

Usage Rights & Scope

License agreements should specify the usage and scope of the IP rights involved, including the duration of the agreement, what approval rights are necessary, and how the IP can be used. It is important to have these items explicitly delineated and agreed to by the licensee—otherwise, the licensor may find its rights being used in a way that it may not approve of. If rights are assigned, then it will be in the new owner's, or assignee's, discretion as to how to use that IP without any restriction from the assignor.

Endorsement deals also contain usage and scope provisions. Stephen Curry, for example, signed an endorsement deal with Under Armour in 2013, right after his Nike contract ended. Under Armour was given certain usage rights to Steph's IP under that agreement for a fixed time. We know the initial deal was likely for only two years, because in 2015, it was announced that he had signed a contract extension through 2024. The contract may provide for further extensions if certain monetary benchmarks are met. Chef Curry for 3!

Trademarks

Trademarks are one type of IP that can be assigned or licensed. When licensing a trademark, the licensor must have some approval rights in its use to ensure that it meets the trademark owner's standards. For example, when Nike's lawyers negotiated the collaboration deal with Travis Scott's lawyers, Travis's lawyers likely secured approval rights for the use of his trademarked Cactus Jack logo on the sneakers.

Sometimes sneaker brands and collaborators create a new trademark in the course of a deal. If this will be the case, the agreement should detail who will own the trademark—will it be the brand, collaborator, or will the trademark be jointly owned?—and how each party can use the trademark.

In a sneaker license or endorsement deal, the brand will typically license the rights to use a trademark from the owner in connection with a sneaker. For example, Nike, in its deal with Off-White for "THE TEN" collection (and additional sneakers that followed), obtained a license to use the Off-White trademark in connection with all sneakers, apparel, and related marketing materials.

In a work-for-hire agreement, a brand may enter into an agreement with a designer to assist with the creation of a trademark. In this case, the brand will ensure that the agreement grants it all of the IP rights in the trademark.

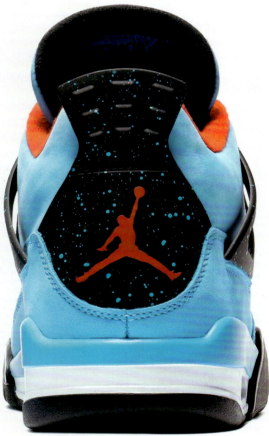

Copyrights

Copyright is another type of IP that can be licensed or assigned as part of a sneaker deal. This IP right is treated the same as others, with the specifications set forth in the agreement. For example, Reebok obtained multiple licenses for copyrighted works from the estate of famed artist Jean-Michel Basquiat for several sneakers.

On the other hand, hypothetically, if Prada were to commission American graffiti artist Futura to create a unique piece of art for its America's Cup sneaker, it might hire Futura as an independent contractor, specify in the agreement that the artwork be treated as a work for hire and that in exchange for his compensation, he will assign the copyright to Prada. Prada would also want to make sure Futura signs any documentation required to support Prada's ownership of the work and effectuate its assignment. Such cooperation language is typically included as part of any work-for-hire or assignment agreement. Futura actually worked with Nike on a couple of Dunk SBs. Whether the deal was a work for hire or not is not publicly known, but it is possible.

If the design is part of a collaboration, both parties may want to have an ownership interest in the designs. In this case, various details must be agreed upon from the outset. These may include where they can be sold, who can sell the design, whether the designs can be licensed, how long the goods with the design should be sold in the marketplace, who is responsible for policing the copyright, and how each party will be compensated.

Patents

Patents can be assigned or licensed as well. Typically, patent applications are filed in the name of the inventor and then assigned to the company. In the same way as trademark and copyright licensing and assignments, when a patent is licensed or assigned, a party secures the rights to use that patent.

In a sneaker license deal, an individual or company that owns the patent would license to another company or individual the right to use that patent in a sneaker. For example, hypothetically speaking, say that an individual creates an innovative utility patent that allows sneakers to change colors based on the climate, and Puma wanted to incorporate the technology in upcoming sneakers. Puma would have to obtain a patent license from the owner of the patent. If the patent license is part of a collaboration, the owner of the patent would likely still retain ownership rights, and Puma would have a license to use it during the term of the deal. Royalty percentages and terms would have to be negotiated. On the other hand, if Puma wants to purchase the rights to the patent, the parties would enter into an assignment, wherein Puma would retain full ownership rights in the patent and be able to use it without any limitations.

Source: Reebok

Source: Stadium Goods

Name/Likeness

Individuals have a right to control how their names and likenesses are used, often referred to as the right of publicity. This right is especially important with endorsement deals involving celebrities or athletes who are highly compensated to wear certain brands' sneakers. If a brand will be working with celebrities, athletes, or other influencers, it will need to obtain the rights to use that person's name and likeness. States have different rights of publicity laws, some more stringent than others, so be sure that your name or likeness usage is compliant with any state laws and to utilize this clause properly.

In 1987, Nike was sued in a right of publicity case by Apple Records, the Beatles' record company. Seeking over $15 million in damages, Apple alleged that Nike had misappropriated and exploited the band's persona and goodwill without permission. Nike was shocked, because it had paid more than $250,000 for the license to use the 1968 classic recording of "Revolution" for its latest and indeed "revolutionary" ad campaign. The license was lawfully obtained by Nike from Michael Jackson, who owned the song's publishing, and EMI-Capital, which owned the copyright. Nobody thought to ask the Beatles, though. In turn, the band was appalled at the commercialization of a song that meant a great deal to the political climate at the time of its release. "Revolution" addressed a time when civil liberties, racism, opposition to the Vietnam War, and feminism were all on people's minds. When the Beatles saw an advertisement using its song to sell athletic products, they were outraged. The Beatles' attorney, Leonard Marks, issued a statement saying, "[t]he Beatles position is that they don't sing jingles to peddle sneakers, beer, pantyhose or anything else." (Beer and pantyhose we get, but sneakers?) The case settled out of court for an undisclosed amount, so we are not sure what happened in the end, but it is safe to say the Fab Four were likely not sneakerheads.

Trade Secrets

Trade secrets are business methods, customer lists, formulas, and other information that is not publicly known. Sneaker brands, designers, and others in the sneaker business all treat trade secrets with the utmost care. There should be a confidentiality provision in any sneaker deal that states that all parties are obligated to keep all trade secrets (along with all other confidential information) confidential.

It is prudent to have all parties involved in the sneaker deal sign an NDA when discussions begin if confidential information will be disclosed. The NDA will cover the initial discussions and ideation of a sneaker deal all the way through the finalization of the deal, and generally extend past the expiration of the deal as well. Therefore, the NDA will ensure that trade secrets are kept confidential no matter what, even if the deal never comes to fruition.

Compensation

Advances

An advance is money that one party pays the other, with the expectation that the party that paid it will recoup (or regain) that amount from future revenue made in connection with the deal. In other words, an advance is essentially a prepayment for future royalties or compensation that the other party may earn. There is some risk for the individual or company paying the advance, because if the deal does not generate enough to equal the advance, the advancing party loses the difference, and the receiving party is generally not on the hook for any unrecouped amounts. Once an advance is fully recouped, the parties typically split profits based on agreed-upon percentages.

Advances are the norm in the music industry when artists sign contracts with record labels. For example, before Kanye West dropped his debut album, *The College Dropout*, which released in 2004, Roc-A-Fella Records signed Ye and gave him a $150,000 advance. It ended up being a pretty smart investment on Roc's end. It recouped the advance quickly and both parties made millions. Kanye's line in "Touch the Sky"—"I went to Jacob an hour after I got my advance, I just wanted to shine"—now makes sense, doesn't it? For endorsement and collaboration deals in the sneaker industry, advances are commonplace for designers and celebrities. If the designer or celebrity has considerable clout, it will be easier to negotiate a sizable advance. On the other hand, if the designer or celebrity is less known, an advance may be difficult to negotiate.

Royalties and Other Compensation

Royalties are a share in the revenues that a particular deal generates. With some sneaker deals, but not all, it may be possible to negotiate a royalty from the brand. Royalties in a sneaker deal typically range from 5 to 10 percent of sales for designers, collaborators, and other parties with significant involvement. The definition of sales will vary, but usually it includes gross sales minus taxes and returns credited to consumers.

If applicable, once an advance is recouped, the agreed-upon royalty split will kick in. If there is no advance, the royalty split will be effective from the start date of the deal and payable at certain intervals throughout the year. Not all sneaker deals include royalties; some involve other payment structures, such as flat fees and one-time payments. A famous example of this is (we know, another Kanye example—must be YZY SZN) Kanye West's deal with Nike. It is well known that Kanye was unhappy with his deal with Nike due to, among other things, Nike's unwillingness to pay him a royalty on the sale of every sneaker he designed. Presumably, Nike was only willing to pay Ye amounts that were not contingent on sales. As a result, Kanye left Nike and joined adidas for what was reportedly a much better deal—and the rest is sneaker history.

Bonuses

Some sneaker deals include bonuses for the licensor, designer, collaborator, celebrity, or another party. Athletes with endorsement deals sometimes receive bonuses for winning championships. Likewise, designers who work for sneaker companies may receive a bonus for a top-selling sneaker. Other milestones and benchmarks can be included in a sneaker deal as well. Bonuses should be considered when negotiating a sneaker deal.

Retros/Re-Releases

Another often-overlooked consideration when negotiating a sneaker deal is including terms about retros and future re-releases of sneakers. It is hard to think about what might happen with a sneaker ten to twenty years after it is made, but as we have seen in the case of many iconic sneakers, they can be re-released over and over again. Thus, if applicable, whatever agreement you are negotiating should specifically mention retros and re-releases, and what the payment terms will be for such items.

Design Approval

In multimillion-dollar sneaker deals, a lot is riding on the design. If it is not well received by the public, it could be a disaster. But do some designers get carte blanche over their sneaker design, or does the company have any say? (Who at Puma is going to tell Rihanna they disagree with her latest design? Not us!)

What about an endorsement deal that is part of collaboration? In 2018, Virgil Abloh collaborated with Nike on the Air Max 97, designed specifically for Serena Williams as part of her "Queen" collection and the fiftieth anniversary of the US Open. Serena has an endorsement deal with Nike, but did she have any approval rights over the 97 design (and the other sneakers included in the collection), or was she just grateful that Virgil blessed her with the beautiful elemental rose upper, gradient midsole, and neon zip tie? After all, she had to wear them at the open, and there is always a possibility that she would not like what she was given to wear by Nike. Sadly, we did not see the contract, so we cannot be sure, but a good lawyer would have tried to include approval rights in Serena's endorsement agreement.

Source: Leonard Zhukovsky / Shutterstock.com

Source: Stadium Goods

Back to the collaboration: who gets final say over the design? If final approval rights are not explicitly specified in the agreement, the two collaborators might find themselves at an impasse over which is better—Vibram or gum soles, lace locks or aglets? And what happens if the disagreement cannot be resolved? Many approval clauses contain language that grants approval rights provided "such approval shall not be unreasonably withheld." This means that if the party with approval rights cannot be reasonable, the other party can proceed to the manufacturing stage. Finally, when collaborating or commissioning a design, language should be added that states the design must be commercially viable or does not include some design element that is too expensive to manufacture. Otherwise, you could end up trying to produce a diamond-encrusted toebox or a plutonium-filled midsole. Madness! The agreement should also cover quality control in manufacturing the sneakers. Quality control ensures that the sneakers are being manufactured in a satisfactory manner and specifies what measures can be taken in the event that the quality is subpar. Standard quality controls generally include the ability for the parties to inspect the manufacturing sites and examine samples and prototypes to verify that the sneakers are being made according to acceptable standards.

Distribution

As we discussed in chapter 4, distribution is an important aspect of the sneaker business. It is therefore critical to consider the manner and method of distribution when negotiating sneaker deals. Where will the sneaker be sold? What distribution channels will the sneaker be sold through? Will the sneaker be sold in stores and online? What stores will get the sneaker? Will the sneaker end up in discount outlets if it does not sell?

Sales and distribution channels are mediums used to sell and distribute products. E-commerce and retail stores are the main sales channels sneaker companies use. Sneaker companies can distribute to wholesalers, retailers, or directly to consumers. No matter what the distribution and sales arrangement is for a sneaker deal, it should be detailed in the agreement. Shipping, delivery deadlines, and other relevant timelines should also be detailed in the agreement.

Retail

When negotiating a sneaker deal, it is also important to specify which retailers, if any, will receive the sneakers. If the designer or collaborator is well known, the sneakers will be highly coveted (and probably limited and exclusive); as a result, you may want the sneakers sold only in high-end and notable retail stores. If a designer or collaborator is still on the come up, you may want the sneaker in as many stores in order to increase exposure and sell as many pairs as possible.

E-commerce

Nowadays, e-commerce is king. People can shop online at their convenience on their phones, tablets, computers, Alexas, and other devices. Sneakers are no different. Companies including Nike (SNKRS app) and adidas (adidas app) have capitalized on ways to sell products online that extend beyond the traditional website. In addition to selling sneakers on their websites and apps, many sneaker companies also distribute to retailers that sell sneakers through their own digital outlets. Kith, for example, sells every top sneaker brand's products on its website and app. Limited sneaker releases are sometimes sold through digital raffles, lotteries, and other means. It is important to ensure that all of these things are considered and included in a sneaker deal.

Discount and Outlet Stores

When a sneaker does not sell out, the leftover pairs are commonly sent to discount and outlet stores. As a designer, celebrity, or collaborator, it is important to consider whether you would want the sneaker to end up in such a store. Many times, popular individuals would prefer that they do not, because it could potentially diminish their brand. For example, it is probable that designer Stella McCartney did not want her Stella McCartney + adidas Originals Stan Smith vegan leather sneakers in discount and outlet stores. Her sneaker retailed for $325, so the license agreement with adidas likely specified premium distribution channels only.

Marketing and Promotion

On July 23, 2019, rookie basketball phenom Zion Williamson signed a $75-million deal with Nike and Jordan Brand. Zion announced the deal by posting a teaser video to his Instagram account. In September of the same year, Jordan Brand launched its global "Unite" campaign, in which Zion was prominently promoted just before his first season with the New Orleans Pelicans. These are just two examples of the many clever and well-timed advertisements that we see from Nike and Jordan Brand's marketing and promotional team.

Source: Nike

Sneakers are big business, so every major sneaker license and collaboration deal should cover marketing and promotion. Each deal should state how much money will be allocated to marketing, and who has approval rights over the final marketing and promotional materials. Many of these multimillion-dollar deals also require exclusivity as part of the promotion clause. For example, during the deal term, Nike might want to ensure that Zion wears only Nike athletic products and certainly not any of its direct competitors' goods.

Appearances are also frequently negotiated as part of marketing and promotion provisions. In April 2019, adidas signed an agreement with Beyoncé to relaunch her Ivy Park athleisure brand. The agreement likely contained provisions setting forth how Beyoncé would contribute to jointly market and promote the brand. For example, adidas might want to specify that Beyoncé is obligated to appear at a certain number of events per year, perhaps performing while wearing adidas x Ivy Park products.

Source: adidas

Source: adidas

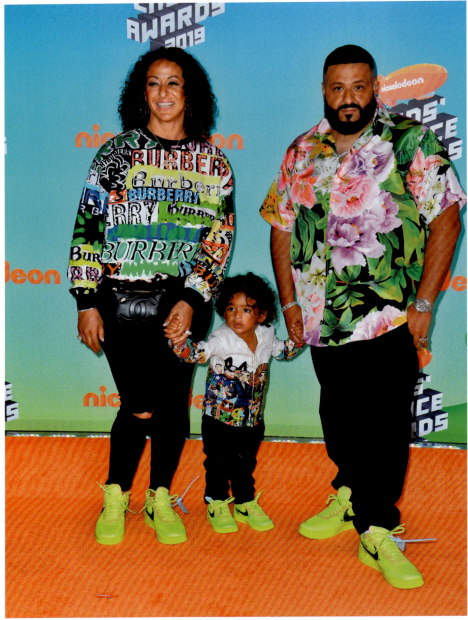

Source: Featureflash Photo Agency / Shutterstock.com

Last, in today's age of influence and social media, we note that marketing and promotion clauses frequently contain product seeding allowances. This means that upon the release of a new sneaker, a certain number of "promotional pairs" will be "seeded" to the athlete, celebrity, and their friends, family, and other influencers with the intent of helping to "grow" the brand organically. Anyone who follows DJ Khaled on Instagram knows he is famous for showing off the array of free goods Nike regularly sends him, his wife, and two sons, Asahd and Aalam. "Still in the meeting!"[32]

---

[32] Note: when celebrities, influencers, and others are sent sneakers, and the individuals post about the sneakers on social media, there may be certain Federal Trade Commission (FTC) disclosures requirements mandated by the FTC that are required. We covered this in more detail in chapter 6.

Counterfeiting

Prosecution

In order to make counterfeiting claims under the Lanham Act, it is very important to have trademark registrations in the United States. For purposes of counterfeiting claims, you will need a trademark registration for the goods that are being counterfeited. Trademark registrations are also necessary to register with customs, which will help stop counterfeit goods from entering the country and often necessary to get counterfeit and infringing goods removed from social media sites and online platforms. In a sneaker deal, as a collaborator, endorser, licensor, celebrity, or other figure, you want to ensure that the sneaker company takes counterfeiting seriously.

Enforcement

Enforcement against counterfeiting is also extremely important, especially in the sneaker business. Companies spend large sums each year to stop the sale of counterfeit goods. They register their trademarks with customs in hopes that the agency will stop the importation of counterfeit goods into the country. Companies also send investigators to investigate stores around the country and the world. Cease and desist letters are sent and litigation ensues. When negotiating a sneaker deal, you want language to ensure that the brand will be vigilant in stopping counterfeits.

Costs

The agreement should designate who is responsible for the costs of anti-counterfeiting measures. If you are a licensor, collaborator, endorser, designer, or celebrity, you are going to want to try to pass the costs of anti-counterfeiting to the sneaker company. On the other hand, if you are the sneaker company, in all probability you are going to attempt to share these costs with the other party.

Employment

Employee versus Independent Contractor

When a company negotiates a sneaker deal with a designer, celebrity, or athlete, it is important that the agreement depict the nature of the relationship. Will the individual be treated as an employee or independent contractor? (For more on this distinction, see chapter 7.) A designer who works for Versace, for example, might be treated as an employee, but a collaborator who owns his or her own design company might be treated as an independent contractor. In either case, there will be important tax implications, so the relationship should be spelled out.

Work for Hire

When Dennis Dekovic, Mark Miner, and Marc Dolce left Nike to join adidas (see "Trade Secrets" in chapter 7), team three stripes likely put assignment language in its contracts so that it was clear that any designs created by the designers in the scope of their employment relationship were automatically assigned to adidas. If there is any doubt as to whether something will be considered a work for hire or not, it is always best to obtain a written assignment.

Confidentiality

Confidentiality is a major part of every sneaker deal. As covered in chapter 7, confidentiality is essential to keeping the terms of a deal secret and nonpublic. When a sneaker brand solicits a major designer, celebrity, or athlete and offers them a huge sign-on bonus, it wants to make sure that the amount is kept confidential so the brand is not compromised on the next deal that it negotiates. Similarly, sneaker brands want to make sure that these individuals, who will now have access to their facilities, resources, and other proprietary trade secrets, keep what they see quiet. A strong confidentiality clause is, therefore, key.

Term & Termination

As discussed earlier in this chapter, the term of an agreement dictates the length of time that the agreement is active. For collaborations, the term is generally limited to the amount of time it takes to release one sneaker but could be longer depending on who the deal is with and how many collaborations are contemplated. For licenses, the term is typically for a limited time as well. Work-for-hire agreements also have a limited term. When the work is complete, the agreement terminates; however, in the case of work-for-hire agreements, the IP would belong to the company in perpetuity after the work is complete, rather than to the person who was hired under the work-for-hire agreement.

Extensions & Renewals

Even agreements with specified terms can include extension and renewal clauses. Sneaker brands like to have the option to extend the agreement if the sneaker performs well. If you are the other party, unless you have a lot of clout, it is unlikely that you will have the right to extend the agreement once it expires. Some agreements have automatic renewal clauses, which extend the term for a set time once the original term of the agreement expires. Typically, with these clauses, both parties have the option to terminate the agreement prior to it automatically renewing.

Terminations

For Cause

A termination for cause means that one party terminates an agreement due to an adverse act, or inaction, by the other party. These are generally included in all agreements and should definitely be included in sneaker deals. Reasons for termination can include materially breaching the agreement, willful misconduct, failing to adhere to the obligations set forth in the agreement, or gross negligence, among others. Terminations for cause are typically useful in endorsement deals, where the brand cannot control what the celebrity or athlete does in their personal time. If their actions damage the reputation of the brand, a termination for cause will give the company an "out" from their obligations under the contract.

For Convenience

A termination for convenience gives a party the ability to terminate the agreement for any reason and at any time, although the party may have to provide a specified number of days' notice. These clauses are favorable to the party that has the ability to terminate for convenience and adverse for the party that does not. As a result, all parties prefer to have the ability to terminate for convenience. Although sneaker companies can usually successfully negotiate to terminate for convenience, it is unlikely that it will allow the other party this option unless that party is highly successful and known.

Morals Clauses

A morals clause is a provision that prohibits certain behavior by a party in connection with an agreement. Prohibited behaviors can include acts that are criminal, bring about public disrepute, contempt, scandal, or ridicule, involve drugs or moral turpitude, and others. Sneaker companies like to have these clauses in the agreement to help protect the brand's image, especially when dealing with celebrities and athletes. However, sneaker companies can also engage in these behaviors, and as a result, as the other party, you want to push to make the morals clause mutual, since you have a brand to protect as well.

Congratulations on making it this far—you are on your way to becoming an OG sneaker lawyer! Remember, you do not need to go to law school or be a lawyer to arm and empower yourself with the basics of these legal principles. We hope what you learned in these chapters will inspire you to be more knowledgeable about law, business, and life in general. We firmly believe that learning can be fun when applied to what you love. But we are not done yet! We have one more chapter left, and we saved one of the best for last. So let's jump into our final chapter on Reselling and Counterfeits.

SNEAKER LAW

Reselling & Counterfeits

"There are sneakers that cost more than an iPod."

—STEVE JOBS

No sneaker business book would be complete without a comprehensive look at the massive resale industry. Currently estimated at around $2 billion, the sneaker and streetwear resale market is expected to reach $6 billion by 2025. So if you feel like it might be too late to get into the resale game, think again. There is still plenty of money to be made, and in this chapter, we're going to explain what reselling is all about and how you can get in on the action.

We have separated the reselling portion of this chapter into three main sections: (1) Reselling and Reseller Basics, (2) How to Acquire Inventory, and (3) Flipping (or reselling) Your Inventory. We then shift gears and conclude the chapter with an in-depth look at the counterfeit industry, which any good consumer and reseller should know about—not only to avoid buying fake sneakers but also to preserve the integrity of the sneaker business. Whether you're a seasoned reseller or looking to flip your very first pair, let's get cooking!

Reselling & Reseller Basics

There are many intricacies to the sneaker reselling business; the deeper you dive into it, the more complicated it gets. But from a broad perspective, the process of reselling kicks is quite simple. It begins with buying a pair of sneakers and ends with selling them to another willing buyer—hopefully, for more than you paid.

First, some basic terminology. In any business, the number one priority is to generate profits. Profits are dependent on the amount of sales revenue a business generates after deducting the costs of doing business. The goal in reselling, therefore, is to cop (or acquire) kicks at the lowest price possible and then flip (or sell) them at the highest. Achieving both is easier said than done.

Types of Resellers

A reseller is someone who purchases one or more pairs of sneakers not for personal use but for profit. Some resellers sell sneakers they don't want to wear just to make enough money to pay for the ones they do. Others have no intention of keeping their inventory for personal use and look at sneakers only as commodities to be bought and sold. We have broken resellers into three groups, according to their resell volume.

First, there are the low-inventory resellers, the little fish, who resell sneakers in fairly small amounts. These are individuals usually just starting out in the resale game, trying to make a quick flip off a few pairs of sneakers. Maybe they are trying to build toward a legitimate resale business, or perhaps they justa have a few pairs that they never wore and want to make some money. Nonetheless, as a low-inventory reseller, they do not acquire large quantities of sneakers. When a release is extremely limited, these individuals typically have a much tougher time obtaining pairs and might land one or two at the most.

Second, there are the mid-level resellers, the sharks, who buy and sell inventory in moderate amounts. These resellers have often been in the resale game for a while. For any given release, these individuals can obtain anywhere from three to ten pairs or more. They may not make reselling their main job or priority but instead use it as a side hustle. Some mid-level resellers have a handful of people working with or for them, hoping to cop as many pairs as possible and take their business to the next level. They will eat the little fish for lunch.

Then there's the third and final kind of reseller, the whales. These are the biggest creatures in the sea: the seasoned vets, online brokers, and brick-and-mortar businesses, known by everyone in the sneaker world. These resellers will eat all the sharks and smaller fish in one swoop, managing to get their hands (or fins) on many pairs of every release and then charging a premium on the flip. Sneakerheads and other individual buyers go to these resellers when they need a specific pair because of their reputation, large inventory, accessibility, and reliability. They can generate millions in sales, have teams of people working for them, and are connected in every facet of the sneaker business, including direct contact and leverage with the sneaker brands, wholesalers, and retailers; many have retail stores of their own.

Now that you know about the different creatures in the resell sea, let's look at the rest of the ecosystem: how to acquire inventory, sell it for a profit, and what to look out for along the way so you don't get eaten alive.

Acquiring Inventory

You cannot get into the reselling game without first buying or otherwise acquiring inventory. There are a variety of ways to get your hands on sneakers. The process can go from fairly inexpensive and painless to extremely expensive and downright frustrating, depending on the release. Whether you wear your sneakers or just plan to flip them, anyone who loves sneakers as much as we do knows how upsetting it can be to anticipate an exciting and well-marketed sneaker release only to take an L by learning they sold out in minutes. How, then, can you get your hands on these highly coveted kicks? Some say it's luck of the draw, whereas others seem to have the secret sauce. In this section, we hope to shed some light on the process of buying sneakers so that you can get some fresh pairs and start making money in the resale game.

Copping at Retail

The fastest way to Air Max out your profit margins and give them an UltraBoost is to cop as many pairs as you can at retail. In case you need a refresher on our discussion about distribution channels in chapter 4, retailers are near the end of the distribution chain, acquiring goods from manufacturers or wholesalers, then selling directly to the consumer. For example, the New Balance store in London is a retailer and the Foot Locker app is an online retailer, or e-tailer. When preparing to buy sneakers from a retailer, you will need to know the following: (1) whether the sneaker you want is a GR (general release), sold in mass quantities, a limited release, sold in relatively small quantities, or something in between; (2) which retailers will have the pair that you want in stock; (3) how many pairs each customer can purchase (some releases are restricted to one pair per customer); and (4) what time and date the sneakers drop. The answers to all these questions can usually be found on the brand's website or the upcoming release section of any major sneaker blog (see chapter 6). Some answers are more elusive than others, depending on the sneaker and the hype around it.

Next, you need to get ready for the drop (release date). As discussed, depending on the release, how many pairs were made, and how large the demand is for the sneaker, copping on the drop date can vary in difficulty.

In-Store and Camping Out

Obtaining the new kicks at retail prices can be done a few ways. The first is the old-fashioned way: go down to the store before it opens, wait in line, and hope to secure a pair before they sell out. This sounds relatively simple, but as you can imagine, lines can be long and stock is often limited. Sometimes pure pandemonium can ensue around an in-store release. In 2005, the night before Jeff Staple and Nike released the Pigeon Dunk SB, there were already a dozen people waiting outside Staple's NYC store, Reed Space. By the morning of release day, there were over 150 people in line. Twenty people were arrested after the doors opened, and Reed Space had to safely escort people through the back door just to make sure they didn't get their kicks stolen before they got home. It was pure bedlam, and this would not be the last time there was chaos at an in-store release. We'll cover more on this in our "Violence in Sneakers" section later in this chapter.

At one point, camping out to beat the lines was the only method to obtain highly coveted sneakers. As the hype around releases became more prevalent, lines got longer and crowds more unruly. In light of the violence and crowd containment issues, many stores have ended campouts and release products only via raffles, which we'll discuss next. Some stores, like Supreme, still permit campouts. But even Supreme has canceled campouts on some of its most limited product releases due to pandemonium, violence, and oftentimes, the police getting involved. For those sneakers that still release in-store, the top resellers will often hire people to stand in line for them. Some resellers even have a team of people working the streets, across multiple states, and on multiple releases! As you can see, lining up and buying sneakers in-store is still an effective way to acquire kicks at retail, but it is often competitive and sometimes dangerous.

Raffles

Because of the hype that surrounds releases and problem with bots (more on these later), many sneaker companies and retailers have resorted to raffling off or holding drawings for the products either online or in-store. In-store raffles require customers to come to the store and sign up for the raffle. Even raffle lines can be extremely long. For example, on May 9, 2019, from noon to 6:00 p.m., the NYC sneaker retailer Concepts held a raffle for the Air Jordan 1 Retro High Travis Scott, and the line spanned several city blocks. Only a small percentage of the people who waited in line for hours actually won the raffle—it's NOT lit! If you are one of the lucky ones and manage to hit a sneaker raffle and cop for retail prices, you have to go back to the store to pay for and pick up your sneakers. The stores usually have a specific window to complete the purchase, and if you are not able to make it in person, you forfeit your kicks.

Online raffles, or drawings, require you to sign up on an app or website for a chance to buy a pair of sneakers, sometimes for a fee or by guaranteeing advance payment in full. These are usually limited to one entry per consumer. If you win, you will either be allowed to have the sneakers shipped to you or go into the store and pick up in person. No lengthy lines or violence to worry about with online raffles, but the odds of winning tend to be far lower, since you are competing with a larger group of people who can easily enter the raffle from their phone instead of taking time out of their day to purchase in person—and you have bots to compete with.

Sneaker Brand Apps

The last option for purchasing sneakers via retail is through a dedicated app. Companies including Nike, via the SNKRS app, and adidas, via the adidas Confirmed app, offer stand-alone applications that can be downloaded to your smartphone and serve as a way to purchase most branded products and new releases. Again, because of the vast number of people who have downloaded these apps and try their luck at copping, it has become increasingly hard to win on them. Anyone who has tried to cop a limited release on SNKRS knows just how frustrating it can be to log in on a Saturday morning, hit "Purchase" less than a second after the sneaker drops, and find them sold out before you even had a chance.

How can you increase your odds? There's good old-fashioned luck of the draw, and then there's bots. Bots are to sneaker resellers what steroids are to athletes—they can give the players a massive advantage over everyone else on the field. Intrigued? Read on!

Bots

Bots are automated software programs designed to perform specific tasks. Used across many industries for different purposes, they serve to replace or imitate human actions. Bots are typically created by computer programmers, developers, and coders and involve complex code. Bots began to emerge on the internet in 1988 and have advanced in technology, functionality, and capabilities incrementally year after year.

Bots made their way to the sneaker business in 2012. Sneakerheads were fed up with not being able to purchase exclusive and limited sneakers; release after release would sell out in seconds, and people looked to bots to gain an advantage. Sneaker bots started out as Google Chrome extensions used as a way to automatically purchase exclusive and limited sneakers online. By installing the extension and inputting the desired size, the sneaker would automatically be added to an individual's cart the moment it released. This gave users an edge over others trying to purchase manually. Advanced versions later allowed users to input their shipping address, billing address, and payment method and have the extension automatically add the sneaker to their cart and attempt to purchase it. As the news of these spread, many began using similar programs, and it became harder to purchase highly coveted sneakers even with the extension. As a result, savvy resellers hired computer programmers, developers, and coders to create more sophisticated sneaker bots.

Sneaker bots became a phenomenon, each bot stronger than the last. In addition to the bots themselves, proxies, servers, fast internet connections, and other technologies became necessary to cop exclusive and limited sneakers, which is still the case today. Elite sneaker bots can purchase hundreds or even thousands of pairs during a given release, whereas lower-level bots may be able to purchase a pair or two, depending on the release and demand. There is immense competition around who can get their hands on the best bot. There are scores out there, and this has made it tough to purchase exclusive sneakers even with a bot.

Sneaker bots have become big business for not only resellers but for the owners of the bots as well. Bot owners generally sell subscriptions to their bot, and if it is successful, they can make a lot of money. For example, in 2017, right before the release of the Supreme x Air Jordan 5, it was reported that the owners of the bot EasyCop sold 500 subscriptions for $595 each, which totaled close to $300,000. Not too shabby.

Sneaker bots are controversial. Some sneakerheads don't mind bots, as they provide an opportunity to obtain exclusive and limited sneakers, whereas others think they are a cancer to the sneaker game. When it comes to reselling, whatever your stance, it is imperative nowadays to have an effective sneaker bot to help you purchase coveted sneakers online. Otherwise, you will have to explore other ways of acquiring inventory that we discuss in this chapter.

Add-to-Cart and Preorder Services

Shortly after bots entered into the sneaker business, add-to-cart services were born. Resellers no longer had to physically purchase sneakers and resell them. Instead, the service, while using a bot, could simply add the sneakers to a customer's cart. The customer would then be able to check out and purchase the sneaker on their own. Add-to-cart services charge a fee for adding the sneaker to the buyer's cart.

Add-to-cart services later transformed into preorder services, where the bot would not only add the sneaker to a customer's cart but automatically purchase the sneaker for the individual as a traditional bot would. In this case, however, the customer does not have access to the bot itself. With preorders, someone pays one of these services a fee, gives the service their payment and contact information as well as their address, and the service inputs this info into the bot and then attempts to purchase the sneaker for them. If the preorder service is unsuccessful, as long as it is legit (it is always prudent to make sure that the company is reputable), the customer receives a refund. For example, Yeezy Mafia runs preorders for YEEZY releases. Generally, days before the release, Yeezy Mafia opens up preorders and, depending on how limited the sneakers will be, opens up a certain number of preorder slots. To secure a preorder, customers must pay the fee, input their desired size, shipping and billing address, contact information, and payment information. If the preorder is successful, congratulations, you just secured a fire new pair of YEEZYs and will receive a confirmation email! If not, don't trip; Yeezy Mafia will refund the fee that you paid.

How Companies Fight Bots

Since the inception of bots, sneaker companies and bots have been in a cat-and-mouse game. Time after time, sneaker companies implement changes to stop bots. The bots then adapt to overcome those changes.

When bots first began to rise in the industry, sneaker companies did little in response. Nike was one of the first companies to act, enlisting an anti-bot team that used various means to detect whether a sneaker order was placed by a bot or a real person. If Nike thought that an order was placed by a bot, they would cancel it. They also designated Nike employees who would, at times, contact profile owners who placed orders using bots. Sneakerheads may remember the infamous Nike employee named Meg, who would call, email, or sometimes even permanently ban people who used bots from shopping on Nike's site. Although these anti-bot measures from Nike were a good start and other sneaker companies followed suit, many bot-placed sneaker orders went undetected with no repercussions.

Sneaker companies continue to implement more effective measures to fight bots. These include CAPTCHAs that need to be solved, images with keywords within the image, IP address bans when suspicious activity is detected, and others. Although these methods may deter the use of bots temporarily, the bot coders quickly adapt and are ready to go back to war by the next hyped release.

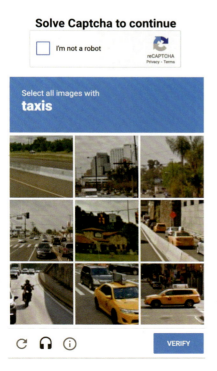

Some sneaker companies have gotten creative when it comes to stopping bots; in 2018, during the release of the Off-White x Nike Air Presto, Kith cleverly replaced the link to the Prestos with the Air Jordan 1 in wheat/gum, a sneaker that was priced at $80, a 50 percent markdown since it was collecting dust on the shelf. Bots were tricked into buying the Jordans instead of the Prestos. In fact, one bot user purchased $1,700 worth of the Jordans! Did Kith refund that bot user or any others? Nope! They told all buyers that it was against their policy to cancel or modify orders once they are placed. In that instance, it is safe to say that Kith beat the bots.

Online raffles and drawings, which are used to prevent chaos in stores, are also a common strategy to combat bots. People who wish to purchase the sneaker must enter, and winners are randomly selected. While entering the raffle or drawing, consumers usually enter in all of their payment and contact information, and if they are selected, the sneakers are automatically purchased and shipped to them. However, in true sneaker bot fashion, bots have been built to give people an advantage over non-bot users for raffles and drawings, too; these bots generally submit large volumes of entries, giving the bot user a higher chance of winning. Nike's SNKRS app, for example, holds drawings for hyped and exclusive sneakers. Being selected in these drawings is exceedingly difficult for manual users who submit one entry, which is how the drawing is supposed to function. But bots that automatically enter the drawing multiple times give their users a better chance of acquiring that sneaker.

Legislation is another tool that's been deployed to combat bots. In 2016, under President Obama, the Better Online Ticket Sales Act (BOTS Act of 2016) became law. The BOTS Act made it illegal to use bots to purchase tickets for concerts, theatrical events, sporting events, and other events on ticketing websites, effectively banning all ticketing bots. Some states, such as California and New York, have passed their own laws banning ticketing bots. Despite these laws, many people continue to use ticketing bots. If federal or state laws are enacted to prohibit the use of bots to purchase sneakers, it would be devastating to bot users and many resellers. It is likely that some people would still try to use bots to purchase sneakers, but it would in all probability significantly curtail their use. Will we see some form of legislation banning the use of sneaker bots? Only time will tell. Admittedly, though, whether you would be for or against such legislation, it would be pretty cool to watch members of Congress debating sneakers!

Cook Groups

Another way to acquire sneaker inventory is through cook groups. These are private group chats that provide exclusive information related to sneaker releases and reselling, including information related to early links, bots, where to purchase sneakers, plugs, and more. These groups typically require a monthly or yearly membership fee to join and are hosted on online communication platforms such as Discord or Slack. Many cook groups are exclusive and allow only a certain number of members to join. Some cook groups are invite-only, and applicants have to be approved by the group admins. Joining a good cook group can definitely increase your odds of purchasing limited and exclusive sneakers.

Buying on the Secondary Market

Buying sneakers on the secondary or resale market is another way to acquire inventory. Oftentimes when a hyped sneaker releases, the low-inventory resellers (the little fish) want to make a quick buck and flip the sneakers as quickly as possible. Because of this, resale prices are generally lower right after the release date. When this happens, some resellers buy the sneakers at initial resale prices as an investment, hoping that the sneaker will increase in value over time. For example, when the Nike Air Yeezy 2 in Solar Red dropped in 2012, the resale value was approximately between $1,500 and $2,000 right after it released. Flash forward to 2020, and the sneaker's resale value is roughly in the $5,000 to $6,000 range.

Source: Stadium Goods

When buying sneakers on the secondary market, it is of the utmost importance to make sure that the sneakers are authentic and not counterfeits (which we will discuss later in this chapter). Remember our Legal Sneakers example from chapter 2? When buying sneakers to either resell or wear, you don't want to get duped by fakes. It is always advisable to purchase sneakers from reputable sellers and companies. As we will discuss shortly, there are many trusted resale platforms that will ensure the sneakers you purchase are authentic.

The Plug

If you know, you know. For the lucky ones, the chosen few who are well connected in the sneaker game, there is the last and final stop on the cop train—the plug. The plug is often a term used with intentional vaguery but typically refers to a person "on the inside" who has access to pairs at retail, at a significant discount, slightly over retail price, or sometimes even for free. The plug is the holy grail of sneaker connects, which is why anyone who has a plug guards that person's identity with their life. After all, no plug wants to be bothered by random people asking for free kicks! Plugs can come in many forms: celebs and VIPs who get pairs for free, brand employees who have access to friends and family accounts, workers at retail stores who get their hands on pairs on or before release date and are able to "backdoor" pairs to their friends, resellers who can cut you in on a deal, and more. Even the most connected people can't compete with a sneakerhead who has access to the right plug. Come release day, there are only so many pairs; if you're not plugged up, you might just miss out. For all the plugs out there, be sure to hit us up!

Strategies to Prevent Resale

Many sneaker companies are staunchly opposed to the resale industry and have taken measures to stop the game. In the case of exclusive and limited releases, some retailers require the customer to put the sneakers on and wear them out of the store. You can't resell sneakers if they are worn! (Well, you can, but like a new car driven off the lot, the value of a sneaker significantly decreases once it is no longer DS.) For example, in 2018, Jordan released the Jordan 1 Retro High "Not for Resale." On the midsole of the silhouette, the words *NOT FOR RESALE* were featured in bold, and the words *WEAR ME* were written on the tongues.

Source: Stadium Goods

Source: Stadium Goods

Some retailers took the concept literally and required that customers wear it out of the store. But resellers still got their hands on the unworn sneakers and did the opposite of what the midsole said to do.

Another clever example of sneaker companies attempting to prevent reselling involves the YZY QNTM release during the 2020 NBA All-Star weekend in Chicago. In true YEEZY fashion, Kanye trucked in an entire fleet of tanklike Sherp ATVs off his Wyoming ranch to drive in procession through the streets of Chicago's West Loop. The vehicles randomly stopped and handed out pairs of the QNTM for free but with a catch. Anyone who wanted a pair of the QNTMs and were lucky enough to find a tank had to take the kicks off their feet (in the freezing cold) and trade them in for the YEEZYs. At the time, the QNTM sold for well over $1,000 on the resale market, so by making the individuals trade in the sneakers that they were wearing, YEEZY left them no choice but to wear the QNTMs (unless they were cool with getting frostbite). In effect, this helped prevent these people from reselling the sneakers.

Despite these examples, it really is a fruitless endeavor for sneaker companies to prevent resale as a whole. The game is at the point of no return; it has turned into a massive industry that continues to grow exponentially. And don't let sneaker companies fool you; the resale industry benefits them just as much and maybe even more than resellers. Resale drives demand and hype. When there is so much demand and hype in connection with a brand, not only are their sneakers going to sell out, but it drives massive publicity to the brand itself. This can help drive ancillary sales in an insurmountable way; limited releases for some pairs means widespread sales for GRs. E-tailers also benefit because the demand and hype drives people to their stores and websites. Again, ancillary sales could follow. Despite all of this, sneaker companies are still on the fence about reselling. Which side are you on?

Flipping Your Inventory

Congratulations—you secured your sneakers and now you need to flip them for a profit. There are many options, and the differences between them are important, especially if you want to make the most money possible per flip. Luckily for you, we're going to lay it all out in this section. We begin with a look at the major resale platforms. These are the multimillion-dollar enterprises, where as long as you have the money to spend, you can get your hands on just about any pair that you want. Then there are the smaller stores, which we refer to as mom-and-pop shops, because they are usually independently owned and operated. Finally, there is the old-school method of selling hand to hand, either in person or through online platforms like Craigslist, popular social media platforms, and others.

Some selling platforms are only online, while others have physical stores in one or more major cities. Some charge resale or broker fees, which can severely cut into your profits. Depending on where each store or warehouse is located, there may be shipping fees and taxes, which also cut into your profits. Some have trained authenticators, who provide consumers with peace of mind while making it harder for fraudulent resellers to pass off fakes. Finally, each one has different methods of processing payments, which is important to know if you want to get your money at some point. Now that you know what to look out for, let's look at some of the different resellers in the game.

Major Resale Platforms

Stadium Goods

Co-founded in 2015, Stadium Goods is one of the biggest sneaker resale platforms in the game. With both a physical and digital presence, Stadium Goods sells sneakers to all corners of the globe. In 2018, Stadium Goods received a financial investment from LVMH Luxury Ventures and was later acquired by the online retail powerhouse Farfetch for $250 million. Today, sneakerheads can drop off their DS kicks in person at one of the SG Market Centers for authentication and, if found to be legit, list their pairs for consignment at a price of their choosing. You can also ship your sneakers to the SG Market Center. Once listed and sold, Stadium Goods will pay you 80 percent of the final sales price, net of their 20 percent resale fee.[33] Stadium Goods boasts a massive inventory, so if you want a pair, chances are you can find it here.

Urban Necessities

Established in 2014, Urban Necessities is a consignment sneaker and streetwear shop that also purchases some sneakers outright as long as the price is reasonable. Offering shopping online and at its flagship store in Las Vegas, Urban Necessities allows resellers to either bring in their kicks to its physical locations or ship the sneakers to them. Either way, they authenticate the sneakers and agree on a price for consignment or an outright purchase. For sneakers on consignment, Urban Necessities takes a 10 percent fee from the final sales price.

---

[33] This, and all other resale platform percentages, were up to date as of the writing of this book but may be subject to change.

Flight Club & GOAT

Founded in 2005 in New York City, Flight Club is the OG sneaker consignment shop. Flight Club truly revolutionized the sneaker resale game. Today, Flight Club has physical locations in New York City, Miami, and Los Angeles. Flight Club also has an online marketplace. In order to consign with Flight Club, you can bring your sneakers into any of its locations, where staffers perform legit checks to verify authenticity, or you can ship your sneakers to them. Once your sneakers have been verified as authentic and listed on Flight Club's platform, you will receive 80 percent of the final sales price, and Flight Club will keep the rest.

In 2018, GOAT, an online sneaker and streetwear marketplace, merged with and acquired Flight Club. As a part of the deal, both companies raised $60 million in funding. The acquisition price was undisclosed. When the deal occurred, the two companies adecided to operate as separate brands but since then, have combined certain resources and technologies to optimize across both companies. GOAT is strictly an online resale platform that allows you to create an account and list new and used sneakers for sale. Once there is a sale, the seller ships the sneakers to GOAT to verify authenticity. If the sneaker is verified as authentic, GOAT then sends the sneaker to the buyer. If the sneaker does not pass the verification, it is sent back to the seller and the transaction is canceled. If you are in good standing with GOAT, meaning that you don't have seller cancellations or sneakers that failed verification, the minimum commission fee is 9.5 percent plus a $5 seller fee for US residents. If you have issues with verification and cancellations, the commission fee can increase anywhere from 15 percent to 25 percent on sneakers sold on the platform. When receiving funds through ACH direct deposit or PayPal, GOAT charges an additional 2.9 percent fee.

StockX

What started in 2015 as the first online stock market for sneakers has rapidly grown into a marketplace for all things hyped, including streetwear, handbags, watches, trading cards, and other collectibles. What separates this reselling company from the rest is that users can view a history of transactions for every item, giving savvy sneakerheads the ability to track and predict market trends for their goods, just as with the stock market. Unlike other sneaker resale platforms, StockX gives the buyer an option to bid on sneakers if they feel that they can influence a seller to bring their price down. This method allows for some online bargaining between buyer and seller. But if you really want that pair, be careful because a third-party buyer can swoop in at any time and "Buy Now." Resellers can flip only brand new, in-box pairs, and some sneakers will be returned if the box is damaged.

Although StockX is primarily an online platform, it does have one permanent physical drop-off station in New York City and has opened "pop-up" shops in Los Angeles and London. StockX buys and ships internationally and offers a fairly foolproof authentication process. Sellers have to send their pairs into one of StockX's warehouses, where if they pass the test, they are tagged as "Verified Authentic" and shipped off to the happy buyer. For new sellers, there is a 9.5 percent transaction fee, which can be reduced to as low as 8 percent once you meet sales thresholds. StockX also charges a 3 percent payment processing fee.

Grailed

Named after "grails," or extremely hard-to-come-by sneakers and other fashion items, Grailed's online-only platform launched in 2014. Grailed offers authentication services, but unlike other physical authenticators, Grailed only runs online checks, determining authenticity by scouring the seller's posted photos. Authenticating a product virtually can be challenging, but Grailed seems to deal with this consumer concern by offering a money-back guarantee for both buyers and sellers. For resellers looking to make a higher profit margin, Grailed charges a flat 9 percent commission fee on sales. Unlike some other reselling platforms, Grailed also allows users to list both new and used kicks for sale. Looking for a gently worn pair of OG Jordan 1s from 1985? Or maybe you've always wanted Louis Vuitton Trainers but don't want to pay retail, so you'll settle for ones that have been worn only once or twice? You might just find what you need on Grailed!

eBay

Perhaps the oldest online auction and shopping site, eBay is now a digital household name. Although eBay has no physical presence, it offers a robust bidding and buying process and has no restrictions on whether sneakers need be new or used. In an effort to drive more sneaker sales through the platform, as of December 2019, for any sneaker sold at $100 or more, eBay has eliminated all North American seller fees, which used to be 10 percent of the final sales price. This is massive for resellers looking to keep all their profits, but unless you are a trusted reseller with a good feedback rating, you will have a hard time convincing buyers that you are a legit seller. eBay has no authentication system, so you have to be able to spot fakes on your own, something that can be extremely tricky online, especially if the seller is careful about concealing flaws or variations. With that being said, there are great deals to be found on eBay, given the lack of fees and ease of the buying and selling on the platform. Happy bidding!

Kixify

Founded in 2013, Kixify is a sneaker marketplace that is strictly online. Resellers are able to sell sneakers directly on the platform by uploading images of the sneaker and setting the price. Buyers can then purchase the sneaker for the asking price or make an offer. When a sale occurs, the seller ships the sneakers directly to the buyer, and because of this, there is no authentication process. Thus, when purchasing sneakers on Kixify, it is important to inspect the images of the sneaker and ensure that the seller has good feedback. However, Kixify also offers a Kixify Select program that guarantees authenticity. With orders placed through Kixify Select, orders are fulfilled by partners that are verified by the company. For sneakers sold through Kixify, the company takes an 8 percent fee from the final sales price.

The RealReal

Founded in 2011, the RealReal is a luxury consignment platform where sellers can consign luxury goods, such as clothing, handbags, accessories, jewelry, and of course, sneakers. The RealReal has an online platform and ten physical stores across the United States, including locations in New York, Los Angeles, Miami, San Francisco, Chicago, Dallas, and Washington, DC. Sellers wishing to consign with the RealReal can either drop off their goods at one of the company's locations or can request a consignment kit, which includes instructions on how to ship the items they wish to consign. Like its name suggests, the

RealReal prides itself on a rigorous authentication process to ensure that all items are real. For sneakers priced at $145 or less, the RealReal takes 60 percent of the net sales price; for sneakers priced between $146 and $195, the RealReal takes 50 percent of the net sales price; and for sneakers priced at $195 or more, the RealReal takes 20 percent of the net sales price.

Round Two

Founded in Richmond, Virginia, in 2013 as a vintage clothing store, Round Two now has several brick-and-mortar locations across the United States, in cities such as New York, LA, and Miami, each with its own impressive stock of sneakers, streetwear, and luxury goods. Round Two's buying process is pretty straightforward: you bring your pairs in, and if the store is interested, they'll make you an offer and pay you cash for your kicks on the spot. You can also earn a bit more on your item if you're willing to take store credit, which can be useful for buying more pairs. It's not great for amassing cash. There really is no predicting how much they will pay unless you walk in, so sales can be challenging, but cash on the spot can also be nice. Interestingly, one of Round Two's owners, Sean Wotherspoon, has designed several highly coveted and resold sneakers, including the Air Max 1/97 Wotherspoon, the ASICS Gel-Lyte III Sean Wotherspoon x Atmos, and the adidas Superstar Sean Wotherspoon.

Mom-and-Pop Shops

Now that you know about the biggest resale platforms, you know that there are a multitude of options, each with pros and cons. But what about the smaller companies—the little mom-and-pop shops, independently owned and operated, often with only one location? All across the globe, these sneaker resale stores are operating with much success despite the competition from their corporate counterparts.

These small but nimble businesses either resell sneakers on consignment or will buy your product outright. They may have limited inventory, little to no resale fees, and little to no method of authentication, other than taking the owner at their word. Some do not even have a store but make their money on the sneaker convention circuit or by opening temporary pop-up shops in vacant commercial space.

Regardless, this way of doing business was the genesis for most of the players in our previous section. There are too many to name. You may have a favorite mom-and-pop spot in your local town or city that could be on the verge of becoming the next Stadium Goods. Who knows, maybe after reading this book, you may want to open your own resale shop. If so, shoot us a note, and the next time we're in your town, we'll come check you out, maybe even cop some heat for the low!

Hand to Hand

Another way to resell sneakers is through hand-to-hand transactions. Resellers schedule in-person meetups with buyers and exchange the sneakers for cash or online payouts through apps such as Zelle, Venmo, Apple Pay, PayPal, and the Cash App. Popular ways to initiate these types of transactions include digital mediums such as Craigslist, social media platforms such as Instagram, Facebook, and Twitter, and at sneaker conventions.

When it comes to Craigslist, a site that features classified advertisements and forums where people can sell or request products and services, resellers can post sneakers that they have for sale in their geographical area, and buyers can then contact the reseller to purchase the sneakers. If both parties agree on a price, they can schedule a meetup to conduct the transaction. This arrangement is similar to selling sneakers on Instagram, Facebook, and Twitter; through these platforms, resellers can post sneakers for sale, find a buyer, and schedule a meetup to sell the sneakers in person. There are also copious amounts of sneaker transactions on social media where the reseller ships the sneakers to the buyer after being paid, instead of meeting up in person. In fact, this is how the majority of resellers sell sneakers on social media. You can refer back to chapter 6 for a detailed breakdown on buying and selling sneakers on social media.

Also as explained in chapter 6, sneaker conventions are large events where sneakerheads can buy, sell, and trade sneakers from brands, resellers, and others. Oftentimes, resellers purchase booths at these conventions and display all of their inventory. This is a good way for resellers to showcase the kicks that they have for sale and hopefully sell a good amount of their inventory.

Unfortunately, as we will discuss in the next section, reselling sneakers through hand-to-hand transactions has its dangers.

Violence in Sneakers

"Your Sneakers or Your Life" was the banner title of a 1990 *Sports Illustrated* cover featuring a story about a fifteen-year-old boy who was murdered for his Air Jordans. Years later, violence is still prevalent, one of the unfortunate consequences of the resale industry's hype, demand, and potential for profit. According to an investigative report from GQ, about 1,200 people die per year from violent acts involving sneakers. The next two subsections are dedicated to the unfortunate acts of violence that have occurred during (1) release dates for highly anticipated sneaker drops and (2) resale transactions. We mention these examples, not to glorify but to educate readers on what they can do to avoid similar occurrences in their own sneaker exploits.

Release Date

Historically, hyped and exclusive sneaker releases mean long lines and people camping out for a chance to purchase. As discussed earlier in this chapter, the reality is that not everyone waiting in a long line for a coveted release will end up getting a pair. Because of this, arguments and conflict can occur, and things can escalate to extreme violence. There have been many instances of release date violence. On December 24, 2011, 2,000 people at a shopping mall outside San Francisco were promptly sent home when a gun went off and canceled the release date for a pair of Air Jordan 11s. That same release date, Seattle police had to use pepper spray to break up a melee between customers, four people were arrested in Atlanta, fights broke out in Kentucky, and glass store windows were shattered in North Carolina. On February 23, 2012, a riot broke out at an Orlando, Florida shopping mall, when a crowd of over 1,000 people became unruly while awaiting the release of the Nike Air Foamposite One "Galaxy." Each year, particularly around the holidays and Black Friday, we hear stories of this kind of sneaker violence surrounding in-store releases. Fortunately, sneaker brands are taking action, allocating extremely limited pairs to online drops only or setting up raffle systems to control crowds and the "first come, first served" method that seems to cause so much chaos.

Resale Transactions

With hand-to-hand sneaker reselling, there is always a chance that violence can ensue. Meeting someone you don't know in person can be risky for both resellers and buyers. Sadly, there have been murders, beatings, and muggings when people meet in person to buy and sell sneakers. In April 2020, a teenage woman was murdered in Miami, Florida during a botched meetup to sell three pairs of YEEZYs. The woman was with her boyfriend, and when they arrived at the meetup location, two men approached their vehicle and fired several shots, killing the woman and injuring the man. The men took the sneakers and fled. Thankfully, both were caught, arrested, and charged with murder. In 2016, a reseller posted an ad to sell a pair of Jordans on Craigslist and connected with a buyer. The two planned to meet up in New York City to complete the transaction. As the seller arrived in his car, the buyer pulled a gun, stole the sneakers, and fled. Enraged, the seller chased the thief and ran him over, severing his arm. The seller was charged with second-degree attempted murder, and the buyer was charged with criminal possession of a firearm and second-degree robbery.

Incidents like these are just a few examples of many that have happened when conducting hand-to-hand resale transactions. As a seller or buyer, it is extremely important to be careful and cautious. Always meet in safe public places with other people around, and if possible, get paid before the transaction occurs. Asking for references from the seller or buyer can help ensure that the person you are dealing with won't cause any problems. Let's all do our part to keep everyone safe in the sneaker community.

Counterfeits

Now that you know all you need to know about the reselling game, we'll fill you in on what a counterfeit is and their impact on the sneaker industry.

A counterfeit is defined as a fraudulent imitation of something else, a forgery. According to the International Anti-Counterfeiting Coalition (IACC), "counterfeiting is a federal and state crime, involving the manufacturing or distribution of goods under someone else's name, and without their permission. Counterfeit goods are generally made from lower quality components, in an attempt to sell a cheap imitation of similar goods produced by brands consumers know and trust."[34]

Counterfeits can be found in all industries. Goods such as nonathletic shoes, apparel, bags, pharmaceuticals, cosmetic, skincare products, toys, electronics, software, cigarettes, and automobile and airplane parts are all regularly counterfeited and sold to consumers. According to the US Customs and Border Protection, there were 4,728 seizures of footwear in 2018, which amounted to 14 percent of the year's total seizures. This is second only to apparel and accessory counterfeits, which amounted to 18 percent of total seizures. It is clear from these staggering numbers that counterfeiting is a major problem in the sneaker industry.

What Is the Harm in Counterfeiting?

Counterfeiting is a multibillion-dollar industry. US Customs and Border Protection officers and the Department of Homeland Security (DHS) seized counterfeit goods valued at approximately $1.5 billion at US borders alone in 2019, and it is a much larger global problem. According to the Organisation for Economic Co-operation and Development (OECD), as of 2019, counterfeits accounted for approximately 3.3 percent of all global trade. The DHS reported seizures of counterfeit products at US borders have increased tenfold over the last two decades, and a recent OECD report[35] detailed a 154 percent increase in counterfeits traded internationally—from $200 billion in 2005 to $509 billion in 2016. Much of the increase in counterfeit goods is due to the rise in online shopping channels.

Why should you care? What's the harm in buying fakes of your favorite kicks? The brands make enough money anyway, right? Wrong! Counterfeiting is a big problem, not just for the companies but for everyone.

Of course, counterfeiting places a financial strain on the companies that legitimately manufacture the goods. The lost sales could correlate to lower wages, job eliminations, and potentially higher prices for consumers. But counterfeiting also hurts society as a whole.

Counterfeit goods are typically made using cheap and sometimes dangerous materials that can put consumers at risk. If you are sick, would you want to take counterfeit medication? Would you want to feed your baby counterfeit formula? What about washing your hair with counterfeit shampoo? It is easy to see how these goods could harm consumers.

You could also be putting yourself at risk by buying from counterfeiters. Do you want to trust a counterfeiter with your credit card and shipping information? This could put you at risk for credit card fraud and even identity theft. Purchasing counterfeit goods could put your device at risk if the counterfeiters put a virus on it or scrub your data when you access their site.

Counterfeiting has also been linked to funding organized crime, drug trafficking, child labor, and even terrorist activities. So think twice before buying those Feezys; your purchase could be funding illicit activity that would physically harm yourself and others.

Source: Jordi C / Shutterstock.com

---

[34] International Anti-Counterfeiting Coalition, https://www.iacc.org/resources/about/what-is-counterfeiting (last visited Sept. 1, 2020).

[35] Organisation for Economic Cooperation and Development Library, https://www.oecd-ilibrary.org/governance/governance-frameworks-to-counter-illicit-trade_9789264291652-en (last visited Sept. 1, 2020).

What Is Being Done about Counterfeiting?

On January 24, 2020, the DHS issued a report to the president titled "Combating Trafficking in Counterfeit and Pirated Goods," which addressed the growing number of e-commerce marketplaces that create increased opportunities for the online sale of illicit goods.[36] Shortly thereafter, on January 31, 2020, President Trump signed an executive order aimed at preventing counterfeit goods from being sold on e-commerce websites.

---

[36] Department of Homeland Security, https://www.dhs.gov/sites/default/files/publications/20_0124_plcy_counterfeit-pirated-goods-report_01.pdf (last visited Sept. 01, 2020).

The DHS report made clear that government action is not enough. Brands need to police their IP to stop counterfeit goods, and e-commerce sites need to establish policies and procedures to prevent the sale of counterfeit goods. Let's take a look at some of the things brands can do to prevent counterfeits.

Enforcement by Sneaker Brands

Sneaker brands spend a lot of time, money, and energy fighting counterfeiting on several different levels. They will often hire investigators and lawyers to track down counterfeiters and stop them. Sometimes cease and desist letters are sent, counterfeiters are subjects of civil lawsuits, lawyers work with investigators and authorities to seize counterfeit goods, and even criminal action is taken against the counterfeiters. Counterfeiting is so prevalent that for many brands, when you get rid of one counterfeiter, another one pops up somewhere else.

Sneaker brands can also register their trademarks with customs in hopes that counterfeit goods will be stopped by customs agents at the port upon entering the country. Companies spend significant time and resources training customs agents on how to spot branded counterfeit products. If the goods are stopped before being offered in the marketplace, it saves time and energy going after the illegitimate retailers. For example, in 2012, after a lengthy investigation into the smuggling of counterfeit products from China to the United States, the DHS Investigations Division and other law enforcement agencies were able to seize over $325 million in counterfeit goods, including sneakers, purses, and other goods from brands such as Nike, Coach, Louis Vuitton, UGG Australia, and others. The goods were seized at the Port Newark-Elizabeth Marine Terminal, a major shipping hub for overseas manufacturers. The investigation revealed that the conspirators were submitting fake documents with the shipping containers that contained the counterfeit goods. Twenty-nine people were implicated in the counterfeiting ring and faced criminal charges. The ringleader of this operation ultimately received ten years in federal prison.

Often, conspirators hire customs brokers, who are private individuals or firms licensed by US Customs and Border Protection, to prepare customs forms for shipping containers, providing them with false documentation that misrepresents what the shipments really consist of. Sometimes these customs brokers are complicit in the crime, and sometimes they are actually swindled by the counterfeiters.

Brands have often been successful in taking down websites that sell counterfeits. For instance, in 2015, adidas and Reebok were successful in taking down scores of websites selling counterfeit products by bringing an action in federal court in Florida, and managed to obtain $5 million in damages from each of the counterfeiting defendants.[37]

There are less costly options than litigation for brands seeking to police their trademarks against counterfeiters. If counterfeit goods are being offered on an online marketplace (such as Amazon or eBay) and the brand has trademark registrations for the trademarks being used, they can typically get the counterfeits removed from the marketplace relatively swiftly. Getting the information for the seller required to stop them can be complicated, however, and can still require legal intervention to be most effective. Some brands even stop selling their products through online retailers to help regulate where their products are sold. For instance, in 2019, Nike stopped selling its products directly on Amazon, and in 2020, the brand announced that it would pull its accounts from other major retailers, including Zappos, Dillard's, Bob's Stores, VIM, and more.

In response to loss of business from Nike and potentially others, Amazon launched a Counterfeit Crimes Unit in June 2020 to fight counterfeit products on its website. Amazon claims that the new unit will make it easier for the company to file civil lawsuits, aid brands in their own investigations, and work with law enforcement officials in fighting counterfeiters.

---

[37] adidas AG et al. v. ADIDASHOODIE.CO.UK et al., 2015 cv 62132 (S.D. Fla. 2015).

Social Media Ads for Counterfeits

In addition to online marketplaces, brands are having an increasingly hard time fighting and stopping rampant counterfeiting on social media. If you have been on social media, you can attest to this. When scrolling through Instagram, Facebook, or Twitter feeds, it is common to see accounts selling counterfeit sneakers. For example, on Instagram from 2016 to 2019, the fashion industry experienced a 171-percent increase in the number of counterfeit accounts, and a 341-percent increase in posts that featured counterfeit products. It is therefore important to shop with caution when buying sneakers on social media. If a page looks sketchy or too good to be true, it probably is! If you see sold-out sneakers for sale or sneakers for less than the retail price, you are likely looking at counterfeits. As a result, the safest option is to shop with legitimate and trusted brands, sites, stores, sellers, and resellers.

What Does the Future Hold for Sneaker Counterfeits?

Sneaker brands will likely be in a constant state of tension with counterfeiters, in the same way they are with bots, for a long time. The minute a brand takes down one counterfeiter, another one emerges. Brands are finding new and innovative ways to regulate their factories, control their supply chain, and insert proprietary, anti-counterfeiting materials into their goods as a way to distinguish and distance their authentic products from fakes. At the same time, counterfeiters are becoming savvier and can have access to the same materials, machinery, and tooling as the factories that make the authentic goods, making it increasingly difficult to tell the difference between a real and a fake. There are also massive segments of consumers who would rather pay a reduced price for counterfeit sneakers than full price for an authentic pair. Some believe that social media and the pressure on young consumers with limited income to obtain these highly publicized, aspirational lifestyles is also driving demand for counterfeits.

It remains uncertain what the future will hold for both reselling and counterfeits; the wild west of the sneaker world is highly deregulated and unpredictable. Both cause a certain amount of chaos in the world of sneakers and both drive an insane amount of revenue to secondary markets. We look forward to continuing to monitor the resale and counterfeit worlds and seeing how they evolve. Remember, keep your margins high and watch out for fakes!

Concl

usion

Source: Stadium Goods

"Let everyone else just keep going. Don't about stopping un don't give much thou Whatever come

"...ll your idea crazy... ...top. Don't even think ...you get there, and ...ht to where 'there' is. ...just don't stop."

—*PHIL KNIGHT, SHOE DOG*

If you are reading this, congratulations! You should now consider yourself an expert in *Sneaker Law,* **and we consider you a part of the Sneaker Law family. We sincerely hope that you enjoyed reading this book as much as we enjoyed writing it and that you learned from it.**

Our goal for this book was to educate sneakerheads and non-sneakerheads alike on the many facets of the sneaker business that, until now, have never been written about all in one place. As we were growing up as young sneakerheads and continuing on into our adult lives, we started to really learn the inner workings of the sneaker industry and realized a book like this simply did not exist, or that its topics were taught in a way that could be more exciting. With *Sneaker Law*, we set out to fill that void and present complex business and legal concepts in a way that is not only practical but also cool! v

To recap, together we went on an exciting journey, starting with the history of sneakers and ending with the highly lucrative and elusive resale biz. In between, we covered exciting topics like design, manufacturing, distribution, and marketing. And *Sneaker Law* wouldn't be complete without the Law of Sneakers. All of these topics were specifically designed to empower anyone with a desire to step up their sneaker business game.

If you learned anything valuable from this book, we consider our mission accomplished. But the sneaker business is rapidly evolving, and we all must keep a close eye on the sneaker industry as it zooms forward.

As authors of this book, our jobs continue as well; looking to the future, we are already hard at work on the second volume of *Sneaker Law*. So stay tuned for the V2 drop!

$99.00
ISBN 978-1-7357820-0-3
59900>